FOOTSTEPS ACROSS THE CONFEDERACY

Missouri, Kentucky and Tennessee

Dave Comeau

HERITAGE BOOKS
2006

HERITAGE BOOKS
AN IMPRINT OF HERITAGE BOOKS, INC.

Books, CDs, and more—Worldwide

For our listing of thousands of titles see our website
at
www.HeritageBooks.com

Published 2006 by
HERITAGE BOOKS, INC.
Publishing Division
65 East Main Street
Westminster, Maryland 21157-5026

Copyright © 2006 Dave Comeau

Other books by the author:
*Footsteps Across the Confederacy:
Virginia, West Virginia, and the Carolinas*

All rights reserved. No part of this book may be reproduced or transmitted in any form or by any means, electronic or mechanical, including photocopying, recording or by any information storage and retrieval system without written permission from the author, except for the inclusion of brief quotations in a review.

International Standard Book Number: 978-0-7884-3583-3

For Those, Past and Present, Who Have Made a Difference by Saving Hallowed Ground

Table of Contents

Introduction ix

1 Missouri: The Fight for the People   1

2 Kentucky: Land of the Pioneers   61

3 Tennessee: Virginia of the West   119

Bibliography   277

Index   279

Illustrations

Missouri	Following Page 60
Kentucky	Following Page 118
Tennessee	Following Page 276

Maps

Missouri	2
Kentucky	62
Tennessee	120

Introduction

This second book is a continuation of my journey as I search for a deeper understanding of the Civil War by visiting sites where conflicts had taken place. After having had my interest piqued by reading about the war, I then decided that I wanted to visit some battlefields, in order to obtain a more thorough appreciation of how these struggles had unfolded, and thus how they aided in determining the final outcome of the war.

Listing out all of the battles that I was aware of at that time, I grouped them by state, and determined to visit a couple of these states. I thought that this would give me an opportunity to walk those hallowed grounds, to see in person the types of terrain that had been fought over, where the folds of the land or thick woods had hidden troops, where generals had faulted or rallied their men as the battles unfolded, and how the landscape had played a role in the outcome. But what I was not prepared for was the emotions that I experienced as I walked the battlefields, or the thoughts that passed through my mind as I tried to comprehend the experiences of the soldiers while they struggled with each other over the fields and within the woods. Thus, what had started out as a way to spend vacations by visiting places in new states that I had not been to before, turned into a desire to see every battlefield where some type of action had taken place. I wanted to become aware of every place where men of both sides had fallen, to pay my respects, and to try to ensure that what they had done there would still be remembered these many years later.

Thus, over a period of six years, my vacations consisted of traveling to different states and visiting as many Civil War battlefields as I was aware of. During those seven summers, I took 18 trips, covering 24 states and the District of Columbia. Initially taking two excursions per summer, by the third year I expanded my trips to three per year. Most of these were taken during the summer, between June and September, but some of my traveling occurred at other times of the year.

The first book covered the initial two-year period, 1994 and 1995. The states visited during those years were South Carolina, Virginia, West Virginia, and North Carolina. Those trips basically comprised the Eastern Theater of operations during the Civil War. The next year, 1996, which is covered by this book, I moved westward, traveling through Missouri, Kentucky, and Tennessee. This region could be considered the upper portion of the Western Theater of operations. The trips were taken during the summer, in the months of June, August, and September.

By this time, I had four references that I used to identify potential battlefields to visit. These were: *The Civil War*, a Time-Life series of 28 volumes; *The Atlas of the Civil War*, edited by James McPherson; *A Tour Guide to the Civil War* by Alice Cromie; and the web site of the National Park Service, which listed 384 of the most significant battles of the Civil War, as identified in the Civil War Sites Advisory Commission Report. I would also supplement my list of battlefields, when possible, from such things as state travel guides and books found in local bookstores.

Identifying battlefields was one thing. But actually tracking them down could be quite an experience. During my first two years of travel, most of the battlefields that I was looking for were contained within National or State Parks, or I found as roadside highway markers, and were fairly easy to discover. But as my list evolved from consisting mainly of large battles to including smaller battles, actions, and skirmishes, I then had to start to ask people for directions to sites that were more remote, or not even marked. This brought me in contact with some interesting people, who in some instances, were able to give me insights about the battle, or their own interpretation, which added to my knowledge of a specific fight.

Before traveling to a state, there were initial tasks that had to be performed. The first one was identifying all of the sites to be visited, and putting them in some sort of orderly fashion, so that I could get to all of the battlefields that I wanted to in the least amount of days. Having a good idea by this time of how many battlefields that I could visit in a day, which varied by the size of the battle, I then grouped the sites, based on geographic location. The number of groupings then determined how many days that I would need in order to visit all of the sites on my list. Additional days were usually added for insurance, to cover such things as inclement weather and to ensure that I hadn't underestimated the time that I would end up spending at each battlefield. From the determination of the total number of days necessary for a trip, I then could do such things as book accommodations, flights, and car rentals.

Airline travel and car rentals were required for trips of over 1000 miles. That is the usual range that I have set up in order to reach a state by car, covering that distance over a two-day period. Anything beyond that range, then I fly to my destination state, and thus, also require a rental car. For the trips covered in this book, I flew to Missouri and Kentucky, and drove to Tennessee. I could have driven to Kentucky, but in order to keep the length of that trip to within one week, I flew there, thus saving a couple of extra days that would have been dedicated to driving. In the case of Tennessee, the two-day range of driving would allow me to reach the eastern portion of the state. Thus, I selected to drive there, doing a counterclockwise circuit of the state in order to start and end my visit at the eastern end.

This book then, is an attempt to pass on the knowledge that I accumulated, and the information that I discovered, during my summer of exploration in 1996.

Missouri:
The Fight for the People

June 8-15, 1996

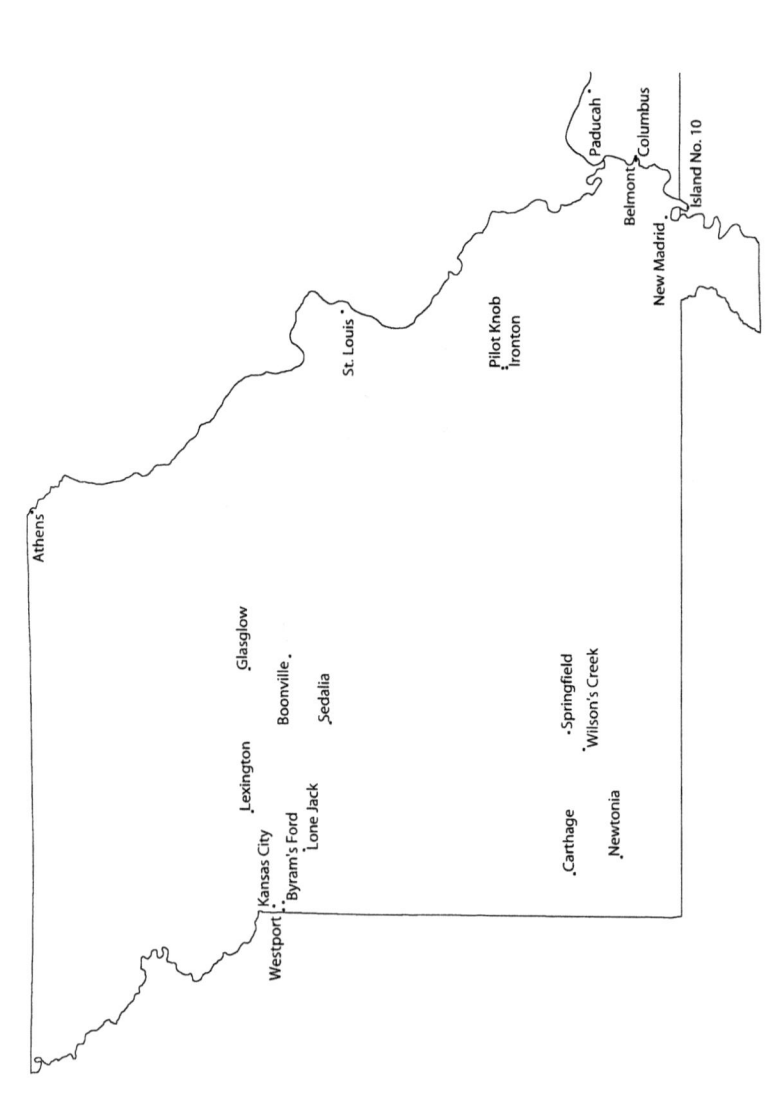

Over the last two years, I had walked the battlefields of the east: the shorelines of South Carolina; the coastal battles of eastern North Carolina; the blood-stained fields of Virginia; and the mountains of West Virginia. These trips had given me a better understanding of how the events of the war unfolded in that region. Now, it is time to concentrate on the battles of the west.

I am not as familiar with the western battles. The majority of the fighting during the war seemed to be concentrated in the east, with a focus on defeating the Confederate Army of Northern Virginia. But, I am aware that a number of major battles had also taken place in the west, with consequences as bloody and devastating as the fighting in the east.

The east of the past still remains the east, which seems an obvious point. But, the west of Civil War times, that untamed land far removed from the civilities of Washington, New York City, and Philadelphia, was not the wild west of Kansas, Colorado, and Arizona, which comes to mind today when the west is mentioned. No, the west of the Civil War was Kentucky, Tennessee, and Missouri, today's heartland of America. Except for California and Oregon, on the west coast, and Texas, the organized states that made up the United States ended on the western border of the Mississippi River: Louisiana, Arkansas, Missouri, Iowa, and Minnesota. All of the land to the west of those states was territory, containing small communities and settlements. The populations of those territories were not yet large enough to form separate states.

The first state in the western campaign that I want to visit is Missouri, where some of the early battles in the west had occurred. This confrontation was not surprising, since skirmishes between pro- and anti-slavery forces had been happening in that state for years before the Civil War started. As well, skirmishing had taken place between forces in Missouri and Kansas. So, with all of that brewing, it is not surprising that with the formation of official armies at the beginning of the war, it would not take long for the two sides to clash.

Mapping out the sites that I want to visit where battles and skirmishes had occurred, I realize that two separate campaigns had taken place in the state. In the east, all of the battles were concentrated along or close to the Mississippi River. These mainly involved Federal General Ulysses Grant and his pursuit of control over the Mississippi River. The other battles happened in the western part of the state, along the Kansas border. These involved attempts by the Federals to push the Confederate army into Arkansas from around Springfield in 1861, and the raid of the Confederates from Arkansas along the Missouri River to Kansas City in 1864.

Since I set my radius from the city in which I am staying to about 120 miles, or two hours of driving, my itinerary will involve staying in four cities: St. Louis; Springfield; Kansas City; and Columbia. My travels will thus form a triangle. The plan is to travel south from St. Louis along the Mississippi River to the battles that Grant had fought. I will then move southwest to Springfield and visit the sites of that region. Next, I will head north along the Kansas border to Kansas City and the clashes of 1864. Lastly, I will turn back to St. Louis, stopping at the towns along the way where battles had unfolded. Expecting that I will not be able to complete visiting all of those battlefields in one day, I plan to stop at Columbia at the end of the first day after leaving Kansas City, then continue on to St. Louis the following day.

The trip is to take place over a one-week period, Saturday-Saturday. If everything goes according to plan, i.e., the weather cooperates and the amount of time I estimate that it will take me to visit each site is correct, then I should be done on Thursday afternoon, giving me Friday to explore the city of St. Louis. Since

Missouri is more than a two-day drive from Ottawa, I will fly into St. Louis on one Saturday, and fly out on the next Saturday.

Wanting to be close to the interstate highways and away from St. Louis, in order to avoid rush-hour traffic in and out of the city, I select a motel in Creve Coeur. This will give me easy access to Interstate 55 and southeast Missouri, and Interstate 44 to Springfield. On my return to St. Louis at the end of the week, when I want to explore the heart of the city, I decide to stay at a downtown hotel. I will select my other accommodations after my arrival at each of the other cities. This will allow for any changes in plans that I may have to make because of weather conditions and/or time constraints. My flight will arrive in St. Louis in the early afternoon. This will allow me plenty of time to pick up my rental car, find my motel, and get settled in.

Saturday, June 8

The flight to St. Louis is uneventful. I pick up my car and proceed to locate my motel. Creve Coeur is a suburb on the west side of the city, along Interstate 270. I depart the airport, which is in the northwest part of St. Louis, and head west a short distance on Interstate 70, until I reach the interchange with Interstate 270. I then turn south.

Entering the suburb, I easily find the motel, which is next to the interstate, and settle in. I spend the evening becoming familiar with the sites that I will be visiting the tomorrow. One thing that I notice while identifying the locations in the road atlas is that there are a large number of cities and towns along the Mississippi with French names. Being Canadian, and of French descent, I know that the French had come down into the Mississippi River Valley during the early part of exploration of the new continent. I am also aware that these settlements had not lasted long under French dominion. Thus, I am surprised to find that so many French names have been retained after all this time by the towns and cities of the area.

Sunday, June 9

The day has dawned with heavy rain. The forecast calls for variable showers on a front that extends north-south along the Mississippi River. Currently, rain is occurring in St. Louis and in the very southeast corner of the state. There is no precipitation at this time between these two areas. My itinerary today is in the southeast, along the Mississippi River. Some of the points that I want to stop at are not showing rainfall at this time. My hope is that I will be able to visit them before the rain starts, or, for the other places where it is now raining, that it will stop before I get there. With this wishful thinking, I set off.

The first stops are actually sites for battles outside of the state of Missouri. My next planned trip is to be to Kentucky. Already having planned a preliminary outline of the sites that I want to visit in that state, I have found that they can all be visited from the central point of Lexington. Except one. This is Fort Anderson in Paducah. Paducah is about 260 miles from Lexington, but only 30 miles from the Mississippi River. It would be a long trip from Lexington for a site that I might or might not be able to find. So, I have added this site to my Missouri trip and thus, my first point of interest is to be in Kentucky.

I head southeast on Interstate 270 and connect with Interstate 55, turning south onto it. Traveling down this highway towards my first stop, I notice that the landscape is hilly, with an abundance of rock outcroppings, which the highway cuts through. This is not the type of terrain that I have been expecting. I had thought that the Mississippi River valley would be very flat, with the river cutting a wide swath out of the surrounding countryside during times of flooding. But, this is not the case. Although I am not right along the river, I find that the land to the east, between my location and the river, rises somewhat abruptly, instead of a gradual increase in elevation. The land consists of a mixture of forests and open spaces, with the forests not appearing to be dense.

At Cape Girardeau, I exit the interstate and turn east onto State Highway 74, driving the short distance into the city. I cross the Mississippi River into Illinois, heading east on State Highway 146 to the intersection with State Highway 3. The terrain that I encounter here is more of what I had expected to see. The land is flat and very low, with a number of fields that are next to the road currently flooded. Although the rain has held off since I left St. Louis, as I had hoped for, the clouds are very low and gray. At State 3, I turn southeast, driving 30 miles to Cairo. Just north of the town, I intersect with US Highway 51 and veer south into the town.

Cairo had no significance during the war as far as battles were concerned. But it was a staging area for Grant's forces during his campaigns. So, even though I do not stop here, I am glad that I have the opportunity to visit the community, as it is mentioned often in the descriptions of the western war strategy.

Just south of Cairo, the highway turns east and I cross the Ohio River at its confluence with the Mississippi to enter Kentucky. I now drive south on the east side of the Mississippi River for five miles to Wickliffe, where I turn northeast onto US Highway 60. I continue on to Paducah, which is another 30 miles.

Arriving in Paducah, and not knowing exactly where Fort Anderson had been located, I follow US 60, which brings me downtown and to the Visitor Center. Unfortunately, the Visitor Center is closed. Just down the block though, there is a museum. Although I am aware that it is not related to the Civil War, I might be able to find out where the fort had been situated. To my disappointment, this too is closed. So, I decide to drive around the downtown area to see if I can find any markers. I figure that the fort must have been located close to the river, so I concentrate on this area of the city.

The only information that I have on the fight here is that on March 25, 1864, during one of Confederate General Nathan Bedford Forrest's raids, that one into Tennessee and Kentucky from Mississippi, he demanded the surrender of Fort Anderson. The Federal commander refused and Forrest attacked, but was repulsed.

After traveling around the vicinity of downtown for about half an hour, I cannot find any markers. So, I decide to move on. It has started to rain heavily, another reason why there is no point in staying here any longer. I hope that my next stop, farther to the west, has had the rain pass by it by now.

That point of interest is the State Park of Columbus-Belmont Battlefield, located just outside Columbus, Kentucky. From Paducah, I travel southwest on US Highway 62 to Bardwell, where I turn onto State Highway 123. This road continues southwest and brings me out at the park in Columbus, next to the Mississippi River.

It is still raining when I arrive at the park. Knowing that there is no ferry to cross the river to Belmont, I decide to stay here and see if it will stop raining soon. My next stop is Belmont, just on the other side of the river. But to get there, I will have to go in a roundabout way either by a ferry at Hickman, to the south, or by driving north back up to Cairo and crossing the bridge there. I will probably not be back on this side of the river because of the extra time involved. Even if I do have to come back down this way tomorrow, I want to visit this site today, while I am here. Besides, it is raining just as much on the other side of the river at Belmont and so, I would not be able to do much at that site either.

After about an hour, the rain stops. So, I get out of the car to wander the grounds and see what is here to discover. It turns out that the Confederates had built a fort here, Fort DeRussy, high on the bluffs above the river. Walking up to the bluffs, I peer across to the other side of the river, and the spot where the Battle of Belmont had taken place on November 7, 1861. The fort here had given supporting artillery fire to the Confederates who were under attack on the other side of the river. Reinforcements were also sent from here across the river by boat as the battle progressed.

Just back a bit from the bluffs sits a large boat anchor and a portion of link chain. The anchor and its supporting chain had been hauled up the cliffs by the soldiers and dug into the ground. The chain, each link weighing 20 pounds, was stretched from the heights of the fort, down the cliffs and across the river, and tied to two trees on the other side. The chain was supported by crates that floated in the river. This allowed the chain to be raised and lowered to allow boats through. The chain though, was quite a hindrance to Union boats wanting to sail up to, or past the fort, and thus, a direct attack on the fort was never attempted.

The attack by Union troops at Belmont was first thought to be a feint for an attack on the fort. However, after the initial Union success at Belmont, it was realized that it was not the fort that was under attack, but the Confederate troops themselves on the far side of the river. This was when it was decided to send reinforcements from the fort to counterattack, which forced the Union troops to retreat back to the boats that had brought them south from Cairo.

It has started to rain again. I decide that I have seen as much as there is here and head out to the next site: Belmont. Since I have already come through Cairo earlier in the day, and it seems to be approximately the same distance to circle around to Belmont via Cairo or Hickman, I decide to go south to Hickman and cross the ferry there. This decision requires me to take State Highway 58 southeast to Clinton, where I connect with State Highway 123 on the west side of town and continue to the south. A short distance along this road, I turn south onto State Highway 239, as State 123 heads westward. At Cayce, I turn to the west onto State Highway 94, which brings me back to the river at Hickman.

I head straight to the river, but do not find any signs to direct me to the ferry. Driving around the small town for a few minutes, I stop to ask for information about the ferry. I am informed that the ferry stopped running here in 1994. I explain that my road atlas indicates that there is a ferry here and inquire as to whether that means that another will be starting up again. The answer is no, there are no plans to have a ferry run here again. Oh well. I guess I can't expect road maps to catch everything.

Now, I have to determine my best way to get back to Missouri. Looking on the map, I see that there are no other places close where I can accomplish this. The closest spot is Cairo, 40 miles to the north. This turns out to be the only spot for the entire length of the state of Kentucky along the Mississippi where I can cross. It is now late afternoon. I conclude that it will take too long to go back up to Cairo and then down to Belmont. Besides, even if I do go to Belmont, there is no guarantee that it won't still be raining once I get there. So, I decide to return to St. Louis, scrapping any more attempts to visit battlefields today.

I retrace my route from Hickman to Cayce on State Highway 94, where I turn north onto State Highway 239. Veering back onto State Highway 123 at the intersection of the two roads, I arrive at Clinton. But this time, I continue north on US Highway 62 until I reach Cairo, where I cross the Mississippi back into Missouri. Heading west, I connect with Interstate 57 after a few miles, which brings me to Interstate 55. Turning north, I drive towards St. Louis, about two hours away. All this time, it has been raining, and continues to do so until I reach the outskirts of the city.

I have spent almost the whole day out of Missouri. There had been sites within Missouri that I had wanted to get to today, but circumstances had prevented me from reaching them. So, I return to the motel and remap my schedule for the next day.

Monday, June 10

Today had originally been planned as nothing more than a travel day from St. Louis to Springfield. But with changes required to my plans because of the weather yesterday, I have decided to go back south first to finish with the sites that I had not had a chance to visit on Sunday. Then, I will go on to Springfield. Since this day was only scheduled for driving, and I had no sites to visit along the way, it doesn't really matter how late I arrive in Springfield.

Unfortunately, it is still raining this morning, with the forecast for showers all day. My modified plan is to go to Pilot Knob first, continue south to some sites around New Madrid, and then head west to Springfield. So, I start out for Pilot Knob, hoping for the same results as yesterday: that as soon as I get outside of St. Louis, it will stop raining.

I start out of St. Louis the same way as yesterday: on Interstate 270, heading south. But just before I reach the interchange with Interstate 55, I turn off onto State Highway 21 and drive towards the southwest, for Pilot Knob is west of the Mississippi River. This highway will take me to the town, about 75 miles away.

It isn't long before I encounter mountains. These are the Ozarks. I discover two things that I didn't know about the Ozarks. First of all, I hadn't realized that the Ozark Mountains are located in Missouri. Second, that they are so close to St. Louis. I had always seen the Ozarks associated with hillbillies, but did not associate Missouri with either hillbillies or the Ozarks. But, this is one of the reasons for traveling to different parts of the United States: to discover the various regions that make up the country.

After spending close to two hours driving up and down mountains, I come into a wide valley: Arcadia Valley. It is in this valley that Pilot Knob is located. Arriving at the small community, it is still raining, as it has been for most of the way from St. Louis. With no indication that it is going to let up soon, I have to now decide whether to take a chance and move on to the southeast to New Madrid, or to give up on the day and continue on to Springfield. With the weather the way that it is, and having the possibility of driving an extra two hours to the south just to discover that the rain has not ceased, and that I will have to go back there later anyway, I decide not to take that chance and turn towards Springfield.

The weather forecast stated that it would be clearing in the western part of the state later today and spread eastward. So, I figure that if I continue with the rest of my itinerary and head west now, by the end of the week, the weather will be sunny in the eastern part of the state as well. Since I have an extra day on Friday, I will then use it to finish visiting the sites in the east that I have not yet toured, sacrificing the opportunity to become more familiar with the city of St. Louis.

I remap my route from here to Springfield, identifying the roads that I will need to take, and begin my trek westward. Initially, I continue southward through the mountains on State Highway 21. After more than an hour, I arrive at the intersection with US Highway 60, near the southern end of the state, and turn westward. I am still about 150 miles from my destination, which I will reach by staying on this highway.

I arrive in Springfield late in the afternoon. As predicted, the skies started to clear as I drove westward. Not having booked a motel here in advance, the first thing that I have to do is find one. It does not take me long to spot one that interests me, on the southeast end of the city, and next to US Highway 65. Since the sites that I want to visit in the area are to the southwest of Springfield, staying at this motel will allow me to avoid contending with morning traffic by driving across the southern part of the city.

Tuesday, June 11

A day finally starts with the sun instead of precipitation. Hopefully, the rest of the trip will be under the sun, since I can't afford any more lost time. The first site on my list is Wilson's Creek, located about 10 miles southwest of Springfield. I get on Battlefield Road heading west and follow the signs to the battlefield.

Arriving at the park, which is a National Park that is supervised by the National Park Service, I stop at the Visitor Center. Here, I watch a short narrative laser light show that describes the battle, then I pick up a map of the driving tour. The driving loop is about five miles in length and contains the entire field of battle.

Wilson's Creek, the stream, runs in a north-south direction, splitting the park in two. Almost all of the battle occurred on the west side of the creek. Unfortunately, the battlefield is now not exactly as it appeared during the fight in 1861. At that time, the area was mainly open ground, with a scattering of oak trees and some bush. Today, most of the site is forested, although the Park

Service has begun a program to place the land back to how it existed in 1861.

The battle took place on August 10, 1861, when Union troops marched out from Springfield in hope of surprising a superior number of Confederates camped at Wilson's Creek. Rain during the previous night allowed the Federals to move undetected up to the Confederate encampment. Part of the Federal force was split off in a flanking movement. Moving to the east and south, this force was to attack the Confederates from the rear as they concentrated their efforts on the main Federal army to the north.

The Confederates were camped on both sides of Wilson's Creek, near the foot of a large hill that rose to the north. This prominence would become known as Bloody Hill. Early in the morning of August 10, the Federals started up the north slope of Bloody Hill and met Confederate resistance. But very quickly, this opposition was overwhelmed and the Confederates started to stream down the southern side. The Confederate commander, General Sterling Price, saw this and was informed that the Federals were at the top of the hill. Reforming these troops, and adding reinforcements, he started back up the hill to attack the Federal position.

Meantime, upon hearing the shooting atop Bloody Hill, the detached Federal force, which had made its way around to the southeast of the Confederate encampment, began to shell the Confederates from high ground, creating chaos amongst the tents. This force then crossed the creek and pushed northward towards Bloody Hill. But as Price focused his main effort on the Federals atop the knoll, he sent others to the south to contend with the detached Federal force.

Price ordered attack after attack on the Federal position atop Bloody Hill. But each one was repulsed, partially due to the greater firepower of the Federal artillery. Meanwhile, to the south, the Confederates reorganized and counterattacked the Federal detachment. With supporting artillery, the Confederates overpowered the Federals, who retreated from the field and made their way back to Springfield. The triumphant Confederates then turned to help their brethren on Bloody Hill.

For five hours, the battle had been raging atop the knoll. The Confederates attacked again. In an attempt to halt this movement, the Federal general, Nathaniel Lyon, led a counterattack and was killed. With casualties mounting and the army leaderless, the

Federals decided to commence a withdrawal, supported by the artillery. Presented with this continuing firepower, and because of exhaustion, the Confederates did not pursue.

The first stop on the tour is Gibson's Mill, located in the northeast section of the park, on the east side of Wilson's Creek. A trail leads from the road down to the mill and house site that had been built next to the water. At the time of the battle, this area was open fields and cornfields, with a layer of trees covering the creek. Today, this whole section is forested with the deciduous trees of the region. The path moves west from the road to the creek, then follows along the bank southward to the mill. A descriptive marker indicates that this route was used by early settlers going to and from the mill.

As I am walking through the woods towards the creek, I start contemplating. How many early settlers had trodden through this forest before me, as I am doing now? How often did they trek to and from the mill? Would they have met fellow pioneers along the way, or would this have been a solitary trip through the peace and quiet of the trees, as it is for me today.

While I am walking along and pondering these things, trying to picture in my mind what daily living would have been like for those people and what did they experience in those times, I am startled by the rustling of leaves. It is too large of a noise to be a bird or a squirrel. I know those sounds after spending so much time on battlefields within woods. I turn quickly to the direction of the sound. It is a deer on the other side of a small stream that runs next to the path at this point. The deer moves back from the stream a few paces, stops, and eyes me to see what my next move is going to be. But, I just stand still and watch this animal, waiting to see what it will do next. After a few moments of a standoff on both accounts, it scurries off into the brush and I walk on. This encounter has made me feel like one of the settlers: walking solitarily along, enjoying the solitude of the place, and coming face-to-face with the wildlife of the region. This is probably something that would have happened to the pioneers on a regular basis.

Continuing on, I come to the site of Gibson's Mill. The land rises slightly from the creek to higher ground away from the water. It was along this area, just to the south of the mill, that part of the Confederate army had set up its camp in what was then open ground.

Returning to the car, the next stop is the Ray House and cornfield, to the southeast of Gibson's Mill. The cornfield, marked by a rail fence, is now overgrown with shrubs and bush, but some open land is still visible. The Confederates had set up more camps here amongst the fields. The cornfield was contested early in the morning. As the main Federal force moved south towards the crest of Bloody Hill, some units crossed the creek to attack the Confederate encampment here. But the Federals were repulsed and pushed back across the creek. This was the only fighting to take place on the eastern side of the creek.

The Ray House is set atop a hill that overlooks the cornfield below, and the land on the other side of the river that rises to become what is known as Bloody Hill. From this vantage point, Ray would have watched the series of events unfold before him. The house was used as a hospital during and after the battle.

The next point of interest is southwest of the Ray House. Walking up a hill to the east of the park road, an overlook exists that surveys the battlefield. Unfortunately, the brush and trees here are now tall enough to block my view of the landscape.

Crossing the road and walking along a path to the northwest, I come to the trace of the Wire Road, which ran between Springfield and Fayetteville, Arkansas. On the west side of the Wire Road is a steep knoll. Climbing this wooded mound, I discover a cannon, indicating the position of the Pulaski Arkansas Battery. This high ground gave a good view of the battle unfolding on the next hill over, Bloody Hill. The battery fired continuously into the ranks of the Union troops as they first attacked the Confederates atop the crest, then later, as the Federals defended their position on the high ground. This enfilading fire helped halt the Federal advance and gave the Confederates time to reorganize at the bottom of the slope after the initial shock of the attack. Even though the gun placement is described as being amongst trees, even during the battle, there must have been enough of a view from the top here in order for the guns to have been fired. However, today the field of fire is blocked by a wall of trees. I am amazed at the ability of these artillery troops, who, in response to the attack, quickly pulled the guns up this steep knoll, through the underbrush, set them up, and started firing at the enemy. This feat was not a trivial one.

Descending the hill, I then walk south along the Wire Road. Today it is unused, but the tracks worn into the dirt remain, with grass attempting to grow in the area between the tracks. Here, a field of wild grass grows on either side of the road, making this part of the site similar to the time of the battle. Ahead of me is a row of large shade trees. This growth hides Wilson's Creek. I follow the path into the woods and cross the water.

Emerging from this growth on the west side of the creek, the land again opens up into a flat grassy terrain with hills in the near distance. A marker by the road, on the west side, indicates the site of the Edwards Cabin. Here, Price had set up his headquarters at the foot of the hill that was to become known as Bloody Hill. The rest of the troops were camped along the edge of the creek. It was here that Price first learned of the attack by the Federals. Hearing a commotion from the far side of the hill, he turned to see his men fleeing down the slope towards him. He reorganized his men here, while the Arkansas Battery fired at the advancing Federals, and attacked back up the hill.

While I stand here looking up towards the top of Bloody Hill, a grassy rise topped with a crown of trees, I try to picture the site that Price may have seen while attempting to ascertain what was developing before him, perhaps as he sipped on a cup of coffee at that early morning hour. Confederate troops probably scurried down the hill through the tall grass of August, some losing their footing and rolling for part of the distance, with no order to this downward race. Then, the site of Union troops would have appeared at the crest, following in their wake of Price's retreating men.

I return to the car and move on to the next stop, at the very southern end of the park, and just on the west side of the creek. Here, I come to the point of Sigel's second position. Federal General Franz Sigel is the one who had suggested to Lyon, on August 9, that he could take some troops around to the southern end of the Confederate line and attack their rear, while the main force attacked from the north. The point here was the north end of a stubblefield. I assume that it was a cornfield from which the corn had already been taken. To the north of this field was a cornfield. The land here today consists of grass, with a few clumps of woods scattered about in the distance. The field is not flat, but descends eastward down to the creek, and rises slightly in the distance to the south. It was here that Sigel moved his troops to, after shelling the Confederates from high ground on the east side of the creek.

I look over in the direction of Sigel's initial position, to the southeast, beyond Wilson's Creek. The land rises quickly to a large hill. It is now covered with trees, but the hill was open land at the time of the battle. Attacking down the western slope, the Federals routed the Confederate cavalry positioned there, crossed the creek, moved into the stubblefield to the south of my position, and realigned to attack towards the north. At the point where I am, the Confederates set up artillery to try to stop the Federal advance. Unable to accomplish this, they moved farther to the north, followed by the Federals.

Continuing north in Sigel's footsteps, I come to his final position on a hillside that descends down to Skeggs Branch. The park road crosses the Wire Road at this spot, southwest of Price's Headquarters. The open fields that Sigel had just crossed change here to woods. The Confederates counterattacked from this forested terrain, first halting the Federal advance, then forcing them to withdraw. Because of the woods here, it is impossible to see the terrain to the north; probably the same problem that the Union troops encountered as they advanced northward to this position.

Following the tour road, I drive northwest to the main area where the fighting occurred. The first stop is where Guibor's Confederate Battery was located, at the southern base of Bloody Hill. From this position, the Confederate artillery dueled with the Federal guns on the crest of the hill, and supported the four attacks by the Confederate infantry up the slopes. The landscape here is a menagerie of tall grass, shrubs, and bushes, with clumps of trees scattered throughout. Across this terrain, the Confederates would have marched, trying to take the high ground occupied by the enemy.

The next stop is Bloody Hill itself. A separate brochure is needed here, which describes the points of interest on a walking tour. The parking lot is on the west side of the crest of the hill and I start the tour by heading east.

The first point is the placement of Totten's Union artillery, which supported the battle taking place on the hill. Another battery to the east of this one assisted the skirmish that was taking place on the east side of the creek. The guns here would have had a clear view of the field. They would have first supported the Union advance, then aided in the defense of the hill, as the Confederates repeatedly tried to retake this ground. Today, low shrubs allow me to get an idea of the landscape that these troops defended, but woods in the distance prevent me from getting a complete picture of the terrain over which the fighting occurred.

Moving farther east, I come to the point where Union troops came under the fire from the Pulaski Battery, located on the east side of the creek. The land here is now wooded, and I cannot view the position of the Confederate artillery that was positioned in the distance.

A bit farther to the east is the middle of the Union line, which stretched to the creek in the east and equidistant to the west. This line was attacked three times by the Confederates, and some of the most intense fighting occurred at this point. This area is now forested. This makes it difficult for me to understand how the battle unfolded here.

Walking to the south, I come to the marker that indicates where General Lyon was killed during the battle. This occurred as the Confederates assaulted the Federals atop the hill for the second time. Lyon's death resulted while he was leading troops into the battle. Again, because of the wooded area that the path now passes through, it is hard for me to comprehend how the events unfolded here.

A bit farther to the south is the next marker, which is from the Confederate point of view. Three futile times they advanced against the Union line. However, as from the Federal position, the woods here prevent me from making a precise interpretation, and I cannot see the Union line that the Confederates wanted to attack.

Continuing south through the woods, I come to a clearing at the crest of the hill. Glancing over the tops of the tall grass into the valley below, I see the Edwards Cabin, set beside the Wire Road. Down the slope of the hill towards the cabin would have been the path followed by the retreating Confederates in the early part of the morning. What I see before me would have been their view as they scurried towards the bottom. General Price would have been standing below, watching this mass of confusion coming his way, before rallying the troops for a counterattack. On the far side of the Edwards Cabin, the land slopes upward to a set of low hills, today completely covered by forest. The terrain between Bloody Hill and the Wire Road is covered in grass, probably similar to the type of vegetation during the battle.

Following the path to the west, along the brow of the hill, I get a slightly different view of the valley below, where the Confederates reformed in order to attack back up the hill. This reorganization would have unfolded in front of the Union soldiers standing here, as they waited atop the hill.

Moving back to the north, and into the woods, I arrive at an area where the heavy fighting had left behind the wounded of both sides, scattered across the hilltop. Today, small spindly trees give a cover of protection from the elements of the weather. But at the time of the battle, there would have been no protected cover to speak of. The open ground would not have protected the wounded soldiers from the battle, nor from the elements. Commotion and chaos would have swirled around them every time that a new Confederate attack erupted. Because neither side had expected the number of casualties that resulted from this battle, the wounded soldiers endured suffering for many hours after the fight before they were finally attended to.

Farther to the north, I come to the western edge of the tree line that now covers the top of the hill. From here, grass covers the ground to the west, although there is a smattering of trees as the land slopes slowly upward to crest in the near distance. Over the ridge from the west had come a Confederate cavalry attack to hit the Union right flank, positioned here. With the help of Totten's Federal artillery, placed to the rear of this position, the cavalry onslaught was quickly halted and repulsed. This was the only major cavalry assault during the battle.

The Confederate cavalry attack allowed the infantry to retreat from its second assault and reform for the third furious attack on the Union position atop Bloody Hill. The final point on this circuitous walk is the position hit by the Confederates during the third assault, just to the north. The terrain here is similar to that where the cavalry assault had occurred: the land in front of the Union line rising slightly, covered mostly with grass, but with a few trees scattered across the landscape.

Leaving Bloody Hill, the final stop of the tour is the area to the north, where the Union troops first positioned themselves to advance upon Bloody Hill, and at the end of the day, passed by here during their withdrawal from the battle. Standing at the Overlook and glancing to the north, I see a line of trees in front of which the Federal troops would have congregated and formed up, then advanced southward across in front of me and on to Bloody Hill. To the south, in the distance, is the slope down which the Confederates retreated from Bloody Hill after being confronted by the mass of men that had just moved passed this spot. It is difficult to make out the lay of the land there because of the coverage by trees.

Moving a short distance east from the Overlook, I come to the spot where the Union troops set up to cover the retreat. This high point, now a grassy area with a wooded patch growing in the near distance, has a great view of the surrounding landscape. It is an ideal position from which to watch the maneuverings of the enemy, and to be aware of the potential for an attack from the Confederates. This threat never materialized, as the Confederates were as low on ammunition as the Federals.

Finishing the tour, I go back to the Visitor Center to browse through the books on display. While here, I start a conversation with one of the rangers. It is during this discussion that I learn that the park is to be converted back to the type of vegetation that covered the battlefield during the time of the clash. He indicates that there has been some debate over whether to change the park into the vegetation of the prairies before the arrival of the white man, or into the vegetation at the time of the battle.

He says that prairie grass was not just one type of grass, but that many different varieties of it covered the plains during the time that it was inhabited by the buffalo and the Indians. Many of these different grasses also flowered at various times of the summer, creating a multiple hue of colors waving in the breeze. The ranger says that this grass was very tall. I tell him that I recall reading about having to be on a horse in order to rise above the tall grass. I add that it would be very fascinating to have an area converted into the landscape of days gone by, and be able to experience something that no longer exists naturally. But, I tell him that my preference is that that should be done at another location, or at a spot on the outskirts of the park that does not include parts of the battlefield. For me, I would elect for the park to be put back into the same condition as it was during the battle. I want to be able to experience and visualize the terrain and landscape that the men had to fight over and across, as the battle unfolded on that day so long ago. That is part of the reason why I visit these sites.

On the subject of terrain, I tell him that I am surprised that the landscape on the western part of the state is not flatter. Since we are quite near to the Kansas border, I expect that there is prairie on the other side of it. This is still a concept though, since I have yet to visit Kansas. I am surprised as well, at the amount of hills that I continue to encounter. He replies that the land flattens out more as I approach the Kansas border, but that the prairies develop farther to the west of the Kansas line. So, I will have to wait to visit Kansas itself before I get to encounter the flatness of the plains.

Leaving Wilson's Creek about noon, my next point of interest is Newtonia. I head west on County Road 182 to Republic, where I connect with US Highway 60. I turn southwest onto this road. After about 30 miles, the highway veers to the west. I continue for about another 10 miles, until I come to County Road M, and turn south.

During my travels through the state, I have continuously seen markers for highways that are designated with letters instead of numbers, something that I had not experienced before. Upon some investigation, it is my understanding that these highways are connector roads that are links between the main highways. For example, I have turned off of US Highway 60, heading south on County Road M. This road will link me to State Highway 86.

Reaching State 86 after three miles, I turn east and drive about a mile to the small town of Newtonia. The highway makes a sharp 90° turn to the south on the western edge of the community, but I proceed straight and enter Newtonia.

There does not appear to be a business district to the village, just a grouping of small houses with yards. I find the main street and drive along it looking for any markers that would indicate that a battle had taken place here. But I do not find any. There is also no one outside of any of the houses or on the streets from which I can get any information. The place seems deserted, although there are cars in the driveways and clothes are hung on the lines, giving me an indication that people do live here.

So, not finding any markers here, I decide to head back out to the highway and follow it south for a short distance. Perhaps the skirmish that I am looking for had actually taken place on the outskirts of the town instead of in it. A few hundred feet after turning back onto the highway, I see a large stone marker on the east side of the road and pull over to investigate. It is a commemoration to the battles that had taken place here.

As it turns out, there were two engagements at Newtonia, not just one. I am aware of the first one, which was fought on September 30, 1862. The Confederates, having left the state in late 1861, re-entered it from Arkansas in August 1862 and settled around Newtonia. The Federals sent a force from Fort Scott, Kansas to repulse the Confederates from the state. Initially, the Federals were successful in driving the Confederates before them. But Confederate reinforcements arrived, and the Federals were pushed back. With the appearance of more Federals, they attacked again. However, more Confederates then entered the fight, and the Federals were driven from the town. The Confederates then withdrew back into Arkansas and the Federals re-entered the town again on October 3.

The second battle here was fought on October 26, 1864. The Confederates were retreating from the state after their loss at Westport, earlier in the month. Pursued by the Federals, they attacked the resting Confederates here. While some Confederate units held off the Federals, the rest withdrew into Arkansas. With the arrival of Federal reinforcements, the Confederates were forced to break off the fight and withdrew as well.

The battles would have been fought in flat open fields, which are used today for grazing cattle. Large individual trees break up the skyline, about ½ mile in the distance. Otherwise, the land trails off to meet the sky. The flatness of the land here is definitely more evident than it had been around Wilson's Creek. This location would have made it quite easy to maneuver troops around during the two skirmishes.

The last stop on this day is to be Carthage. From Newtonia, I stay on State Highway 86 and head west until it crosses US Highway 60, about eight miles. I turn north onto this highway, continuing in that direction on State Highway 59, as US 60 turns to the east. Thirteen miles along this road brings me to the intersection with Interstate 44, where the highway that I am on changes to US Highway 71. A few more miles northbound and I arrive at Carthage.

As I enter the town, a sign indicates the way to the Battle of Carthage State Park, which is located on the east end of town, on East Chestnut Street, next to a branch of the Spring River. In the park, I find a large board with a map that describes how the battle unfolded. The park turns out to be the end point of the battle; it had actually started nine miles to the north.

The battle took place on July 5, 1861. Federal Colonel Franz Sigel had a detachment camped to the southeast of Carthage. Notified that the Confederates were approaching the town from the north, Sigel decided to attack them before they reached it. About nine miles north of Carthage, near Corn Creek, the Confederates waited atop a ridge for the Federals to approach. After an hour of dueling between the artillery, the Federals attacked. Even though the Federals began to break the line, Sigel became aware that the Confederate cavalry had moved to his rear and, concerned with this maneuver, he ordered a withdrawal. The Confederates pursued and a running battle took place back to Carthage, where it continued in the streets.

Here at the park, Sigel set up his final defensive position before retreating back to Springfield. On the west side of the park, the land is flat and contains a grassy area, which has been cut out of the woods. It was in here that the Federals had set up their defenses. Across the river, on the east side, a rock cliff of about 20 feet in height creates a terrace upon which the Federals placed their artillery. The terrace is now shrouded with trees.

Having gotten a good idea from the battle description of how the battle had unfolded, I note the significant spots where fighting took place. With these notes, I set out to view the highlights of the skirmish in reverse order.

Carthage is situated on the south side of the Spring River. As the Federals crossed the river from the north and retreated through the town, street fighting took place when the Confederates pursued them. Quite a bit of the fighting occurred around the Courthouse. I reach this building by driving west on East Chestnut Street, turning north onto Lincoln Street, then west again at East 4th Street, and driving for a couple of blocks. It is a large castle-like three-story structure, made out of white stone and dwarfing the shade trees that ring it.

I next want to get to the bridge that crosses Spring River. To do this, I turn north onto Main Street and immediately west onto 3rd Street, driving the few blocks until it ends at South Garrison Avenue. Here, I turn north and after a few more blocks, reach West Central Avenue, which I turn west onto. At the intersection with

North Francis Street, I turn north again. This brings me to the bridge at the river. The Federals had set up defenses on the south side of the river as a delaying action. The river here does not appear to be too deep.

I continue north and cross the river. I am now on 15th Street and looking for Buck Branch Creek, the last line of Federal defenses that were set up before their retreat back to Carthage. The landscape out here is mainly flat, with very slight rises and declines in the terrain. So, looking up the road into the distance, I can see about two miles ahead of me to where the road crests. Keeping my eye on that spot, I soon reach the knoll. Buck Branch Creek is at the minor depression that occurs between this crest and the next hill to the north. It is very small, and I almost miss it since its flow under the road does not even warrant any type of bridge. The land here is open farmland on the west side of the road and a clump of woods grows on the east side. The creek seems like an insignificant point at which to set up defenses, but on the other hand, it is the only discernible feature in the area.

Continuing northward, my next point of significance is at Dry Fork Creek, which is the subsequent stream that I come to. The creek is larger than the previous one, and again, occurs at a slight depression in the land. This spot appears to be a better place to set up a defensive position, and the Federals did use this as their first line.

About ½ mile before the end of the road is the initial Union position, before they advanced against the Confederates. The Confederate line can be viewed in the distance from here, at the crest of the small rise. The land around the Federal staging area is covered with brush, giving an indication that it may be swampy within the growth. The Federals lined up within the vegetation, using it as cover. The Confederates waited for the Federals to emerge from the brush before firing upon them.

The last stop is where the road ends. The land continues to rise a bit to the north. It was along this crest that the Confederates set up their line and waited for the Federals to attack. Holding the line, the Confederates stopped the attack and as the Federals retreated, the Confederates followed them in the running battle that ended nine miles away in Carthage.

This ends my itinerary for the day. It is now mid-afternoon, and the sun has been with me all day. I want to stay tonight in Kansas

City, from where I will start my touring in the morning. So I need to connect with US Highway 71, which will take me north to that city. US 71 is a short distance to the east. I turn east onto another County Road M and drive across the flat open land until I reach the main highway. I turn north and commence my two-hour journey to Kansas City.

Upon arriving in Kansas City, I drive around the southern portion of the city, having a very difficult time finding and selecting a motel in which to stay. Eventually, I do select one, just beyond the southern limits of the city and pull in.

Wednesday, June 12

The previous evening, as I was mapping out where I needed to be to start my touring today, I initially thought that the motel where I was staying was out too far. But, as I identified my points of interest, I discovered that I was closer to my desired starting point than I had expected. The plan for today is to visit the battle site at Westport, if I can find it, and then start my way eastward, back towards St. Louis, through the heartland of the state, meandering back and forth across the Missouri River as I go.

From the maps that I have, I know that the Battle of Westport had occurred along Brush Creek. I also know that Wornall's Lane ran through the center of the battlefield. On a current map of Kansas City, I have located Wornall Road. Assuming that these two are one and the same, I head west from my motel on Bannister Road to Wornall Road, then north to Brush Creek.

At the top of the hill just before I descend to Brush Creek, I find a marker pertaining to the battle. I now know that I am on the right track. It is marked as Tour Stop 6, and as part of the description, the marker indicates how to get to the next Tour Stop. So, all I have to do is find the Tour Stop 1 marker to begin the tour.

Thus begins a frustrating search that will last over an hour. Descending the hill, I find Brush Creek at the bottom. Today, a park lines both sides of the creek, with cement walkways along the edge of the water. This is certainly quite different from how the creek would have appeared during the time of the battle. Lining the path next to the water, on the south side, are a large number of high-rise apartment buildings. On the north side of the creek, the buildings appear to be from a previous era. It turns out that this section of the city is the old town of Westport. As I drive around it, I notice that quite a few of the blocks around the creek have retained the buildings of yesteryear; although probably none of these structures existed during the time of the battle. Judging from the map that I have, the town of Westport had been about 1½ miles to the north of the creek.

Driving back and forth around this area, I cannot locate any of the tour markers that I am looking for. I think that perhaps the Visitor Center might have some information on the battle. Unfortunately, when I locate the Visitor Center in my road atlas, it turns out to be downtown, at Main and 12th Streets. So, off I go to the downtown core.

Surprisingly, the traffic and parking in the core is light and I have no problem parking nearby. The Visitor Center gives me a brochure on a walking tour of the Battle of Westport and a photocopy of a description of the battle. On reviewing the brochure in more detail, I discover that it has to do with a battle that occurred along the Big Blue River, not Brush Creek. Now I am more confused, and still have to find out how to begin the tour at the Brush Creek site. So, back I go to Brush Creek. Not being able to find out any more information on the battle, I finally decide, in frustration, that I will have to deal with the information that I have.

In mid-September 1864, Confederate General Sterling Price had come out of Arkansas to raid into Missouri, and had hoped to spark a general uprising against the Union occupation of the state. He had moved from the southeast part of the state up to the capital at Jefferson City, then turned westward to Kansas City. A Federal force was formed in the west to extinguish this raid, while at the same time, another Union force pursued Price from the east. The western Federal force blocked Price's way into Kansas City at Westport.

The Battle of Westport took place on October 23, 1864. The Union force was positioned on the south bank of Brush Creek, with their backs to the creek. The Confederates attacked from the south early in the morning. But the Federals counterattacked, initially driving the Confederates back. The two sides battled each other across the creek for the rest of the morning. The Federals found a path up a ravine to the west and were able to flank the Confederate line. While fighting was taking place in this vicinity, Price learned that the Federal force coming from the east had defeated his rearguard at Byram's Ford and were crossing the Big Blue River, creating another force on his opposite flank. Thus by early afternoon, Price ordered a withdrawal, and began his march back towards Arkansas.

From the map that I have, I know that the Union forces had set up their lines on the south bank of Brush Creek, with their backs to the creek. Although this site is now part of the city, I believe that the surrounding terrain has kept its overall features over the years. The creek is at the bottom of two steep hills: the one on the south side of the creek ascending more quickly than the one on the north side. Looking up the street in a southward direction, I am able to get an idea of how the landscape was. At the top of the hill is where the Confederates would have formed their line of battle. The Confederates attacked down the hill and into the Union lines. However, the Federals counter-charged and drove the Confederates back up the hill.

At the top of the hill where the Confederates had attacked from, the land flattens out, but continues to ascend slightly through a series of rolls. Just south of where the hill crests from Brush Creek, a marker on the campus of the University of Missouri at Kansas City indicates the position of the Union artillery, after the Federals had pushed the Confederates back from this position.

Heading south on Wornall Road, Loose Memorial Park is on the west side of the road. Near the north end of the park is a marker describing a Confederate cavalry charge across this terrain towards the Union guns positioned in the distance. Since the area is now a park, the landscape is mostly lawn, interspersed with large shade trees. Although this is not how the land would have looked on the day of the charge, I suspect that the lay of the land probably is similar to the way it was then. As stated earlier, the ground descends slightly towards the Union gun position, but there is a small depression in the land that the Confederate cavalry would have had to gallop through before reaching their goal. For a cavalry charge to take place here, I surmise that the land would have been open grassland. The Union cavalry came to the defense of the artillery and beat back the attack.

At the south end of the park, a set of artillery pieces indicates the Confederate line after being pushed back from the crest of the hill by the Federal advance. Looking north from the line, the land is mainly flat with a few slight depressions. Across this open area, the

Federals would have advanced against the Confederate position here. What broke the line though, was not the frontal attack, but the flanking assault on the Confederate left.

A bit farther to the south is the Wornall Homestead, which was originally built on a 640-acre plot of land. As the Confederates retreated southward, this area became the center of much of the fighting. The house now sits on a small lot; all that is left of the original 640 acres. The red-brick house is a two-story structure. Four large white pillars line the front entrance. This would have been considered a grand farmhouse at the time that it was built, and obviously, the Wornall family was wealthy.

Directed to a few other markers farther to the south of the Wornall Homestead by the markers that I have been reading along the way, these identify some of the Confederate positions as they retreated along Wornall Lane, but are of no real significance. They are mainly at street intersections, and it is difficult to imagine how the land would have appeared back then.

So, I finally get an understanding of how the Battle at Westport had unfolded. As I mentioned, the brochure that I was given at the Visitor Center pertains to the other battle that took place on October 23, at Byram's Ford. I now set out to find that site.

Byram's Ford is near 63rd Street, at the Big Blue River. The Wornall Homestead is next to 63rd Street. So, I return to this house and turn onto the street. I head east for about three miles and reach the area where the fighting occurred.

The brochure that I have, which includes a map, is difficult to make out because it is a photocopy, a very poor one, and most of the map is black. But, I am able to figure out that the area that contains the markers is where 63rd Street crosses the Big Blue River. On the west side of the river, I turn north onto Manchester Trafficway, and then east onto East 60th Street. This street brings me to the markers, now in an industrial area.

The brochure calls this the Big Blue Battlefield, but it is also known as Byram's Ford. There is supposed to be a walking tour of this area, and I can make out some of the numbers on the map that corresponds to descriptions on the other side of the brochure. But the map is so dark that I can't see most of the tour. Since it also appears that most of the fighting took place around this high ground next to the ford, I believe that I have found where the main action was, and it is not necessary for me to try and follow the tour.

Here on the west bank of the river, the Confederates had set up a defensive position to block the second Union force that was coming from the east. The inability of the Confederates to hold off this second force was part of the reason why Price decided to give up the battle at Westport and retreat.

A small patch of wild grass and flowers beside a railroad track contains a marker indicating this spot as The Meadow. On this high ground above the river, the Federals struck at the Confederate defenders. The day before, October 22, 1864, the Confederates had crossed from the east side. The Federal western force that was defending this crossing were pushed back by the Confederates to Westport, where the Federals then set up a defensive position along Brush Creek. The next day, the Confederate rearguard, which had remained here to halt the Federal force that was chasing them from the east, was then attacked. These Confederates were in turn pushed back from the ford. Because the ground close to the river is very rugged and covered by vegetation, I cannot get close to the river, or where Byram's Ford was. So, I content myself with what I have found here at The Meadow.

Unfortunately, because of the confusion with brochures, and the time that it took me to try to obtain information on the battles here in Kansas City, I estimate that I have lost about two hours. But now, I am ready to move on to my next stop. From the *Missouri Travel Guide* that I received before my trip, I had identified some sites to add to my original list. Most of these, I will visit during the rest of the day.

The first one is Lone Jack, situated about 10 miles east of metro Kansas City. Since I am already on the east side of the city, it should not take me long to get there. Returning to 63rd Street, I turn east and drive about two miles, until I reach State Highway 350, where I veer to the southeast onto it. After eight miles, I arrive at Interstate 470, and the road that I am on becomes US Highway 50. I continue on US 50 as it turns to the east. I now leave the city, later than I had originally expected, and drive across the flat land. Very shortly, I arrive at the small community of Lone Jack, on the south side of the highway, and turn off.

Union troops were sent to the small town of Lone Jack in August 1862, and were attacked by Confederate units on August 16. The battle took place on the main street, lasting for five hours, as the two sides fought back and forth across it. The focal point became two Union guns that had been set up on the east side of the street, where a Civil War Museum now sits. The guns were captured, and regained again four times during the fighting. The Federals finally retreated from the town.

The community, probably no bigger now than at the time of the skirmish, consists mainly of the main street with a number of houses lining both sides, and a few side streets. As I mentioned, the Civil War Museum marks the spot where the majority of the fighting occurred. I enter it, pick up a brochure of the battle, and view the exhibits.

The museum describes not only the battle that took place here, but also other major battles that occurred in Jackson County. A map of the state in 1862 shows all of the little communities that had sprung up by then. Each one contained a small population that the two sides wanted to control, and try to sway into supporting their effort and cause. So, skirmishes broke out at almost every one of these small towns, insignificant in themselves, but serving the bigger purpose of trying to sway the populace into coming over to their cause.

As I look at the map and all of these small settlements, I picture in my mind the little houses and farms scattered sparsely throughout this part of the state, and think of the loneliness that the families must have endured. Even in small towns like Lone Jack, only a few families lived here. What isolation must they have experienced in their daily existence, living on this flat mostly treeless land? Of course, being from the 20th century, I have never had to experience what these frontiersmen had to put up with. Certainly, I believe that isolation would have been more predominant in the last century; there were not the large numbers of people gathered in large cities then, as there are today. Remote communities would have been the norm. So I believe that the people had more of an acceptance of it.

Stepping back outside of the Civil War Museum, I find that the back part of the grounds, to the east, contains a small cemetery. At the time of the battle, a hedgerow existed here, and this was where the Union troops had set up their artillery. Most of the fight took place around the attempt by the Confederates to capture the guns, and the prevention of that by the Federals. The town limit to the east seems to end right at the property line of the museum. Beyond the cemetery, the land opens up into grass and wooded areas.

I leave Lone Jack, heading east on US 50, and start cross-country through the cornfields of this flat land towards Lexington, my next destination. After a short distance, I turn north onto County Road F, which I hope will take me up to US Highway 24. The highway does take me to Oak Grove, but somewhere north of it, the road begins to narrow and, as I hoped would not happen, eventually stops at the intersection with another road. What I have not realized is that I am no longer on County Road F, even though I have continued straight north from Oak Grove. The map shows that this road should lead me to US Highway 24, but I guess not in a straight line. Unfortunately, looking east, the direction that I want to go, the road does not look like it leads to anywhere. So I turn west, which causes me to have to backtrack some. But I feel that this is better than going east for some miles, then having the road end.

Traveling west a short distance, I come to County Road H, and turn north again. After a few miles, this road brings me to US 24. So, I didn't have to travel too far out of my way. But, it makes me cautious about using the side roads. From now on, I will only use them for traveling short distances between two endpoints. I now turn east onto US 24, my destination of Lexington is about eight miles away.

I arrive at Lexington by turning off of the main highway onto State Highway 13, heading north. I follow the signs that lead me to the Civil War battle that occurred on the east end of town. State 13 becomes 13th Street, and at Main Street, I turn east. Four blocks brings me to 17th Street and I turn north onto it, driving until I reach the end of it near the river, at the battlefield.

I pick up a brochure at the Visitor Center, which describes the battle and shows the walking tour. I also view some of the exhibits pertaining to the siege that took place as part of the fighting. The battle here occurred between Sept. 12 and 20, 1861.

Confederate General Price, after his victory at Wilson's Creek the previous month, moved on to Lexington, the largest center of population between St. Louis and Kansas City. The Union troops stationed here had built earthworks around the Masonic College. Price surrounded the Federal fortifications starting on September 12, but had to wait for his ammunition wagons to arrive, which did not take place until September 18.

The Fight for the People

The attack on the earthworks started on that day. The Confederates moved forward, using trees and ravines for cover, eventually forcing the Federals back into their inner works, which also caused them to lose access to their water supply. A stalemate developed. On the evening of September 19, the Confederates developed a unique tactic. Since it was September, and harvest time, the fields surrounding the college contained bales of hemp. The Confederates hid behind these bales and fired on the Union defenses. The Federal rifles and artillery caused little damage to the bales. On the morning of September 20, the Confederates started to roll the bales forward. After several hours, they were close enough to rush the defenses. With no food or water, and low on ammunition, the Union troops surrendered at this point.

Leaving the Visitor Center, I walk north towards the Anderson House, noticing on the map that the first few stops on the tour pertain to the buildings and grounds of this property. The Anderson House is located to the west of the college grounds, and became involved in the fighting. Prior to the battle, the house had been designated as a Union hospital; no one was living there at the time. Normally, the designation of this structure would have been respected by both sides. But because of its strategic importance during the siege, the Confederates occupied it and it began to be used by sharpshooters. This upset the Union commander who, in retaliation to this action, ordered the house to be attacked.

Looking at the east side of the house, the back side, and the side that was assaulted by the onrushing Federals, the structure has an L-shape. The main part of the house runs north-south, with the extension on the north end and running eastward. This is a two-story red-brick structure, with two chimneys at each end of the main building, one on each side of the house, and one at each end of the extension. Multiple windows, all the same size, run the length of the house. A verandah exists for each floor, supported by small white decorative pillars. The top verandah also has a railing that extends along its length. A doorway opens onto each verandah; the doors are positioned one above the other. A doorway has also been built on the bottom floor, at the corner of the extension where it attaches to the main house.

Across the lawn that leads from the garden is how the Federal attack would have advanced against this Confederate position. Dodging bullets that were coming from all of the openings on this back side of the house, running as fast as they could to get to their objective, the Union troops were able to storm the house. But they only held it for several hours. Scars of the battle can still be seen on the walls and brickwork of the Anderson House. The land around it contained gardens and an orchard, through which the Union troops moved on their way to the dwelling. Some of the men who charged over this ground never made it past the soft earth that they tramped upon on their journey towards the house.

Crossing to the east from the Anderson House to the grounds of the Masonic College, I pass through a dip in the land that exists between the two points. The ground where the college stood is a flat plateau that is large enough only to contain the college grounds. The land all around it falls off, except for the small roadway that leads onto the grounds from the south. The roadway circles the perimeter of the land here. The college building no longer exists. Where the land crests around the boundary of the grounds, and starts its descent, is where the Federals would have built their entrenchments.

Walking around the perimeter, next to the defenses, it is difficult to get an understanding of what the soldiers stationed here would have witnessed, as the Confederates approached from behind the protection of the bales. Woods now come almost up to the top of the hill, blocking my view of the surrounding countryside. During the time of the battle, all of this vegetation would have been cleared away, as the land was used mostly for farming. In the northwest corner of the compound, the Confederates attacking up the slope were met by Union troops who left their trenches and attacked down the hill, resulting in the only hand-to-hand fighting that occurred during the battle.

Completing the tour of the battle here, I depart Lexington the same way that I entered it: on State Highway 13. Leaving the path of the Missouri River, I want to travel southeast to my next destination: Sedalia. So I continue southward on State 13, back into the farmland of Missouri. Just beyond the intersection with US Highway 24, the road that I am on turns to the east, then veers to the southeast, before continuing to the south again. After about 30 miles through the rolling farmland, I come to US Highway 50, on the outskirts of Warrensburg. Here, I turn east onto US 50 and travel another 35 miles over the soft rolling hills of this country to Sedalia.

It is around 4:30 by the time that I reach Sedalia. I see that there are a number of motels on the west end of town as I drive towards the center of it. My original plan had been to stop overnight at Columbia, thinking that that city is large enough to have a variety of motels for me to choose from. But because of my loss of time in Kansas City earlier in the day, I haven't gotten as far today as I had intended. So, since I now see a selection of motels here, I decide to spend the night in Sedalia, and will continue on from here in the morning. My original schedule for tomorrow only had one site for me to visit. Thus, I can add the sites that I did not visit today to the agenda. There are three of them.

But before settling in for the evening, I continue to the center of town. My objective is the Visitor Center. I want to get information on the skirmish that occurred here, if I can. That way, I will be ready to start in the morning, and will know exactly where to go to begin my day. The signs for the center have me turn south onto South Limit Avenue, and I drive for a little more than a mile to the outskirts of the town, where I find the Visitor Center near the fairgrounds. It turns out to be in a caboose.

The lady in the Visitor Center is very helpful; it doesn't appear that she gets many visitors. I explain to her that I am interested in the Civil War and in the battle that had taken place here. She says that she isn't familiar with any fighting that took place in Sedalia; the main attraction here revolves around the railroad. She does seem to have heard that there was a battle that had taken place around the Courthouse, and that I might be able to get more information there. She tells me that she is originally from New York state, but married a farmer from these parts and moved here. She says that she knows a man who lives about 40 miles west of here who is quite familiar with the Civil War, as it pertains to this region. She suggests that she can give him a call, and since this gentleman owns a bed and breakfast, perhaps I can stay there for the night. Although that is very tempting, and it would be very intriguing to talk to someone who can give me details on the battles and skirmishes of the region, I am not keen on going back 40 miles and starting from there in the morning. So, thanking her for her offer, I decline. She is able to give me some brochures though, on some of the other towns that I want to visit tomorrow. Since they contain maps of the towns, I can study them tonight, and be more familiar with where it is exactly that I need to go when I reach those towns. Thanking her again for her hospitality and help, I head back to the western part of town to select a motel.

Thursday, June 13

Starting out today, I head for the downtown area and the Courthouse. Reviewing the brochures last night, it turns out that the main attraction not only for Sedalia but also for all of the other towns around here has to do with the railway. At first, I pondered why so many towns would have the same theme. My thinking was that if one town concentrated on one type of theme, then the others would do something else. Then, I realized that the reason that these towns all had the same theme was because that was probably the reason why they existed in the first place. These towns became stops along the railway, the lives of the community had centered around this enterprise, and without the train, the towns probably never would have come into existence.

From the brochure that I have of Sedalia, there is a small map that identifies four blocks of downtown as being part of the historic district. I assume that the Courthouse will be in this area. So, I drive east on Broadway Boulevard to Ohio Street, where I turn north into the historic district. Sure enough, I find the Courthouse on this street, a small two-story white stone structure.

I look around for any markers that would indicate that a skirmish had taken place here on October 15, 1864, but I cannot find any. The raid had been part of General Price's movement into the state that culminated at the Battle of Westport, later in the month. Since it is before 9:00, the Courthouse isn't open yet. Not wanting to wait for it to do so, with the thought that when it does, no one will be able to give me any more information than what I already have, I decide to move on to my next stop.

This is Boonville. I continue north on Ohio Street, which turns into State Highway 765 near the edge of town. It then merges into US Highway 65, and I drive northward, back towards the Missouri River. After 18 miles across the rolling countryside of Missouri, I come to Interstate 70, and turn east onto it. Another 25 miles brings me to the first exit for Boonville, and I veer off, turning north onto State Highway 5. This takes me the last three miles, and I enter the town from the southwest.

The Fight for the People

Because of the journey that I am about to take in the vicinity of Boonville, it will turn out to be one of those places that will probably always remain etched in my memory. Having picked up a brochure of the town while at Sedalia the day before, a map included in the pamphlet indicates on which streets the battles took place. I know that two battles took place here. The map only shows the downtown core though, so both sites are labeled on the streets where they occurred, with arrows indicating that they are actually to the east of this area.

The first battle of Boonville is located on Locust Street. At the south end of town, State Highway 5 intersects with Main Street, and I turn north onto it, going towards downtown. After a few blocks, I reach Locust Street and turn east. I travel the full length of this street, which turns into Rocheport Road at the edge of town. The road then changes to gravel from pavement, continues to the east, down a long steep hill, ascends another hill, and disappears over the crest of it.

I stop at the beginning of the gravel road, looking at its path over the terrain in the distance. I'm perplexed. I have not seen any markers indicating where the battle had occurred. Able to see over a mile into the distance to the east, I do not see any signs that indicate to me that I should continue in that direction over the gravel road to the battle site. So, I determine that I must have missed the marker on the way out from downtown. I turn around, and head back to the core of the town, driving slower and watching closely for where the site is. I reach Main Street again without having found any battle identifiers.

I think this odd, that I haven't discovered anything. The only thing of note that I have seen is the Boonville Correctional Center, but nothing else of significance. The thought occurs to me that perhaps the battle site is where the Correctional Center now is. If that is the case, then I won't have an opportunity of visit this battlefield. The other possibility that I think of is that the brochure is giving me outdated information, and the battle site is no longer marked. So, I decide to head to the site of the second battle of Boonville, which is situated on Morgan Street, a few blocks farther to the north.

I drive north on Main Street and turn east onto Morgan Street. Near the top of a hill, a short distance from where I have turned onto it, I find a marker on the south side of the street describing the second Battle of Boonville.

It was along this hill, now a residential area, that the battle unfolded. The pro-Union Boonville Home Guard had built some earthworks here, on what was then the east end of town, in order to be able to defend it against pro-Southerners, who lived in the surrounding counties. On September 13, 1861, a group of these Southern sympathizers did launch an attack against the town. But, the local guard was able to stave off this assault.

My review of the environs of this battle does not take long, since it no longer looks like it did in 1861. But, I still have not found the marker for the first battle. So, I decide to stop at the Courthouse, where the Visitor Center is also housed, to see if I can get any information on where that battle site is. I have to go downtown anyway, because my next stop is Glasgow, which is north of the river, and I have to cross the bridge on Main Street in order to reach it.

As I get back into the car at the site of the second battle, I notice a car is stopped at a stop sign at the next intersection to the east. The man inside seems to be watching me closely, and the car is not moving. My rental car has Ohio license plates. I think that maybe this town doesn't get very many out-of-state visitors and that I am something of a curiosity to him. I pass him in the car and turn around in a driveway at the top of the hill, on the north side of the road. The driveway is a long one of gravel that ends at an old brick house set back off of the street.

As I back out of the driveway, I notice a small marker on a pole jutting out of the tall grass. Out of curiosity, I park the car again, and get out to read the sign. The small marker indicates that this was the site of the Hannah Cole Fort; a fort built during the War of 1812 as refuge for the families of the area against Indian attacks. It was named for the first settler of Boonville, Hannah Cole, a widow, and her nine orphaned children.

Looking up from the sign, I then notice that the man in the car is parked on the next block to the west, and on the opposite side of the road. I am now getting concerned. It is one thing to watch a stranger from a distance; it is quite another to start following him. I decide that I will ignore that he is even there, for now, but keep one eye on his movements. He isn't going to make me deviate from my plans of exploring this town. As I look around to get an overview of my surroundings though, I notice that on the south side of the street is the back of the Correctional Center. Now things make sense to me. This man is affiliated with the center. He is watching my movements probably because: a) I am wandering around the back side of the Correctional buildings; b) I have out-of-state plates; and/or c) perhaps I am just posing as a tourist instead of a real one. I guess from his point of view, it is me who is the suspicious character, and not him. With a bit of relief, and smiling to myself at the thought of me being deemed a suspicious character, I get into the car and drive past him back to the downtown section. I also chuckle to myself, as I remember that when I had passed by him the first time, while he was sitting at the stop sign, he had been eating a donut. How could I have missed such an obvious sign of what his line of work was!

Stopping in at the Tourist Information Center, located in the Courthouse, I talk to a very helpful lady about Boonville and the Civil War. I tell that I have been looking for the two Civil War battle sites, but that I have only been able to find one of them. She says that that is because the first battle did not take place in Boonville, but in a place called Merna, which is about four miles east of here. I ask her if anything still exists out there pertaining to the battle, and how can I get there. She explains that the village of Merna doesn't exist anymore, although the remains of an old house, the Derendinger Home, is still there. She adds that a small marker has been placed at the site of the battle. Or at least the house and marker were there the last time that she had been out that way. That had been a few years ago, before the flood of '93. She has no idea in what condition the area may be in now because of it. I tell her that I am willing to take a shot at finding out if there is anything still there, if she can tell me how to get to the spot.

She pulls out a more detailed map of the county, called the Historic Sites Map of Cooper County. This large map indicates the registered historic sites of the county. Included on it are the Derendinger Home and the Boonville Battle marker. She shows me that if I go back out Locust Street and Rocheport Road, my stopping point when I was looking for the battlefield earlier, and continue east for four miles, that I will come to the site. I tell her that I am not particularly interested in traveling four miles on a gravel road if I do not have to, and ask her if there is another way to get there. I can see by looking on the map that there should be other options, if those roads still exist, a factor that appears to have to be included in these parts. She indicates that by going southeast out of town on State Highway 87, and turning east onto State Highway 98, which is before I get back to the interstate, I can travel on paved highway most of the way. I will then have to turn north and travel about ½ mile, at which point I will intersect with the gravel road coming east from Boonville, which exits the town as Rocheport Road. From this intersection, the road continues east for about another ½ mile to Merna, then loops southward back to State Highway 98. I ask her if one or the other of the gravel roads that loops north from State 98 through Merna is in better condition. She says that she doesn't know, but that one is probably no better than the other.

I decide that I will take the one to the west of the site. The one to the east has more curves in it. My thinking is that that one will be more rugged and thus, has a better chance of being cut off somewhere along the way, the flood washing out the road and it was never repaired. The lady tells me that the battle marker is along the railroad tracks when I get to Merna, and that it is a small stone monument. She says that during the war, the river had run right beside the tracks, but over the years, the river channel has moved about a mile to the north. She also gives me a small brochure of the Civil War battles around Boonville. As well as the two skirmishes in 1861, the ones that I am already aware of, the Confederates briefly occupied the town in October 1863 and October 1864. I thank her for her time and information, and off I set on my expedition.

Heading south out of town on Main Street, I follow her directions, and veer onto State Highway 87, Bingham Road. After about 1½ miles, I reach State Highway 98 and turn east onto it. I know that somewhere around two miles, I will have to start looking for a road on the left.

Passing through farmland of corn, as I near the two-mile point, I see that I am coming up to a road on the left that could be it. A street sign indicates that the name of this road is Merna Road, which makes it obvious that I am on the right track. Turning onto the gravel road, the fields of corn are elevated above the height of the lane. I travel north along this road, without being able to view the landscape around me. Climbing a small grade, I arrive at the intersection with the gravel road that comes from Boonville, and I turn east. The road at this point changes from gravel to dirt. It also narrows more, making it difficult for two cars traveling in opposite directions to pass.

Moving on, and now driving on high ground, I come to the top of a hill that I have to descend in order to continue. At the crest, the road enters a thick wooded area that is somewhat dark because the sun cannot penetrate through the foliage. The road has also narrowed by this time into a single lane, and has gotten quite a bit rougher. I stop at the hilltop and peer down to the bottom, about 1/8 mile in length. The road is muddy, and since the sun has not been able to get through the vegetation to dry it, I am not sure how deep the mud is. At the bottom of the hill, I can see that a stream is running across the road, and there is no bridge. My concern is that I will get down to the bottom of the hill, realize that I will not be able to ford the stream, and that the hill is too muddy for me to get enough traction to get back up it.

After a few seconds of weighing all of these factors, I decide to move down the slope slowly, and test how deep the mud is. Of course if the mud is very slick, then I could end up sliding down to the bottom of the grade without having any say in the matter. I had passed a house just after turning onto this road, so it would be a bit of a hike back to there if I do get stuck. Not to mention that this would pretty well ruin the ability of me keeping on somewhat of a schedule if I have to wait and get towed out.

But down I start. After moving a few feet, I press on the brakes heavily to see how much the car digs into the mud. To my surprise, and relief, I discover that the ground is harder than it looks, and is only damp on top. So if I need to back up the hill, I can. But another concern pops into my head at this time. At the bottom of the hill, just beyond the stream, the road curves around the hill to the left. Therefore, I have no indication if the road even exists beyond the curve. I may get down to the bottom, attempt to cross the stream, and then run out of road. But I have decided to find out, so down I go. I am also glad that I have a rental car. For one thing, if I bottom out, it won't be my car that I am doing damage to. The other thing is that my car is a lot bigger and longer. The road levels out quickly at the bottom of the hill, and my car may have had problems with this.

I reach the bottom, and looking now at the stream, I can see that there is a point where I can cross, where the water is shallow. I slowly make my way across the stream in the car. Rounding the hill, the land opens up into a small grassy meadow, which is brightened by the sun. The road here has also changed to sand. As I complete my rounding of the corner, I discover, to my surprise, that I am at the railroad tracks! I have found it! Driving up the short distance up to the tracks, the road ends. But that doesn't matter. I am here. I get out of the car, and off to my left, peeking out of the ankle-high grass, is the marker. I am so elated. I have found something that people aren't even sure still exists. I may be the first person to be out here since the flood took place three years before.

Now, I take the time to observe my surroundings at this remote location. To the north of the tracks, there is a line of trees, beyond which are mud flats, and in the distance, another set of trees. The river proper is somewhere outside of my view, beyond the second set of trees. On this day, the flatlands are covered in a shallow layer of water; the effects of the rain over the past number of days that has caused the Missouri River to rise. The mud flats are probably the remains of the old riverbed. To the east, the tracks run between the tree line, at the mud flats to the left, and the base of a steep cliff of rock on the right, which rises straight up about 100 feet. The top and sides of the cliff are covered in green vegetation, making it difficult for me to see where the cliff stops and the trees start.

It is within this environment that the battle would have taken place. The fighting occurred on June 17, 1861. As the Federal army approached the town from the east, the Confederates congregated in this area to halt them. The Confederates probably set up their defensive line here, where I am standing, to try to pin the Federals within the narrow opening of the train tracks between the river and the cliff. But after about an hour, the Federals overpowered the Confederates, who gave way and retreated westward.

I now head back to Boonville, to cross the Missouri River onto the north side. I will then move on to Glasgow. I am still so pumped up from finding this remote site that I decide to stop back at the Information Center, to inform the lady there of my find. I have to go right by the building anyway, and if there is a spot to park at, I will stop. Since the woman had been so helpful, I want to let her know the condition of the site, in case anyone else is interested in visiting it.

The trip back to town doesn't seem to take as long. Parking in front of the building, I go inside and find the woman who had helped me earlier. I inform her that I have found the marker, and even though the road isn't in great condition, it is passable. She is delighted to here this and tells me that she is a bit surprised that the small marker is still there. She says that there had been a large boulder located on the north side of the river, with carvings in it. The carvings were supposed to have been put there by members of Lewis and Clark's expedition when it passed by here in the early 1800s. After the waters from the flood of '93 had receded, the rock was gone. She adds that the river had cut a channel more than 30 feet deep in the vicinity of the rock, and that divers had been sent down to see if the rock was at the bottom of the river. Nothing was found there, nor has the rock ever been located. I reply that it seems amazing that something so large would be moved by the currents of the river, yet something as small as the Boonville battle marker was left untouched by these forces of nature. Thanking her for everything, I proceed on to Glasgow.

I cross the bridge at the end of Main Street on State Highway 87 and follow it north to Glasgow, about 20 miles distant. The road on this side of the river has more of a roller coaster effect to it than the flatness of the roads on the south side of the river. Also, the landscape here is more forested than the country that I had been traveling through. Just west of Boonville, the river turns north and actually runs by Glasgow in a north-south direction. The highway angles up to the town from Boonville and comes up next to the river again at Glasgow, cutting cross-country instead of following the path of the river.

Even though the highway angles into the town from the southeast, it actually connects to Glasgow next to the river on the southwest edge of town, and at the main street. I enter the town from the south, and travel north along the main street looking for any markers. I do not find any, so I backtrack to the outskirts of town, where the highway crosses Greggs Creek. I have a map of the battle that took place here, and so I am able to find the points of interest on my own.

The battle here occurred on October 15, 1864, the same day as the raid on Sedalia. Confederate General Sterling Price split his forces after occupying Boonville, sending some to Sedalia, and the rest to Glasgow. Greggs Creek flows from the northeast into the

Missori River at the south end of town. Here on the north side of the creek, the Union troops had set up their defenses and awaited the approach of the Confederates, who followed the same route that I did to get from Boonville to Glasgow. The area is flat and grassy, with some trees that follow the path of the creek. The defensive line was about two miles long, and was anchored here on the west side at the Missouri River. The creek at this spot runs perpendicular to the highway; so I cannot follow its path upstream and the line of the Federal defenses. But by going back into town, and driving to the southeast section of it, I can pick up the creek again on the extreme left end of the Federal line.

I return to the town and try a couple of streets that run to the east before I come across Washington Street, which I discover is the one that I need in order to reach the southeast corner of Glasgow. Washington Street becomes County Road 214, and I shortly arrive at Greggs Creek again, this time farther upriver. The road is now a dirt track that does not seem to be used much. During the time of the battle, this would have been a main road, departing Glasgow to the southeast and crossing the creek at this point. But after all these years, it still exists. This road anchored the left flank of the Federal line, which ran westward along the north bank to the Missouri River.

Driving back into town, I try to follow the route of the battle as it unfolded. The Confederates attacked across the creek and pushed the Federals northwest, back into the town. The northeast section of the town is situated on top of a hill, called Herreford's Hill. The Federals retreated up this hill from the southeast, and made a stand at the apex. From that point, the line ran from the hill on an angle back down to the southwest corner of the town, and also continued along the heights to the northeast. The Federals were then driven off of the high ground, and withdrew from the town.

I turn onto 6th Street from Washington Street in order to follow the path of the fighting. The street to my front, rises steeply up the hill, and is now a residential area, as it would have been during the time of the battle. But according to the map, this was the most easterly street of the town then, and therefore, no streets or houses would have existed to the east of 6th Street, as they do today.

At the bottom of Herreford's Hill is a cemetery. I do not know if it was present at the time of the battle. The hill ascends for a distance, levels out slightly, then continues its ascent to the top. As

I look up the hill from the Confederate position, I picture the Union troops slowly backing up it: one instant looking to their rear to keep their footing on the uneven ground; the next looking to their front, firing at the advancing Confederates, surveying the results of their shots and the reaction of their adversaries.

I drive to the top of the hill, where the street ends at Saline Street. I now stand and inspect the site from the Federal point of view. Some of the first arrivals at the top of the hill would have been busy preparing defenses while observing the rest of their comrades scurrying up to this line, followed by the advancing Confederates farther below. This area was probably settled at the time of the fighting. As a matter of fact, to my right front is an old red-brick one-story building that resembles some type of hall and looks like it has been around for awhile. It does not appear to be in the best condition.

Approaching the front of it, I notice that it is an AME church, and was built in 1842. So this building would have had the battle swirling around it on that day in October 1864. There doesn't appear to be any noticeable damage to the structure that resulted from the skirmish, although any devastation could have been repaired over the years. The windows are too high for me to peer in and the doors are locked. Two white doors are located at the front of the church, equidistant from the ends, and from each other. I walk back up to the top of the hill and observe the hillside one more time. Then, I climb into the car to proceed to my next destination: Athens.

Athens is located in the very northeasterly corner of the state. So, my trip there will require a cross-country trek across that part of Missouri. From Glasgow, I need to take State Highway 240 east out of town. This is Saline Street, which I am already next to. About seven miles outside of town, I reach State Highway 3, and turn north onto this road. After 17 miles, I come to US Highway 24 and turn east. I follow this highway as it veers to the northeast, then turns north, until I reach the town of Taylor, a distance of about 70 miles. At Taylor, US 24 turns east to cross the Mississippi River into Illinois, but I continue north, now on US Highway 61. I note that I am now in Mark Twain country. This is the region that Twain would have described in his books. Just west of the town of Canton, 15 miles north of Taylor, State Highway 81 veers off to the northwest, and I follow it, away from the Mississippi River. After zigzagging across the countryside for about 20 miles, the road then turns north. Another 20 miles brings me near the Iowa border, and I start to see signs for Athens State Historic Site. About three miles from the state line, County Road CC heads east four miles to Athens, located on the Des Moines River.

I arrive at the park late in the afternoon, with the sun shining brightly. It does not appear that there are too many people taking advantage of this nice warm day, for the park is mainly empty. Although there are many outdoor activities to do here, the main focus of the park is the remains of the town of Athens, a community that held about 200 homes and was one of the largest towns in the area at the time of the Civil War. Today, it consists mainly of a few remaining buildings that sit along the marked streets of the town. A two-sided sheet of paper that is available at the site shows the layout of the former town, and describes the town and the battle that occurred there.

The land that the town was built on is flat and sandy, but there is a very slight elevation as it moves southwest away from the river. The town was built above the banks of the river, and I would have to walk down a small hill to get to the water.

The battle here took place on August 5, 1861. The Union had organized troops from the area and they were stationed here. A Confederate force of State Guardsmen approached and surrounded the Union troops on all three sides, the fourth side was the river. The Federals held their ground, and eventually defeated the Confederates, who retreated. A granite monument marks the location where some of the fighting had occurred.

Walking from the remains of the town down to the river, part of a stone wall identifies the site of the flour mill that operated here. The quietness that exists here now by the river, next to the growth of trees that line the riverbank, is probably quite a contrast to the bustle of this community during the war years. A dock existed for the unloading of supplies for the town and its surrounding farms, and no doubt, there would have been a lot of commotion to do with the goings-on of the riverside. Coming back from the river, I get a view of what would have been the main part of the town, markers now placed in the sandy soil to indicate the names of bygone streets and their locations.

This completes my itinerary for the day, and I now am ready to start my three-hour trek to St. Louis. Rather than backtracking south on State Highway 81 all the way to US Highway 61, I want to explore a different route to get to US 61. So, I angle southeast using County Road C to arrive just north of Wayland, where I turn south onto County Road B. At Wayland, I get onto US Highway 136, which brings me to US Highway 61, north of the point where it connects with State 81. US 61 follows the course of the Mississippi River, although a short distance inland. I drive along this highway until it intersects with Interstate 70, about 20 miles west of the environs of St. Louis. Turning east onto the interstate, this brings me into the heart of the city and next to the Mississippi River.

I had hoped to spend Friday exploring the core of St. Louis, but weather circumstances earlier in the week have forced me to continue with my Civil War explorations. But after being on the road for almost a week, I am looking forward to a nice relaxing stay at the hotel downtown.

Friday, June 14

Today will involve retracing some of the steps that I had taken during the first part of the week. But this time, they will be under more pleasant circumstances. As I had hoped for, with my decision to postpone this part of my travel until now, the sun is shining, and the temperature is very warm. Even though I am located downtown, my hotel is near the confluence of Interstates 70, 55, and 64, which makes it easy for me to exit the city. I am traveling against the traffic on this morning and thus, have no problems getting out of St. Louis. I head south on Interstate 55, for the first part of the trip follows the route that I had taken the previous Sunday. But this two-hour drive will proceed past Cape Girardeau to my first site: Belmont.

Belmont was the battlefield that I had tried to cross to the previous Sunday from the Kentucky side, and had had problems in accomplishing that task. Now on this bright clear morning, I am heading for that unattainable location, as fate would have it. About eight miles south of Sikeston, I reach the exit for State Highway 80, and turn east onto it. After a short turn to the north, and another back to the east, I am to head straight east on this road until just before I reach the Mississippi River, where I will angle south to the river and the spot where the battle of Belmont is located. The highway is flat, and completely straight, as I pass the fields of corn and various other crops of the area.

I stop in East Prairie for a quick break, then continue on. Leaving this small town, I think about the name. Although this is certainly not the prairie region, the flatness of the land certainly makes this a prairie. But I expect that the reason for the flatness of this region has more to do with the meandering ways of the Mississippi over time than by the land being carved out by glaciers.

As I drive along, I notice ahead of me in the distance an old beat-up pickup truck that is going at about the same speed as I am, thus I am remaining about the same distance behind it as I proceed. Crossing the intersection of this highway with State Highway 77, at a place called Thirty-Four Corner, the complex of the road changes. The smoothness of the highway changes to a rougher blacktop covering. I conclude that this part of the road is less traveled and therefore, does not require the maintenance and smoothness as the previous part of the highway does. The local people must go as far as Thirty-Four Corner, but very seldom anyone goes much farther than that on this road.

I continue on though, driving at the same speed that I have been going all along. I notice however, that the truck in front of me is going slightly slower now, and that I am gradually gaining on it. After a few more miles, I have caught up to the pickup, which is now going quite a bit slower. I'm not sure what to make of this, since the truck had earlier been going at the same speed as I had. It seems as though it has slowed down on purpose, in order to allow me to catch up. I wonder if the driver has recognized that I am not a local because of the out-of-state plates that the rental car has, and that he doesn't want any strangers in the area. I continue to proceed behind him anyway, but cautiously.

At about the same time that I catch up to the truck, we come to a 90° turn to the right. I do not remember seeing a turn on the map. I had expected to drive in a straight line out to the river. I now start to wonder if I am on the right road; if maybe I had missed a marker back at the intersection with State 77 and I am now on the wrong road. At the curve is also a large orange and black warning sign indicating that from this point on is for local traffic only. The truck has slowed for the sign, but continues on. I decide that as far as I am concerned, I am local traffic, and if the pickup is going to continue on, so am I. I will continue on this road for some distance to see where it will take me. I am not yet convinced that I am on the wrong road.

We start down a small but steep hill, now heading in the southerly direction at a very slow speed. Near the bottom of the hill, the truck stops. Looking beyond the truck, I see the reason for this cessation: water covers the road. Road signs with arrows indicate that the highway makes another 90° turn, this one to the left, and then heads on in an easterly direction. So, I am on the right road after all. I wonder how deep the water is, and for what distance it lasts. Maybe if the water is shallow, and is only over the road for a short distance, then I can cross it and continue on my way to the river, and the battlefield. Perhaps this is just a hollow area that we have come down, and the road will move back to higher ground briefly. As I sit pondering my circumstances, and whether I should go around the truck to see what my options are, the driver of the vehicle gets out.

I now wonder whether I should back up and turn around or get out of my car and meet with this fellow. I decide to talk to him, see what my options are, and find out if I can get to the battleground. As I get out of the car, the man is walking towards me. While he is still a short distance away, he calls over to me that I can't get to the other side from here. At first this confuses me. I can't get to the other side of what. Then, I realize that he has probably seen the out-of-state plates on the car. Since they are Ohio plates, he probably has deduced that I am heading back there, and that I want to cross the river. I chuckle to myself at this, and tell him that I'm not interested in crossing the river, just in getting to it. I say that it looks like the river has met up with us, instead of the other way around. By this time, he is beside me, and I ask him how deep he thinks that the water is here, and if there is a chance that it can be crossed. He replies that the water is about four feet deep here. He points to the cautionary turn signs at the curve in the road. There are about four or five of them spread evenly and sticking up out of the water. He indicates to me how far up the post that the water is on one of them.

We are now walking towards the edge of water. He shows me that the signs are at different heights, and he knows the vertical length of each; that's how he knows how deep the water is here. I tell him that this then, rules out any possibility of crossing through the water to higher ground. As we look east, through a row of trees that grows along both sides of the road, he says that the river is slowly receding, but not fast enough for him.

So, I have come in contact with the Mississippi River flooding over its banks. I remember that when I had crossed the river at Cape Girardeau the previous Sunday, there had been quite a bit of water in some of the fields. I had concluded that this was an accumulation of water from all of the rain. But, I guess that it was the river rising over its banks and moving into that low-lying region. I ask him how far it is from here to the river, when it is not in flood stage. He replies that it is three miles. I'm not even close to the battle site, and now realize that I will never be able to reach it. However, I'm also not sure if I would have found anything when I reached the site. I know that there are no official markers there, but I wanted to see the place anyway. I will find out, after returning home, that the reason that there are no markers for Belmont is because the battlefield is now underwater. The course of the river has changed over the years, and the river has taken over the site.

The Battle of Belmont had taken place on November 7, 1861. With the Confederates occupying Columbus, Kentucky, and the small hamlet of Belmont, Missouri, on the western side of the Missisippi, Federal General Ulysses Grant decided to move against this position. His focus would be on the Confederate encampment at Belmont, instead of the strong fortifications at Columbus.

On November 6, Grant moved his force down the Mississippi River from Cairo, Illinois in transports, stopping about six miles short of Belmont. The Confederates were aware of Grant's movement, and sent additional troops over to Belmont from Columbus. But thinking that Grant's main attack would be against the fortress at Columbus, the majority of soldiers remained there.

The next morning, Grant disembarked his troops about three miles north of Belmont. Moving through the woods, the Federals ran into the Confederate defenders, who were positioned just to the north of their camp. The Confederates initially broke through the Federal line, but were pushed back by a counterthrust. The Federal momentum eventually forced the Confederates rearward, into their encampment. There, Confederate resistance broke down and the Confederates retreated to the riverbank.

Believing that the attack had been successful, and was over, the Federals wandered through the Confederate camp, picking up souvenirs. But when the Confederate commander realized that the main attack was against Belmont, and not against Columbus, he began to shell the Federals, who were still mingling about in the Confederate camp. He also sent boatloads of troops across from Columbus to land between the Federals and their boats to the north.

Grant pulled his men back into their units and attacked this new Confederate threat. Eventually able to break through, the Federals headed back to their transports, and safety, pursued by the Confederates. With the Confederates firing at the boats, the transports pulled away and returned to Cairo.

I decide that since I can't get to Belmont, I have some time to stay and talk with this guy for a little while. He is a man of about 5'6", slightly overweight, and has a fair-sized beer belly. He is a jovial and friendly person, and he likes to talk. We now walk back from the river to his truck and lean on the back. All of this time, he has been holding a can of beer, which he has been drinking. Finishing the contents of the one that he has, he leans through the open window of the truck, pulls out a fresh one, and offers it to me. I thank him, but refuse, saying that 10:30 in the morning is still a little early for me to have a beer. He chuckles, opens it, and takes a drink.

He introduces himself as George. I ask him what he does, and he tells me that he is a riverboat pilot. I then ask him if he travels up and down the length of the Mississippi, and he states that he mainly works in this area. He says that he lives on this side of the river, and came down here to see if the water had gone down at all. With the water up over the road, he has to drive 50 miles around to go to work. I tell him that I can relate to the distance that he has to drive under these circumstances, having tried to cross the river from the Kentucky side the previous Sunday. It takes him an extra hour and a half to get to work, and the same amount of time on the return trip, when the river is high. So, he was hoping that it had gone down. He has to go to work at midnight. He had just gotten off work and thought that he'd come to see about the river before he went home to bed.

He asks me where in Ohio I am from. I grin and tell him that the car is from Ohio; I am from Canada. He says that he has always wanted to visit Canada, but has never made it there. He tells me that he used to go up to Minnesota when he was a kid to visit his cousins there. That was as close as he got to Canada. He says that his cousins used to make fun of him because he always said y'all; at which we both laugh.

We then turn back to discussing the river. He points out that we are at a levee. The hill that the road comes down is actually the inner wall of the levee, and now as I look at the side of the hill, I notice that it runs into the distance in both directions. This is something that I would not have come to realize on my own. I had heard about levees situated along the length of the Mississippi, but had never seen one before.

He then tells me a story about the flood of '93; the same year that flooding had occurred on the Missouri River. I remember all the flooding that had affected the state of Missouri that year. As he had stated earlier, the locals knew how high the water was by the curve sign markers and their heights. He says that during the flooding of that year, a local farmer had come up to this point, looked at the signs, and saw where the water was. He figured that the water was up about four feet, but that he was going to try to cross here anyway. Of course, not able to see the road, the trick is to set up the truck so that it is pointed in a straight line, and drive very slowly without turning the steering wheel.

So, off the farmer went to cross the river. But what he didn't realize was that the river had risen so quickly that the marker he thought was for the four-foot depth, was actually for the five-foot depth. The river had already swallowed the marker that he was looking for. Now he hadn't lined up the truck as straight as he had thought either, and he drove onto the shoulder of the road. The shoulder had become very soft because the ground had absorbed a lot of water that was lying on top of it. The weight of the truck caused the shoulder to start to give way, and it started to slide down into the ditch. So he stopped. If he had slid down into the ditch, the truck would have disappeared, because he had one of the smaller Japanese trucks, not a big American truck.

Now he was stuck. He couldn't back up, and didn't dare try to go forward. So, while he waited for some help to arrive, he decided to pass the time by fishing. He pulled out his fishing rod, climbed out of the cab through the window into the bed, and commenced casting his rod. This is how George found him. George said that he had come out to check the height of the river, as he was doing now, and saw what he thought was someone just sitting in a boat fishing. He says that he had to look real close before he realized that it was a truck, so much of it was underwater. So he threw the farmer a rope, and pulled him out with his old Ford here, slapping its side.

I wasn't surprised that he still had the same truck. This brown pickup had definitely seen better days, but I could tell that he was proud of the old vehicle, and would probably never part with it until he had to. The moral of his story is that even the locals are not immune to underestimating mother nature and the river that they all have come to learn to live with.

He now decides that he wants to be sure that the water is exactly as deep as he thinks it is. He is going to drive his truck out into the water to the marker and check the depth. I think that this is more for my amusement, and to prove to me that he knows what he is talking about. I tell him that it is time for me to move on, that I have other places to visit today. We shake hands and I say that I am glad to have met him. I start to move away from the truck. He gets in it and starts it up. He says that he is going to check the depth of the water anyway. I smile and tell him to go ahead. I decide to wait here to make sure he doesn't get into any problems. Down he goes into the water, moving slowly to make sure that he rounds the bend of the road correctly. He reaches the marker. Keeping the engine of the truck revved up, he leans out the window, looks at how high the water is against the door of the pickup, turns to me with a smile on his face, and calls over that it is just as high as he had thought that it was. As he starts to back up, I know that he isn't going to try to get into any mischief in the water, and I head towards my car.

I get in, start it, and back up the hill to turn around. George backs up the hill as well, and with a big smile and wave, turns the truck around and sets off. I smile back, wave, and think to myself that this is quite an interesting character that I have met. I am glad that I had stopped and chatted with him. He had informed me about things related to the river that I would never have discovered on my own. I have also gotten to understand a bit of how the local people live in harmony with the river, and its different moods. I pull out my map to figure out how to get to my next point of interest. When I look up, George's old truck has disappeared from site, and off I set for New Madrid.

In order to get to that town, I return along State Highway 80 to Interstate 55, then proceed south to the New Madrid exit, at US Highway 61. Turning south and approaching the town, I follow the signs for the museum, which turns out to be located on Main Street.

Main Street runs north from the Mississippi River, and the museum is situated a block away from the river.

I park next to the museum. But before going inside, I want to take a look along the river. At the edge of the water is a levee that protects the town from the river. Ascending the levee, a pier runs out into the river, on a perpendicular course to the water. The town is at a bend in the Mississippi, and the course of the water here is east-west, instead of north-south. Walking out to the end of the pier, I find a plaque that describes the action that occurred here during the war.

There were actually two battles that took place in the area: one here at New Madrid; and the other farther upriver, at Island No. 10. Both of these sites were Confederate strongholds that blocked the ability of the Federals to move up and down the Mississippi. So, a Union force was sent against these fortifications to break them. A Confederate fort was located here at New Madrid, and the Federals laid siege to it, including firing on the town from gunboats positioned in the river. The siege started on March 3, 1862, and lasted a little over a week, until March 14. At that time, the Confederates evacuated the fort, and the troops moved upriver to Island No. 10.

According to the plaque, the original town is now gone, swallowed by the river. The new town, still located along the riverbank, is north of the original one. The fort was located along the river on the west edge of town; therefore, it no longer exists either. Looking east up the river, I try to picture the activity that must have occurred here during that time of early March 1862. I imagine the gunboats coming down the wide expanse of the river, rounding the corner in the distance, and moving towards the town to set up for a bombardment.

Turning around towards the town, the pier looks like a continuation of Main Street, as the dock lines up perfectly with it. This is the view that the sailors located on the Federal gunboats would have had as they maneuvered back and forth along the river and fired into the town. Although the town has now changed from the time of the battle, some of the buildings appear to be quite old, and the main part of the town probably has not changed much since it was rebuilt due to the shifting of the river.

Finishing with my observations here along the river, I go back to the museum, to see if I can get some information on Island No. 10.

None of the maps that I have indicate that there are any roads that lead to the vicinity of where Island No. 10 would have been located. But, I know that not all roads are necessarily on the maps. I have already had some experience with this during my Boonville escapade.

Three older ladies are attending to the museum, a small building housing artifacts from the Civil War. I am not particularly interested in viewing the museum itself, since most of the museums that I have been in contain similar types of items. If I visit a museum, it is because it contains a narrative or description for a particular battle that had been fought in that vicinity. This museum doesn't contain anything like that. I inform the ladies that I am interested in getting out to Island No. 10, and want to know if that is possible. One of the ladies, who seems to be more familiar with the surrounding area than the others, informs me that there are no roads that lead out to that area. She indicates that the river has shifted to the north, and that since Island No. 10 was located at the south end of a 180° curve, it is now part of the mainland on the south side of the river. So even if I could get out to the location, I wouldn't be able to tell what part of the present landscape had been Island No. 10.

I know that I can probably get to the vicinity of Island No. 10 if I go to the south side of the river, which is in Tennessee, but I also know that that would not be an easy task. I had already had experience in trying to cross the river. Since it doesn't appear that I am going to get any more information out of these women as to where Island No. 10 was, or how I can get to the vicinity of it, I give up on the idea of being able to reach it.

I then ask them where the Confederate fort had been that was attacked during the battle for New Madrid. One of the other ladies states that the location of the fort is now in the river, so there is no sense in going to look for it. I reply that I would like to see where it was anyway. She doesn't seem to understand that I would want to see the vicinity of something that is not there anymore, so she just keeps repeating that the fort is gone. I tell her that I understand this, but want to get out to the vicinity anyway. She doesn't seem to want to divulge this information, and states that there is no roadway that leads out to the fort. Finally, I give up on this too, thank them for their information, and continue on my way.

The battle for Island No. 10 had occurred in early April 1862, after the Federals had occupied New Madrid. With the army downriver from Island No. 10, a plan was developed to march them farther downriver along the west bank, have the navy transport the troops to the east side, then march towards the Confederate defenses at Island No. 10 from the south. The navy was upriver beyond Island No. 10, and was concerned about running past the Confederate defenses there in order to reach the point where the ships could ferry the troops across the river. So, instead the navy commenced a bombardment of the island. This turned out to be ineffective.

On the night of April 4, 1862, one Federal gunboat successfully ran by Island No. 10, mainly because the Confederates could not lower their guns enough to fire upon the ship. A couple of days later, another gunboat steamed past the defenses. The two gunboats then bombarded the Confederate shore batteries that were situated on the east side of the river, in the vicinity of where the Federal army wanted to cross to. On April 7, the army crossed to the east side of the Mississippi. Realizing that Federal troops were in their rear, the Confederates abandoned Island No. 10 by crossing to the south bank and heading east. However, the Federal army had arrived in the area before this, and captured most of them, although some eluded capture by moving through the swampy ground.

This completes my excursion along the Mississippi River, and my experiences with the ever-changing landscape created by the shifting waters. The last site of the day to visit is to be Pilot Knob, in the Ozark Mountains. I had been there on Monday, but the rains had prevented me from stopping. So, I will return to this site now, this time approaching it from the southeast instead of the north.

From New Madrid, I get back on Interstate 55, and head north until I reach the exit for State Highway 72, just north of Cape Girardeau. I drive northwest on State 72, up into the mountains. Reaching Ironton, about 60 miles from the interstate, I turn north onto State Highway 21 and drive three more miles to Pilot Knob.

At Pilot Knob is Fort Davidson State Historic Site. A Visitor Center is located here, and I go inside to see what it contains. I find a couple of small brochures that describe the fort, and what happened here. I pick these up to help me in understanding the battle.

On September 27, 1864, Confederate General Sterling Price attacked the Federal fort here, after crossing from Arkansas. Fort Davidson was Price's first battle and, losing this one here, he decided that his army was not strong enough to attack St. Louis. Thus, he turned to the northwest. He then made attacks at Boonville, Glasgow, and Sedalia, culminating in his defeat at Westport in late October.

As the Confederates approached Pilot Knob from Fredericktown, which is to the southeast, clashes occurred with the Union army at Arcadia, south of Ironton, and at Ironton itself, on September 26. At daybreak on September 27, the Confederates renewed their advance northward towards Fort Davidson, and the Federals retreated into the safety of the fort. Instead of shelling the fort into submission from the heights of Shepherd Mountain, to the south, and Pilot Knob Mountain, to the east, Price decided on a frontal attack on the southeast corner of the fort.

In 20 minutes, the Confederates lost more than 1,000 casualties. Price then decided on the artillery bombardment that he had earlier rejected. For the rest of the day, the Confederates pulled the guns up the steep mountainsides. But during the night, the Federals withdrew from the fort, and in the morning, a small force that remained behind blew up the powder magazine before departing.

The Visitor Center has a very good narrative of the battle that took place here. The circumstances leading up to the battle, and the engagement itself, are described on a three dimensional platform that shows the landscape of the region. It then uses laser lights on the map to indicate how events unfolded. The brochures also show the features of the fort. Now knowing the local geography, and which pieces of the terrain took part in the episode that developed here, I proceed outside to walk the grounds and interpret the events.

The fort was built on the southwest edge of town. It was constructed in the summer of 1863 to protect Pilot Knob, which was the termination point for a railway that ran back to St. Louis. The Arcadia Valley was rich in iron, and the excavated metal was shipped back to St. Louis. The land here is part of the valley floor, and is quite flat. Mountains surround the fort on all sides though, which made it vulnerable to artillery attacks from the high ground. The fort was hexagonal, and was made of 9-foot earthen walls, supported by wooden planks. A 10-foot wide moat surrounded the fort on all sides. Two long trenches, used as rifle pits, angled out from the north and south walls. A gateway on the east side of the fort was the entrance, and a large cellar-like powder magazine occupied the center of the stronghold.

The outline of the fort still exists. But time has eroded the walls down to a few feet, and the moat is no more than three or four feet in width, and not very deep. A scattering of tall shade trees now grow on the walls. The rifle pits no longer exist, nor does the entranceway. The gateway into the fort is now on the northeast corner. Standing at the opening into the fort, I see a single tree growing near the center of it, with a hole located next to it. It is difficult to tell how deep the hole is today, for it is filled to the rim with water. This hole is the remains of the powder magazine that the Union troops blew up before retreating from the fort.

Walking past the hole and over to the southeast corner, I peer over the wall. This is where the Confederate assault took place, and a Union soldier standing here, as I am, would have been able to watch the advance of the Confederates across the open ground and towards the fort. The ground today is still open, with a scattering of trees in the background. Beyond these trees is a forest, which starts near the base of Pilot Knob Mountain and ascends to the top. The mountain has sides that descend from its peak on a slight grade. The sides do not appear to be steep, and a stroll to the top seems to be able to be done without much effort. It was at the base of the mountain where the Confederates formed before their advance.

Moving over to the west side of the fort, I peer up at Shepherd Mountain. This mountain has even flatter sides than Pilot Knob Mountain. I wonder how many people have trekked up that prominence since the Confederate artillery pulled their guns up the slopes. I am curious as to the view from up there, and how much of the fort can be seen.

Finally, I focus on the hole in the center of the fort, which today resembles a small pond. It is about 20 feet in length, about 10 feet across, and oval-shaped. I ponder at how big the explosion must have been since remnants of a hole still exist here after all this time.

I exit the fort and walk around the outside, trying to see if I can find any remains of the rifle pits, especially the one on the south side. The men in the trenches were more exposed to the Confederate attack, and they ended up taking more of the brunt of the assault. But they held on as long as they could, and were very instrumental in defeating the Confederate advance. Unfortunately, there are no signs of these trenches.

Finishing here, I decide to backtrack slightly to Ironton, to see if there are any markers there related to the skirmishing that occurred the day before the battle at Fort Davidson. I had read that scars from the fighting that took place in Ironton were visible on the Courthouse. Driving the two miles back to Ironton, I arrive at the square in the center of town, which is dominated by the Courthouse.

It is a two-story red-brick building, trimmed in wood that is painted white. Three large windows with rounded tops adorn the second story. The first floor contains two smaller square windows, one on each side of the door. A white cupola sits atop the roof at the front of the structure. A large white beam crosses the front of the building at the roof line. Just to the right of the center of the Courthouse, the bottom of this wooden beam has a semi-circular hole punched out of it. This is the damage caused by a cannonball during the skirmish here.

Backing up to the other side of the street, I take in a more panoramic view of the Courthouse, the surrounding buildings, and the lawn area associated with the Courthouse. The lead elements of the Confederates were met by Union troops stationed here, as the Confederates entered the town from the south. The Union force was pushed back into the center of town, and the skirmish moved back and forth around the vicinity of the Courthouse. The damage done to the Courthouse was the result of the Union artillery, supporting their troops during the fighting. The Federals eventually retreated back to the safety of Fort Davidson.

This completes my tour of Missouri. As I start back towards St. Louis, I review what I have seen and discovered over the week. The thing that I found different about this trip, compared to my other excursions, was that the majority of the fighting in this state had taken place in the towns and villages. All of the battles that had been fought in the east had the objective, at least early in the war, of trying to capture the enemy's capital, and later in the war, of trying to destroy the other army. But the battles out here in the west, I guess more appropriately, on the frontier, had to do more with the capture and control of the towns. Since the size of the armies out here were quite small, and there were never any plans during the war to have large armies roaming around the frontier, the idea seemed to be to occupy the towns. As the people of Missouri were divided concerning their loyalty, I assume that the thought was that if one side had control of a town, it could try to convince the people of the town to favor that side. If this could take place in all of the towns, then the state would become partisan to that side, be it Union or Confederate. The appearance to me was that the troops of the army seemed to be scattered throughout the state to protect the local populace from the other side, and to keep the people swayed to the side that controlled the town. Later in the war, when the Federals occupied most of Missouri, and General Price attempted his raid into the state in 1864, this seemed to be the only time a large army, comparatively speaking, was massed together for an extended period of time. The battle at Wilson's Creek in 1861 was the exception, early on. Even with the Price raid of 1864, the Federals took some time to put together an army that could fight against that army, since the Union troops were spread throughout the state.

One thing that I found disappointing was that in my travels to the different points of the state during the week, I had not come to know more about the war that had taken place between the other forces within the state. This was the border war, between the Southern sympathizers and the Union supporters. This unofficial guerrilla war had gone on for years before the Civil War had started, and there were many people who died during the raids back and forth between the towns of the frontier. I was aware that this type of warfare had taken place, and not knowing much about it, I wanted to get more of an understanding of what had unfolded out here on the frontier. Unfortunately, all of the places that I visited only ever dealt with the formal fighting that occurred between the two armies, or between the Union troops and the Missouri State Militia. I guess this understanding will have to wait for another time, perhaps when I visit Kansas. Or I may just have to read about it. But at least if I have to resort to just reading about the guerrilla tactics, I now have knowledge of the landscape upon which that fighting occurred. The purpose of these trips is to walk and drive over the terrain where blood was spilled, to understand how and why events unfolded the way that they did. These pictures in my memory will stay with me. So as I read about the happenings that took place during this unofficial war, my mind will process the landscape that was associated with these happenings.

I drive northward on State Highway 21, back through the mountains again, but in the reverse direction from which I had done earlier in the week. This time, the sun is shining, and my view of the landscape is better, and prettier. When I had driven down in the rain at the beginning of the week, the low cloud cover had prevented me from seeing much of this mountainous terrain. But this is not the case today, and I am enjoying the view very much.

Because of the weather earlier in the week, and my need to finish visiting Civil War battlefields, I have not had a chance to tour around St. Louis. I had been hoping to explore the city during this time at the end of the week, but things have not turned out that way. But earlier in the week, before heading out to visit the rest of the state, I had heard an advertisement on the radio in St. Louis concerning a free outdoors concert that was to be put on by the city today. The band that is to be performing is Beausoleil, a Cajun band from Louisiana. Although I am familiar with the name, I have actually never heard any of their music. Being of Acadian descent, I feel that this is a good opportunity to hear them. So I had decided that on my return to St. Louis, I would attend the concert, since it is to take place at Union Station, not far from where I am staying. The concert begins at 6:30. Thus, I have to hurry back in order to make it. I calculate that I won't have time to eat, but hopefully I will be able to grab a quick snack before the concert.

Arriving back in St. Louis, I park the car at the hotel and head for Union Station. This is a very interesting spot. The old train station has been transformed into a shopping mall. After I get my bearings, I find out that the concert is actually going to take place on the back side of the station. Wandering outside, I discover an area that houses a lagoon with fountains. Within the lagoon is a stage, on which Beausoleil will perform. There are many people here, and it appears that this concert series is quite popular. Most of the people have brought lawn chairs on which to sit, and there are a number of kiosks where refreshments can be obtained. Getting a drink to quench my thirst on this hot mid-June Friday evening, I stake out a spot where I can get a good view of the band once they start.

The band performs for close to an hour; playing lively music from the bayou. On this night, they have lots of fans right here in St. Louis, including a new one from Canada, who is enjoying his last night in Missouri before returning home.

The trip had not started out on the best footing, but once the weather decided to cooperate, the week turned out to be very eventful. I have made some discoveries, and met some interesting people, well beyond my expectations of finding and exploring the battlefields of the state. But overall, and most importantly, I have continued to add to my knowledge of the Civil War in a most enjoyable way.

Looking southeast from atop Bloody Hill towards Price's Headquarters along the Wire Road, at Wilson's Creek battlefield

Looking north across open land from the Confederate position on the high ground above Brush Creek at Westport

Looking north at the Federal siege position on Masonic College grounds at Lexington

Looking east from the Confederate defensive position at the First Battle of Boonville

Kentucky: Land of the Pioneers

August 3-10, 1996

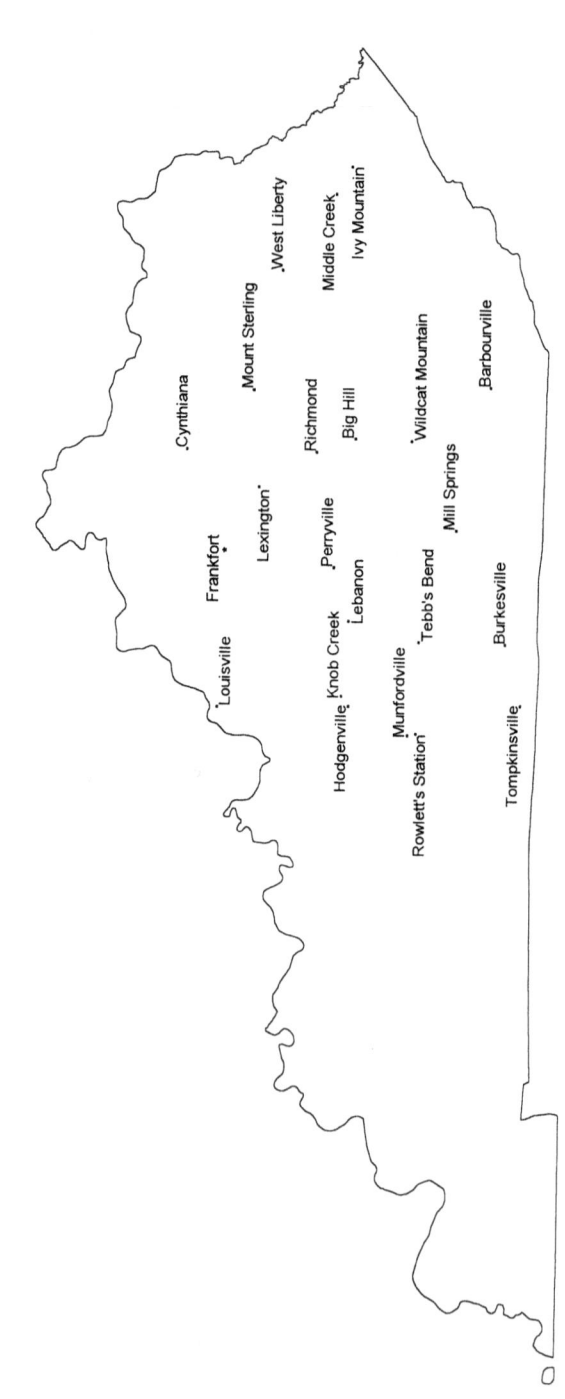

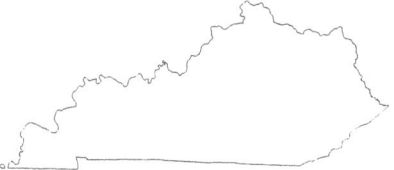

Since I had started going on these Civil War excursions, I had taken one trip in June and another in September. This was partially to avoid the crowds, but also to avoid the possibility of experiencing extreme heat, since I was touring the more southern states. Having enjoyed my other trips so much, I want to continue with my quest of understanding more about the Civil War by traveling to battlefields. To that end, I have decided to add a third trip each year, in the middle of summer. The one this year will be during the first week of August.

The next state on my list, to visit and explore, is Kentucky, the Blue Grass State. As in all of my previous trips, I have not been to Kentucky before, except for a brief excursion, in June, into the western end of the state during my Missouri trip. So, I do not know what to expect once I get there. As usual, the first thing that I need to do is decide on all of the details associated with this trip.

I initially had thought about driving to Kentucky. My range for driving to a destination is about 1000 miles, which I can do over a two-day period. Anything over that, I take a plane. However, since this trip will only be one week, I would have to take two extra days to drive there, and two more to drive back. I would then have to use up more vacation time just for driving, or reduce the amount of time that I will actually spend in Kentucky. So even though Kentucky is within my driving range, I decide to fly.

The plan is to stay in Lexington, which is central to all of the sites that I want to visit. After reviewing my options for flights to Kentucky, I find out that it is easier for me to fly into Louisville, instead of Lexington. This is because there are more flights into Louisville. I figure that renting a car there, and driving to Lexington, will probably take less time than waiting for a connecting flight between the two cities. The added benefit of flying into Louisville is that I will get to experience some of the countryside before getting out and exploring Civil War sites.

As in the past, I review the Civil War sites that I want to visit, and plan them out to ensure that I can fit them all into my allotted time. Or more to the point, I figure out how many days that I will need to be in Kentucky in order to visit all of the sites on my list. But, as I had discovered in the past, knowing where a battle occurred does not necessarily mean that there is any marker there. Or, as I had found out in Missouri, that I can still get to the battle site, as it may now be under water. But, I still create a list of sites that I know of, where battles had taken place. I will try to see if I can find any remnants of that place, either officially as a park, or unofficially, by just discovering the site that may now be a vacant piece of land.

One of the sites on my list that I have already visited is Paducah. As I mentioned, I had been there during my trip to Missouri in June. This was mainly because of the distance that it is from the rest of the sites that I want to visit in Kentucky. As it turned out, I didn't find anything there. So, it was beneficial for me to have included Paducah with my Missouri trip. For me to have driven over 250 miles for naught, would have been disappointing, and would have wasted a lot of time.

Saturday, August 3

Today is to be a travel day. It will consist of flying from Ottawa to Louisville, with a plane change in Detroit, renting a car, driving to Lexington, finding the motel, and settling in. All of this takes place without any incidents. The day is sunny in all locations, and I have a pleasant drive from Louisville to Lexington.

The landscape mostly consists of a series of long slowly inclining hills, except for around the Frankfort area, where there are a number of very steep hills that seem to push right up out of the ground. But the landscape is not particularly like that of rolling hills, which I associate with the Bluegrass Region of Kentucky, until I get close to Lexington. I guess that I was expecting most of Kentucky, except for the eastern portion, which I know is an extension of the Appalachian Mountains, to be that of rolling hills and horses. As it turns out, and as I will find out over the next week, only the middle section of the state contains the rolling hill type of landscape. But, that is one of the reasons that I travel to these states: to discover the various types of terrain that are contained within them.

After settling in at the motel, it is late afternoon. So, I decide to go out and explore my surroundings, to see what restaurants, service stations, and stores are in the vicinity, which I can take advantage of over the week. As well, I just want to learn a little bit about the city. My motel is located in the north end of Lexington, on Newtown Pike. A road called New Circle Road rings the city. The motel is situated at the intersection to these two roads, which gives me easy access to head out of the city in any direction that my need requires, or for easy access from one side of the city to the other, while avoiding the downtown area.

The downtown core of the city is very small, with very few large buildings existing. It appears that the city is in the middle of renovating its center, adding new shops and restaurants. But this change remains in progress while I am here.

Quite a few of the businesses, restaurants, and stores are situated now along the New Circle Road. Two universities reside in Lexington: Transylvania University, and the University of Kentucky. The areas of the city where these universities are located, are catered to by the local businesses there. So for an outsider, it appears that the city is made up of a number of distinct districts, which remain separate from each other, instead of blending together to make up a multi-layered city.

Sunday, August 4

The sun is shining as I start out on my first day of exploring. This day will consist of traveling to a number of sites in the south-central part of the state. My first stop will be the battle at Wildcat Mountain, located just south of Livingston, on US Highway 25. To get there, I head south on Interstate 75, to where it intersects with US 25, about 50 miles.

The landscape starts out as rolling hills and valleys, but by the time that I reach my turnoff near Wildcat Mountain, I have entered a mountainous region, known as the Rockcastle Hills. The mountains here are not particularly high, but very close together.

Reaching the interchange with US Highway 25, I turn off of the interstate onto this road. The road climbs and descends the numerous hills as I move towards my destination. I drive south through Livingston for another six miles, until I see a marker indicating the way to Wildcat Mountain. There appears to be very little population in this area, and the landscape is mainly forested.

I turn east off of US 25, and drive on a single vehicle road through the woods. As I move along at about 10 mph, the fastest that I want to try to go on this path, the road has leveled out. The side of a mountain runs parallel to me, and ascends immediately on my left. I notice a sign next to it that indicates that I am on the Old Wilderness Road, the wagon road used by the pioneers to climb up the mountain. As I continue on, I see many other trails leading off into the forest, on my left. The remains of some of these paths are visible to me underneath the canopy of trees that grow on the side of the prominence. These trails became multiple paths across the mountain. For as more people traveled the road, more ruts developed. Situated amongst mountains, any rainfall created streams that would roll down the road, and eventually wash it away. So every so often, the road would have been moved, or as was more likely to have happened, a new part of the road would have been cut out of the wilderness. This highway, now a small gravel road, was the main route from Virginia, northward from the Cumberland Gap, which led into the heartland of Kentucky. Daniel Boone was one of the first developers and principal users of this roadway.

Continuing on, the road starts its ascent, hopefully up Wildcat Mountain. I say this because other than one sign early on, pointing the way towards the mountain, I have not seen any more markers stating that I am still on the right path. At no time have I been able to get a clear view of the mountain because of the closeness of the land, and also because the trees are blocking my ability to see very far into the distance. The road has narrowed down further, and contains more gravel. But this gravel soon gives way to larger stones and rocks as I climb farther up the mountain. This road is obviously not used much.

As I drive on, it crosses my mind, a number of times, that I have missed the battle site, for I have still not seen any sign telling me that I have reached the battlefield. This thought of having passed the site becomes more evident when the ground levels out again, and I come to a small clearing. A house is located on the left side of the road, against the mountainside, and a barn has been built on the right side. A fence runs perpendicular to, then along the roadside, and it kind of blocks my ability to see beyond it. I am not sure if I am at the end of the road and have entered someone's driveway, or if the road continues on past it.

As I get up to the buildings, I can now see that the road does continue on, and so do I, still not sure if I have passed the battlefield or not. As I drive next to the fence by the barn, I happen to glance over and see a dead snake strung over the top rail. I decide that this probably isn't a place where I want to stop to ask directions. I wonder if the snake has been set there temporarily, and the person who put it there will be retrieving it later, and for what purpose. Is it to be skinned, or possibly eaten? But I press on, and just beyond the barn, the road starts its ascent again, climbing higher and becoming one even less traveled by car.

Nearing the top of the mountain, a sign finally indicates that I am entering the Wildcat Mountain Battle Site. So I have made it. I have not missed the spot after all. It is unfortunate that there are not more visitors to this site, so that the road could be maintained better. But on the other hand, I am grateful that some group has decided that this site is important enough to warrant a road.

It turns out that the distance from the highway is two and a half miles, quite a length. It would have been nice if a sign at the entrance had indicated what the distance was, or if there had been more signs along the way to notify me that I was still headed in the right direction. Traveling at no more than 10 mph along this road, it has taken me about 20 minutes to ½ hour to reach here, which seemed considerably longer when I didn't know how far it was, or what I was even looking for. I will also find out, by looking at a map after returning from this trip, that I have been traveling north to this spot, not east, as I assume while I am here.

At the top of the mountain, there is an intersection with another road, forming a Y-junction. The trees are pushed back from the roadway here, so as I approach the crossroads, the markers are visible against the backdrop of the trees. A stone marker in the shape of a tombstone has been placed at the site. Two smaller rectangular ones are also here, one on each side of the larger one. Also, a large board has been erected that describes the battle that took place here, and some of the history of the site.

A Union camp was built here that straddled the Wilderness Road, the main road from Virginia at the time. The road climbed up Wildcat Mountain from the south, and descended it to the northwest. The road that descends the mountain to the northeast was known as the Blade Road. The camp was set up to obstruct any Confederate activity in the area, after they had taken Cumberland Gap, to the southeast.

The Confederates attacked the Union camp from the south, on the morning of October 21, 1861. This assault was repelled by the Federals. In the afternoon, the Confederates attacked again, but were repulsed for a second time. During the night, the Confederates withdrew back to the south.

The stone markers commemorate the battle and campsite, with the two smaller plaques indicating the regiments that were involved in the fight, one for the Union side, and the other for the Confederates. I expect that the campsite and surrounding area would have been cleared of trees during the time of the battle.

I walk back down the Wilderness Road about ¼ mile, in order to get a glimpse of the spot where first contact was made between the two armies. Glancing off to the east, which at this time I think is south, through an opening in the trees is a small plateau in the distance. This was where the battle started. After the initial skirmish there, the Union troops were pushed back towards the camp. It was there that they held and eventually beat back the Confederate attack.

Walking back towards the camp, I think about what camp life for the soldiers must have been like here before the skirmish. In the evening, campfires would have been lit amongst the surrounding tents, with the men mingling around them. Arriving at the intersection, I glance along the Wilderness Road as it continues down the north side of the mountain, meandering around a corner of brush, and out of my site. I think that it is amazing after all of these years that traces of this old pioneer road still exist. This piques my interest to the early history of Kentucky, and I want to find out more about the terrain of this southern part of the state. Why was the road selected over this mountain? Why has the road now been bypassed? As I think upon the pioneer history of Kentucky, and the people who walked this road over all of those years, I get in my car and head back to the highway.

As I reach the highway again, a trip that doesn't seem to take as long as it did on the way in, I notice a highway marker, and pull over to read it. It states that the Battle of Wildcat Mountain occurred a few miles to the north. The description though, is more on the pioneers that moved through this region, on their way to the open land in the central part of the state. It also shows some of the common routes that were used, when they became frequently used, and why they had evolved. The focus on history in this part of the state appears to be the early settlement of the land by Daniel Boone, and the people who came with him or just after him.

Moving on, my next point of interest is Barbourville, to the southeast of Wildcat Mountain. I continue south on US Highway 25 to London, where I get on State Highway 229. This route, I feel, will give me a more scenic drive than staying on US 25. It also angles down to the southeast, which will cut off some mileage, instead of me continuing south on US 25, then east on US Highway 25E.

The landscape to the south of London is less mountainous and more one of high rolling hills, like a valley where the floor of it isn't level. State 229 connects with US Highway 25E about two miles west of Barbourville. So turning east, I continue on to the town.

There isn't much activity in this small community on this sunny Sunday morning. I drive around the town to see if I can find any markers concerning the battle that occurred here. It had taken place on September 19, 1861. Confederates marched in from Cumberland Gap, to the south, to seize the town, and were met by a small home guard force. The home guards were quickly dispersed by the Confederates, who destroyed their camp, then returned to Cumberland Gap.

I find nothing here. So after enjoying a few moments of the scenery that surrounds the town, I move on. My next stop is to be Mill Springs, along the Cumberland River. While doing my planning for this site, I had a dilemma over where the battle had actually taken place. The fight is recognized both as Mill Springs and Logan's Cross Roads. Mill Springs lies on the south side of the Cumberland River, and Logan's Cross Roads is on the north side. It appears to me that the battle started on the north side, but continued on the south side. I cannot find Logan's Cross Roads on the road atlas, but Mill Springs is there. So, I assume that the major part of the fighting took place around Mill Springs, and that is where I have selected to go. If the battle had mostly been fought at Logan's Cross Roads, then I have no idea how to get there. My other concern is that if I go to the north side of the river, then it puts me out of the way for my last two stops of the day, which are also on the south side of the Cumberland River. The crossings of the river are few and far between. So, I am hoping to find what I am looking for at Mill Springs.

I leave Barbourville on State Highway 6, heading west. For quite a long stretch, I am not sure if I am on the right highway or not, but I know that I am traveling west, so I continue on. One thing that I will find throughout this trip is that the highways of Kentucky are not well marked. I will encounter a number of times where I will either miss the highway that I am looking for, will not find it at all, or will not be sure if I am still on the same road that I started out on. It almost seems as if the state doesn't expect any visitors, that the only people that travel the roads are locals, and they already know where everything is. This will be very frustrating for me at times.

Driving through the mountainous region that resides to the west of Barbourville, I eventually meet up with State Highway 26, which goes north to Corbin. At Corbin, my plan is to get on State Highway 312, which will connect me with State Highway 192, and take me to Somerset. At Somerset, I want to go south on US Highway 27, to State Highway 90. State 90 will take me west to Mill Springs.

Unfortunately, I never do find State Highway 312, and after driving in circles for a few minutes looking for it, I select an alternate route in frustration. From Corbin, I take US Highway 25W southwest, to its intersection with State Highway 90. State 90 heads west, then northwest, then turns back southwest, where it passes by Mill Springs.

This drive takes me through Daniel Boone National Forest, which reminds me a lot of the similar mountainous terrain that I had encountered in Monongahela National Forest in West Virginia.

Although the mountains here aren't as high, I can still tell that I am traveling along high ground.

I arrive at Mill Springs by taking State Highway 1275 north from State Highway 90 at Touristville. Mill Springs today consists of nothing more than a Post Office at a Y-junction, with some old abandoned houses scattered about. It is hard to say how large the town was during the time of the Civil War, or since.

A marker exists right at the Y-junction, which states that Zollicoffer, the Confederate commander, had his headquarters a mile to the south of here. An old house, the Lanier House, is also here, but is not open, and looks like it is abandoned. But I cannot tell if fighting actually took place here, or somewhere in the vicinity. So, I drive around the area for a few minutes to see if I can find any other markers. But there are none.

A side road goes down to the river, and I take it to try to get a glimpse of the other side. Although there is very little habitation here, the road down to the river leads to a water playground. The road ends at the water, and the place is filled with boats, trailers, and trucks that are pulling them. This is now a docking point, and has become very commercial, with a gas station for boats, lots of docking facilities, and people. But what I am here for is to view the other side of the river, where I know that some skirmishing had taken place, and to try to put all of the commotion that is around me out of my mind. I want to think about how this place might have appeared during the time of the battle.

As I will find out after returning from this trip, the battle had actually been fought on the other side of the Cumberland River. In late 1861, Confederate General Felix Zollicoffer had set up a camp on the north side of the Cumberland River, at a place called Beech Grove. In January 1862, a Federal army arrived to the north of the Confederate camp, with plans of attacking it. Instead of waiting for this to occur, Zollicoffer decided to attack first.

Marching through rain and mud, the Confederates assaulted the Federal line on the morning of January 19, 1862. During the fierce fighting that took place as the heavy rain continued, Zollicoffer was killed while leading one of his brigades. Initially taking possession of ground in the center, the Confederate momentum started to fade. This was partially because many of them were using old flintlock muskets, and the powder had gotten wet. After three hours, the Federals counterattacked, and broke through the Confederate left flank. The Confederates then retreated across the river, using a small steamboat and some barges.

Since I have not been able to find anything related to the battle here at Mill Springs, I have to assume that the major part of the fighting had to have taken place on the other side of the river, at Logan's Cross Roads. I know that the Confederates had crossed the river here to escape after the battle, and there was probably some skirmishing in this area. But there does not appear to be any way for me to get over to that side of the river easily. However, even if I do go over to the north side, I am not sure if I would be able to find anything related to the battle. I have no idea where Logan's Cross Roads would have been. So, I content myself with peering over towards the area of the battlefield from the south side of the Cumberland River.

The river here is quite wide, probably about ½ mile. At the time of the fight, the river was swollen from rain. But I do not know if over the years, the river has actually become wider here, possibly because of damming, or if the river is about the same distance in width as in earlier times. The land on the other side of the river consists of what appears to be a dense forest of trees, which comes right up to the edge of the water. That side of the river does not seem to be inhabited at all. I stand here for a few minutes, looking at the land on the other side, and try to imagine the battle taking place over there, wondering if anyone on this side would have been able to hear the gunfire and commotion that was unfolding beyond the other shore. Under the bright afternoon sun, the heat is starting to get stifling. So, it is time to move on.

Getting back on State Highway 90, I continue west. My next stop is Burkesville, about 45 miles from Mill Springs, and on the same highway. As I drive along, I notice that the land in this region is flatter than I had encountered earlier in the day, to the east. The hills are not as high, and there are longer distances of flatness between them.

Arriving in Burkesville, I start looking for any marker as I drive towards the center of the town. A skirmish took place here on July 1, 1863, as Confederate General John Hunt Morgan started his cavalry raid. He had left Alexandria, Tennessee and crossed into Kentucky. His first encounter was here at Burkesville, against a Union cavalry unit. From this point, he continued on northward into Indiana, and then eastward through Ohio. I had been to the spot where his raid had ended, Buffington Island on the Ohio-West Virginia border, in June of last year. Now, I am at the spot where he first encountered the enemy.

In the center of town is the Courthouse, around which the road goes. I figure that if there were any markers pertaining to this skirmish, then they would be here. But I find nothing in the deserted core of this small town. So, I head to my last point of the day: Tompkinsville.

To get there, I continue west on State 90, until it meets with State Highway 100. Turning onto this road, it heads off to the southwest and goes through Tompkinsville. State 100 mainly winds its way amongst the cleavage of the mountains here. They are too close together to create a valley. Thus, the road does not follow a straight southwest direction.

Arriving in the town, I search around the main core to see if I can find any markers. Tompkinsville had been attacked by Confederate General John Hunt Morgan and his cavalry on a raid into Kentucky in July 1862, the year previous to his raid that included the town of Burkesville. The purpose of this raid was to destroy the supply lines of the Union. The town is about six miles from the Tennesee border, and a garrison of Federal soldiers was stationed here.

Not finding any markers in the downtown area, I know that Morgan had started in Tennessee, and therefore would have had to approach the town from the south. State Highway 163 heads south from Tompkinsville. Finding this road, I turn onto it. Sure enough, just a little way down this highway, I find a marker. The land here starts to rise up a hill as it leaves the town, and it seems that it was here where the Union garrison of tents and stores was located.

This completes my travel plan for the day. It is now after 4:00. I turn around to start my journey back to Lexington. Actually, it is only 3:00 here, for I have crossed the time zone into Central Time; something that I will do continuously over the week. But as far as I am concerned, I will run my schedule on Eastern Time, because that's where I will spend most of my trip.

There is no direct route back to Lexington from where I am. So, I will have to travel along two-lane highways in order to reach my destination. From Tompkinsville, I head north on State Highway 163 to Edmonton. Here, I get onto US Highway 68, which will lead me the rest of the way back to Lexington. During this drive, I pass by places that I will be visiting over the next couple of days: Perryville and Lebanon.

There are times along this highway when I don't believe that I am on a main road. As I will experience at different times throughout the week, it appears that some sections of the highways have probably not been updated since the '50s or '60s. Instead of broad shoulders to the roads, bordered by ditches, there are areas where the land comes right up to the road, where there is nowhere to pull off of the highway. During the week, I will hear advertisements on the radio about Kentucky having one of the highest rates of highway fatalities in the country. This I can believe, for if anyone tries to maneuver over these roads at high speeds, there is no way that they would be able to keep control.

One of the unexpected benefits of traveling along US 68 is the scenery as it crosses the Kentucky River, just southwest of Lexington. The roadway leaves the plateau above, and winds its way down the cliffs to the river below. Crossing the bridge and looking down and up the river, I see a waterway that is penned in by high cliffs on either side. The vista here is just awe-inspiring, and I am amazed at the beauty of the setting. Knowing that I will be coming back this way tomorrow, I climb up the cliffs on the other bank and continue homeward. Tomorrow though, I will stop and get some pictures of this sight.

As I drive along, I wonder how long the highway has been here. Certainly at the river, the road has been blasted out of the bedrock to get down to the water, and this is probably a more recent occurrence. But if this road had been the main road to Lexington in the previous century, how did the old highway make its way down to the river for crossing? This is one question that I will not find the answer for during the week.

Monday, August 5

Today will be spent visiting the battlefield at Perryville. If time permits, since I am never sure how long it will take me to visit a site, I will readjust my schedule and continue on to Lebanon, which is about 20 miles to the southwest of Perryville.

Reversing my trip of the previous evening, I head out of Lexington on US Highway 68. But first, I stop at the place where the highway crosses the Kentucky River, to get some pictures of the beautiful scenery that I had encountered yesterday.

The sun is just coming up over the cliffs in the east. The rays touch the water and steep rock face on the west side of the bridge, but not yet to the east of it. Therefore, on the east side of the bridge, the area is darker, and a fog hovers over the water. The west side however, is bright and fog-free. The cliffs do not ascend straight up from the water, but initially leave the river on about a 45° angle. Then they roll back on a less steep angle as they approach the apex, a total distance of probably over 200 feet. All of the rock here is completely enshrouded in greenery. There are only a few spots where I can see that there is actually solid rock beneath this vegetation.

After my brief stop to view nature at its best, I continue on towards Perryville. Arriving at the small town, I go to the Battlefield Site, and head for the Visitor Center and Museum. Here, I pick up a brochure of the park, watch a film that describes the battle, and view some of the items that are on display. Wandering through the section of books that are for sale, I find a booklet called *A Guide to the Perryville Battlefield*, prepared by the Perryville Battlefield State Historic Site. In it is a driving tour outside of the park, which includes parts of the battle beyond the park boundaries, and suggests that I start with the driving tour before doing the walking tour within park. Purchasing this booklet, I start out on the driving tour, to get a better understanding of the battle that unfolded here.

The battle took place on October 8, 1862. Union troops, coming out of Louisville, and commanded by General Don Carlos Buell, headed east to attack the army of Confederate General Braxton Bragg. The main Federal army moved southeast towards Perryville, while a diversionary wing headed east towards Frankfort. Bragg believed that the diversionary force was the main army, and prepared the larger part of his army to defend against it. A lesser army was positioned at Perryville, to attack what Bragg believed was a small Federal diversionary force when it arrived here.

The main Federal army moved towards Perryville on three separate roads, one corps on each. To the north was the Mackville Pike, in the center was the Springfield Pike, and to the south was the Lebanon Pike. During the night of October 7, the corps moving along the Springfield Pike approached Perryville. The area was dry, and lead elements pushed on to Doctor's Creek, west of the town, to get water. On a hill to the east of the creek, and overlooking it, were positioned two Confederate regiments. They fired at the approaching Federals, who retreated for cover. But as more Fedeal units arrived, they were positioned and attacked the Confederates on the high ground, forcing them to retreat back to the main line, about a mile closer to Perryville.

Bragg, thinking that he was still facing a diversionary force, wanted to attack the Federals along Springfield Pike. He placed his men north of the road and up to the Mackville Pike, in an effort to hit the Federal left flank. But as he was doing so, the northern Federal corps arrived along the Mackville Pike. Bragg then repositioned his army farther to the north, mostly north of the Mackville Pike, in order to attempt to still hit the Federal left flank.

In the early afternoon, the Confederates attacked, hitting the center of the northern corps. On the right end of the Confederate line, the initial assault was halted by the supporting guns of the Federal artillery, and the Confederates hid in the woods. Reinforcements then came up, and were also halted by the Federal guns. But the Confederates renewed their attack, reaching the high ground where the guns had been placed, and taking that position. On the left, the Confederate assault was also successful. The Federals then withdrew about a mile to the west.

The Confederates followed up their success, and continued to attack. But Federal resistance on the right halted the assault. On the left, some of the Confederates found a gap between the Federals along Mackville Pike, and those on Springfield Pike, and pushed into this opening. But, a few Federal units were sent from the center corps to plug the gap. However, most of the Federal troops in the center were kept occupied by a small Confederate force on the Springfield Pike.

Late in the afternoon, some Federal units pushed forward on the Springfield Pike, forcing the Confederates from their position near Doctor's Creek, and back into Perryville. The Federals pursued, and street fighting ensued temporarily, until the Federals were recalled back to their original position. In the meantime, the main Confederate attack, on the Mackville Pike, continued. The Federals withdrew again, about a mile to the west, and the Confederates followed. But this time, as nightfall closed in, the Federals were finally able to halt the Confederate attack.

Most of the Federal units remained unengaged during the battle. This was because Buell did not realize that heavy fighting was taking place along the Mackville Pike. A phenomenon known as acoustic shadow, whereby noise does not travel far, was in effect, and the sound of the battle did not reach Buell. Therefore, he did not send available units to where the fighting was. Realizing through the night that he faced a larger force than he thought, Bragg withdrew during the darkness.

The first stop on my driving tour is west of Perryville, along US Highway 150, just over two miles from town. This is the site of the Dorsey House, along what was known as the Springfield Pike. It was Union General Don Carlos Buell's headquarters during the battle. This road was traveled by Buell's III Corps, under General Gilbert. Here on the south side of the road, amongst the rolling hills of pasture, the majority of the soldiers attached to this corps bedded down on the night preceding the battle.

Stop No. 2, to the east, is where Doctor's Creek crosses the road. The Union troops followed the creek northward here in search of water. All of the rivers were low at this time, and some of the beds were dry. The finding of water was of as much importance as finding the enemy.

Doctor's Creek is at the bottom of a small ridge, which runs parallel to the stream on the east side of it. The top of the ridge was known as Peter's Hill. On the east side of Peter's Hill was another small stream, Bull Run. The Union army found water at Doctor's Creek, but Confederate soldiers on top of Peter's Hill were guarding it. The Federals decided to take and hold Peter's Hill, in order to gain access to the water. They pushed the Confederates from the heights, and across the valley of Bull Run, to the next hill, Bottom Hill. This was done by 3:00 a.m. in the early morning of October 8.

Standing atop Peter's Hill, and looking east, the terrain of pasture moves down to Bull Run, which cannot be seen because of the steepness of the hill, and up again to the top of Bottom Hill. The land does not descend and ascend smoothly, but in a series of small folds. Across this open ground, it would have been easy to spot the movements of the other side during daylight. Later in the morning, the Federals moved across this pasture to take Bottom Hill. The Confederates, who were ordered back towards Perryville, relented the hill to the Union troops, who were then ordered back to

Peter's Hill. This is where the III Corps would remain for the rest of the battle.

Stop 4 is located northwest of Perryville, on the Hayes-Mayes Road, formerly known as the Mackville Pike. I have to drive back to town in order to connect with that road. On top of the ridgeline, at Stop 4, was where the left of the main Confederate battle line was formed. It was positioned to attack what the Confederates thought was the left of the Union III Corps, not realizing that the I Corps had come down the Mackville Pike and set up their own line. Here, high above Perryville, the land is mainly flat, with some large but shallow dips. Groups of trees are scattered across the countryside of mostly open pasture, and the Confederate soldiers would probably have been able to see the Union troops that were formed in the distance.

The next stop is to the north, at the bottom of the hill. The H.P. Bottom House was located here, beside Doctor's Creek. On the west side of the creek was where the Federals set up their line. The Confederates charged westward in the afternoon of October 8, from atop the hill, down through the open fields, and into the main part of the I Corps positioned here. Today, this spot is very quiet; there is not even any noise from the still waters of the creek. But at this site in 1862, the thunderous commotion of hand-to-hand combat would have been everywhere across the lawn that exists here now. Within an hour though, the Union troops gave way to the onslaught of the Confederates, and withdrew up the hill to the west of the Bottom House to reform.

Stop 6 is at the crest of the hill above Doctor's Creek, where the Federals reformed after they were driven from the vicinity of the stream. This line did not remain formed for long. For the Confederates continued up the hill after the retreating Federals, attacking them again, and forcing them to move back further to the west.

Continuing west on what was the Mackville Pike, for about ½ mile, tracing the path taken by the Federals, I come to an intersection with Benton Road, and Stop 7. Just east of this intersection, at the remains of the Russell House, the Union troops set up their next, and last line of defense. Across the gently folding fields of pasture, the Confederates advanced. This time though, they were met with stronger resistance from the Union line. The field is completely wide open as it leads up here, to where the

Federal defenses were; a patch of woods lies in the background. The terrain would have created no hiding spots for the Confederates.

Driving northeast on Benton Road, for about ½ mile, I reach Stop 8, the left flank of the Union line of the I Corps, earlier in the day. Here atop a high hill, in the fields above the road, the Federals were more successful at holding off the initial Confederate onslaught than they were around the Bottom House. The Confederates advanced across the open fields of the next hill to the east, which is less elevated than the one that the Federals were positioned on here. This gave them quite an advantage over the oncoming Confederates. But as the Confederates drew close, the Union artillery could no longer depress their guns to fire at the advancing line.

Moving eastward, to the crest of the hill directly below the one at Stop 8, this is Stop 9, the initial Union line at the beginning of the afternoon. This line too, gave the Federals the advantage of high ground over the advancing Confederates, as the one later in the afternoon did, farther to the west. Here though, the Confederates not only had to climb the hill, but move through a wooded area as well, that grows on its side. The woods are not thick however, mainly consisting of deciduous trees. But it still would have presented an obstacle for the Confederate soldiers to deal with. After repulsing the first attack, the Union force moved back to the higher ground at Stop 8, where they prepared for the second assault, later in the afternoon.

At the bottom of the hill, with the intersection of the New Mackville Road, is Stop 10. This is where the Confederate cavalry charged up from the river, to the east, only to be met by a hail of gunfire from the Union left, positioned atop the hill. Running into this hail of bullets, the cavalry turned south onto the road, and headed away from the Federal line.

Turning right, and following the path that the Confederate cavalry had taken, I arrive at the entrance to the park. Returning now into the park, I continue with the walking tour, which is described in the park brochure.

Walking back to the entrance of the park, I come to Post 1. The ground here is slightly elevated from the rest of the land, both in front of me, looking east, and behind me, to the west. Across the road to the east, on level ground that is lower than that on which I am standing, crops are planted. Behind these crops is a line of trees. This vegetation blocks my view of the Chaplin River, and the accompanying cliffs on this side of the water. The Confederates crossed the river and climbed the cliffs in the early afternoon. In the farmland on the east side of the road, they assembled for their advance on the Union line, which would have been located behind me. The rise on which I am standing, would have blocked the view of the assembling Confederates from the Federal troops.

I turn around to face where the Federal line was situated, in the distance. The land slopes down from this hill, then rises again. It was along the rise that the Federals had set up their line. As the Confederates reached this spot, the Union troops, including artillery, opened up with devastating effect. Between this point and the bottom of the hill, the lead Confederate regiment, the 16th Tennessee, lost 200 men.

Walking northwest along the eastern perimeter of the park, to the northeast corner, I reach Post 2. It was here that Confederate artillery set up and fired quite effectively into the Federal ranks, as the Confederate infantry moved forward to attack that line. The land rises gradually from here for about 1/3 mile, towards the Union position. At the apex in the distance, Union cannon are visible. After the Confederate infantry captured that Federal artillery, the Confederate guns stationed here were moved up to that position.

Heading south across the lawn, I come to Post 3. Here, a zigzag rail fence runs along next to me as I near the marker. It would have extended the full length of the park during the battle, and separated a wooded area from a meadow. The Union line was located in the meadow, to the west, on higher ground. The Confederates would have moved through this wooded area in order to reach the fence. A scattering of trees has been planted where the woods used to be. This position is about half way between the crest, at Post 1, and the Union position. At this point, the Confederates still had a distance to cross before reaching the enemy lines. The rest of the way would have been over the open meadow.

Walking northwest, up the hill from the fence, I come to Post 4, known as Parson's Hill. Here, the Union artillery was located, giving a broad view of the landscape below to the east. The guns were placed just to the front of the crest. A clear line of sight across the open land gave the gunners here an excellent position from which to fire into the Confederate ranks, as they advanced from the woods at the fence line. However, as fate would have it, as the Confederates climbed over the fence and moved forward, the green troops of this artillery battery fled, allowing the Confederates to capture this position. This allowed the Confederates not only to bring up their own guns from their position located on the next rise to the east, but also to use these abandoned Union guns against the same men that they belonged to.

Continuing in a straight line that I started after leaving the fence, I come to the park boundary at Post 5, in the northwest, which was the left of the Union line. The men were positioned at the apex of the hill, which levels out part way down, before descending again. The inexperienced men stationed here collapsed and fled westward with the approach of the Confederates.

Moving now in a southerly direction, following along the line of battle of the Union troops, I reach Post 6, in The Cornfield. As the first line of Federals collapsed and moved westward, a second line had been waiting here in reserve, crouched in this cornfield. As the Confederates approached over the crest of the hill, to the east, the Union line stood and fired from within the rows of corn, surprising the unsuspecting Confederates. This however, did not stop the Confederate advance, and the Federal regiment moved back to their defensive line atop the next ridge to the west. That hill is where the Union line stopped the Confederate momentum, and which I had visited previously while on the driving tour.

Standing here in the cornfield, near the west end of it, I face east, as the Union soldiers would have done to fire their volley at the advancing Confederates. Today, the corn that is growing is short, as it is only August. The plants are spaced farther apart than usual, not as I would normally see them, and they do not appear to be planted in rows. I assume that this cornfield looks the way that it would have been on that day in 1862. Since I am not an expert in the ways of farming in the 1860s, I suppose that the corn was possibly sown by hand, thus having this appearance of being scattered about, and not of much density. Because the battle had taken place in October, I also must assume that the concealment of the Union troops had to be more from the height of the crop than from the density of the planting. For standing here, I do not feel that I would be able to hide from anyone, even by crouching down on the ground.

Looking across the cornfield towards the direction of the Confederate advance, a row of large trees marks the boundary of the field. The land here is not flat, but rises up a small mound, then rolls back down again, out of my sight. Waiting here for the Confederates, the Union troops would have had to hold their fire until the Confederate line had crested the hill before releasing their lead, not too far in the distance. For this is not a large cornfield.

Moving westward and crossing the road, Benton Road, I am following first in the steps of the retreating Union troops, and then those of the Confederate army, who pursued them. This brings me to Post 7, atop the hill, where the Union line held against repeated assaults. I have already been here, but in reaching these heights again, I have done so in the same fashion as the retreating and advancing armies had. The first time that I was here, my point of view was from that of the Union troops, who were already stationed here and waiting for the Confederate line to reach them across the open fields that lay below. This time, I have traced the route of the attacking Confederates, seeing the high ground from their point of view.

Walking to the southeast, across the hills and valleys that the land has formed here, I return to the Visitor Center, and Post 8, which is located beside it. This is the Confederate cemetery, where soldiers are laid to rest near where many of them fell, crossing this valley between the high ground to the east, upon which they had initially formed up, and the hill to the west, their goal of the Union position.

This completes my tour of Perryville. It is still early in the afternoon. So, I decide to continue down the road to Lebanon, after a quick bite to eat.

Lebanon is located about 20 miles southwest of Perryville, along US Highway 68. Arriving in the community, I start to look around for markers pertaining to the two skirmishes that took place here: one on July 12, 1862; the other a year later, on July 5, 1863. In both instances, the fights commenced by the raiding cavalry of General J.H. Morgan attacking the town. The larger fight occurred in 1863, against a Union garrison that was stationed here.

Not knowing exactly where to go, I start by driving down Main Street. Having been through here yesterday, I had not noticed any Civil War signs. But I still peer for any markers that may be posted. Nearing the center of town, I find one. This one indicates that during the Morgan raid of 1863, one of Morgan's brothers was killed while the raiders attacked the train depot. So, the battle had not occurred right at the marker.

I decide to drive around to see if I can find where the skirmish had actually taken place. Continuing down Main Street, I don't see any train station. I turn right onto State Highway 55, Spalding Avenue, which heads north out of town. I notice a small area between two streets, like a grassy median that divides a boulevard, except this median consists of gravel. I realize that this was the old railway tracks bed! Turning right again on Water Street, I follow this path back into the center of town. Here, I find the marker for the spot where the battle of Lebanon occurred in 1863. It indicates that as the fight unfolded, the Union troops barricaded themselves in the train depot. After seven hours of battling, the Federal soldiers finally gave up.

Today, the site where the depot was, about two blocks north of the spot where I had found the first marker on Main Street, is a parking lot. The land here that covers the railroad bed is a lawn. But looking off into the distance, I see in my mind the tracks of yesteryear, moving towards the horizon. I also try to picture the commotion that went on here at the train depot, as the Confederate raiders scurried around and attempted to dislodge the surrounded Union garrison.

Feeling good with myself for having used some sound deductions to find this spot, I get into the car to head back to Lexington, having now finished up my adventures for the day. I return again over the path of US Highway 68, traveling this route for the third time in 24 hours.

Tuesday, August 6

Having visited Lebanon yesterday, I have reviewed my itinerary to see how it should be adjusted. Today is to be spent visiting sites within a short distance of the Lexington area. Whereas the previous days had taken me far from my base in this city, today I will be circling around in the vicinity.

Departing from Lexington, I head northwest to Frankfort, by way of Interstate 64. Not knowing exactly where the battle had taken place here, I want to drive to the downtown area, to see if I can find out any information there. So, I follow the exit signs that indicate the way to the center of town. I turn onto US Highway 127, heading north. I am to the southwest of the city.

Located on the Kentucky River, Frankfort is surrounded by high hills. This hilly country exists only around Frankfort, in the central part of the state, and is in contrast to the rolling hills around Lexington, to the east, and Louisville, to the west. At US Highway 60, I turn east. As I near the central part of the city, the State Capitol building is on my right. Seeing a marker for the Kentucky Military History Museum, I decide that that would be a good place to start; the people there should know where the battle had taken place.

The museum is situated on East Main Street. It turns out to be in an old two-story building of red brick, which resembles, to a certain extent, the outlines of a castle. It has been built on the side of a hill. Main Street continues to the east, ascending up the hill and around a corner, away from downtown. This would have been the main road to Lexington during the war.

A marker is located next to the building. It indicates that the museum resides in the Old Arsenal. It was occupied by Union troops, but attacked and seized by the Confederates in September 1862, during the Confederate invasion that culminated with the battle at Perryville. The arsenal was recaptured by the Federals in October 1862, as they moved from Louisville to meet the Confederate invasion. So, this is where the battle had occurred, right here at the site of the arsenal. Thus, it is not necessary for me to inquire inside as to where the battle had taken place. The marker also indicates that a second skirmish took place here in 1864.

Looking north and northwest, the old part of the town is laid out below the site of the arsenal, with a large forested hill located behind it in the near distance. Since the central part of the town appears to be about ½ mile or more to the west, it seems to me that the arsenal was located a bit of a distance from what would have been the focal point of the city town during the time of the war. I would have expected the arsenal to be closer to the core.

Finishing here, and feeling that I will have more time to get in all of the sites that I want to visit today, I drive back over to the State Capitol. As I had passed this structure on my way into town, I was impressed by it. So, I want to take a few minutes and view it in more detail.

The Kentucky State Capitol is on the south side of the Kentucky River, away from the original part of the city. I cross over the bridge, and drive towards the building. The structure turns out to be a replica of the United States Capitol in Washington. A large grassy median runs down the middle of the street that leads up to the building. It contains a myriad of multicolored flowers, arranged in different plots. The outer side of the street is lined with a row of shade trees. The landscaping definitely adds to the stateliness of this grand structure, making this site very picturesque.

After a few moments of serenity at the State Capitol, I decide to see if there are any more markers, possibly located at the Courthouse. So, I drive back across the bridge to the downtown area. I do not find any signs, but what I do discover is a different perspective of the town, and its relation to the arsenal.

As it turns out, the Old State Capitol building is situated on Broadway Street. Looking to the southeast, the street rises partially up the slope of a hill, to connect with East Main Street, right at the site of the arsenal. So, the arsenal was not remotely located to the town. What I was looking at from the arsenal, was newer growth in the town, to the west. The main part of the town during the Civil War, including the State Capitol, was situated at the foot of the hill, guarded by the arsenal. The railway runs right along Broadway Street, and built just to the east of the Old State Capitol, was the train station. So, this would have been the center of activity and bustle during the war. Today, a few shops are located on the west side of the street, opposite the Capitol building. There is very little activity unfolding here on this midmorning. Now having a more thorough understanding of the city during the time of the war, it is time to move on to the next site.

I head east out of Frankfort on US Highway 60, past the Old Arsenal. As US 60 turns southeast on the outskirts of the city, I continue east on US Highway 460. At the east side of Georgetown, I veer to the northeast, onto US Highway 62. Traveling on this highway for about 20 miles, I come to the town of Cynthiana, my next stop.

The town is situated on the east side of the South Fork of Licking River. At the bridge that crosses the river into the town, sits a marker. The marker indicates that Colonel John Hunt Morgan attacked the Federal forces located here on July 18, 1862. This was a continuation of the Morgan cavalry raid that occurred in July

1862. I had already visited his raiding sites in Tomkinsville and Lebanon. His objective here was the railway depot, as it had been in Lebanon. The marker also indicates that Morgan, then a general, was defeated in the town on June 12, 1864. The land here is flat, and a good place for a cavalry engagement to occur. But not knowing if the battle had actually occurred right here at the bridge, I proceed into town to see if I can find any more markers.

Not finding anything along US 62, which heads off to the northeast from town, I return to Main Street, and turn north on US Highway 27. At the north end of town, where the road crosses the railway on an overpass, I find another marker concerning the 1862 raid.

Morgan's force had split up into three groups. The first two crossed at the bridge, back at the previous marker, and attacked the Federal forces in the center of the town. The third force came in from the north, along this road, and attacked the Federals from behind, hemming them in at the railroad depot, which was located near this marker. At the depot, the Union troops eventually surrendered, and Morgan moved on. This was actually the last town that was attacked by Morgan during the raid. After Cynthiana, he started back towards the Tennessee border. I have found no other markers related to the skirmish that occurred here in June of 1864, just the brief note on the marker by the river.

From Cynthiana, I drive south on US Highway 27, which turns southwest at Paris and continues on to Lexington. Coming in along the Paris Pike, the landscape consists of the rolling hills, the type of terrain that I had associated with Kentucky. This stretch includes many of the horse farms that Kentucky is famous for. The scenic beauty of this road is breathtaking: large farms set back from the road, nestled amongst the hills; huge shade trees growing on both sides of the narrow roadway, protecting it from the sun; and stone walls that trace along parallel to the highway. Of course with the rolling hills and darkened road, it makes the drive a bit dangerous, and I have to be aware of cars pulling out of laneways with minimum notification to me that they have done so. But traveling this pike is well worth it, because of the scenery that lies before me.

I have listed Lexington as one of the places where a battle, or skirmish, had occurred, and so a place that I want to visit. Not knowing where the fight had taken place, I to see if I can get some information at the Visitor Center. The building is located at the south end of the downtown core, on East Vine Street. So, I drive into the middle of town and track it down.

The person at the Visitor Center states that she is not aware of any battle that had taken place in Lexington. It had been occupied by the Confederates, but no fighting had occurred here. I thank her for the information, pick up a few brochures, and move on.

Looking through my reference material for a description of the fight that occurred in, or around Lexington, I cannot find any. I have no idea now, where I had gotten the information that a battle of some kind had taken place in Lexington, none of my books indicate that one had occurred here. So, onward I go.

The last site of the day is to be Richmond, about 20 miles southeast of Lexington. I decide that to go from Lexington to Richmond, I will travel on US Highway 25/421, instead of the interstate. The highway was the same route that the soldiers of both armies had traveled on, before and after the battle at Richmond.

The terrain along this route is hilly, but they are ones that are longer and higher than the gentler rolling landscape around Lexington. Since I am on high ground, I can see for farther distances than was the case around Lexington. Unfortunately, the highway connects to Interstate 75 about half way between Lexington and Richmond. This roadway doesn't have the same feel as traveling along the two-lane highway, so I stop observing my surroundings. I begin to wonder what the soldiers must have been thinking about as they marched along these roads. A few miles distant, I am able to get off of the Interstate again, and back on to the old highway. But, I decide just to continue on to Richmond on this warm sunny afternoon, for the two roads run parallel to each other.

I arrive in Richmond by exiting off of the Interstate, getting back on US Highway 25/421, and driving the short distance southeast into the city. I know that a self-guided driving tour brochure is available at City Hall, on Main Street. Thus, this becomes my first stop.

After orienting myself with the map and the sites, I head to the first station. The Battle of Richmond occurred on August 29-30, 1862. In the summer of 1862, two wings of Confederate General Braxton Bragg's army marched into Kentucky. His plan was to draw the Federal army into the open and destroy it, which hopefully would cause the people of Kentucky to side with the Confederate cause. The invasion would end with the Battle of Perryville, in October, at which point the Confederates withdrew back to Tennessee.

The first, east, wing was commanded by General Kirby Smith, and moved before the western wing, which was under Bragg himself. On August 29, Smith's wing descended from the mountains, to the south of Richmond, and into the rolling hills of the central part of the state. Advancing in front of the main force was the cavalry, which was attacked south of Richmond by Federal cavalry. The Federals drove their counterparts back into the main part of the army. The two sides then continued to skirmish until dark, when the Federals withdrew.

By the next morning, the Federal infantry had arrived, and positioned themselves in a line across the Lexington Pike, about seven miles southeast of Richmond. Early in the day, the Confederates moved up to confront the Federal position. But while waiting for all of the units to get into place, the Federals attacked. Concentrating on the Confederate line, the Federals did not pay attention to a reinforcing column of Confederates, which attacked the Federals on their right. The Federals then fell back to their original position. When the Confederates counterattacked, the Federal line broke, and the Federals retreated towards Richmond.

Federal General "Bull" Nelson arrived in Richmond in mid-afternoon, and started to reform his troops at the south end of Richmond, within a cemetery. At 5:00 p.m., the Confederates arrived in front of the Federal defenses, formed up, and attacked. After some heavy hand-to-hand combat in the cemetery, the Federals fled, moving through town to the north. But Smith had sent his cavalry around to the east and north, to get into the rear of the Federals. As the Federals approached the Confederate cavalry position, they were met with artillery fire. More than half of them quickly surrendered.

The driving tour includes stops at some preliminary fighting as well as the main event of August 29-30. The first station is located about 12 miles south of Richmond, at a place called Bighill. Driving out to the first stop, I encounter to my front, the beginning of the Cumberland Mountain range. The first height to be climbed over is named Big Hill.

Ascending to the top of the mountain, over a twisting road, I find Station 1. Here by the roadway, cut out of the forest that covers the mountain, the Confederate cavalry, preceding the advancing army, met the Union cavalry, which was heading south to find them. The fight here took place on August 23, 1862, a week before the battle at Richmond. The skirmish was won by the Confederates, who chased the Federals back towards Richmond.

The highway today is surrounded by heavy vegetation, hardly pushed back from the sides of the road. The highway of that time must have been even more condensed by the surrounding trees. I wonder how two opposing cavalry forces could have maneuvered about atop this dense vegetation, while at the same time fighting their foe. It is beyond my imagination that this could have been accomplished. But somehow, it was done; more effectively I guess, by the Confederates, who were victorious in this fight.

I turn around, since Stations 2 and 3 are situated about two miles north of Station 1. The Merrit-Jones Tavern, Station 2, was located here, a place for overnight lodging along the Old State Road. Wounded Confederate soldiers were brought to this place after the Battle of Richmond. The ones that died were buried in the adjacent Confederate Cemetery, Station 3.

Continuing north, and descending out of the Cumberland Mountains, I come to a marker along the side of the road that is not designated as a Station on the tour. The sign states the same information about the skirmish at Big Hill as the marker atop the mountain.

Here, the land opens up, and is flatter. It must have been a comfort to the Confederate soldiers to finally come down from the mountains, to get on more level and open ground, after having had to traipse up and down over that high ground. The downside to this relief was that they then had to fight.

Standing out on the highway, and looking southward, back towards the mountains, the road is visible for about ½ mile. It then disappears into a valley that splits two mountains. Those mountains rise on either side of the highway, creating a gateway to the heights beyond. Directly behind where the road disappears, but farther in the distance, rises the greenery of Big Hill, like a deterrent to travelers. This mountain cannot be sidestepped, like the two previous mountains in the foreground, but must be tackled and overcome head-on, welcoming the voyager to the mountainous region of Kentucky.

Stations 4 and 5 are located 12 miles north of the skirmish at Big Hill. On August 29, the Confederates crossed over Big Hill, and moved towards Richmond. The Union line was positioned at these stations. The Confederates, encountering these defenses late in the day, decided to wait until the next day to attack.

The Union position was formed along a ridge, which runs perpendicular to the road, on both sides of it. The landscape consists of open fields, with a scattering of trees. A small depression is created between the high ground here, and another hill, about ¼ mile to the south. In order to reach the Union line, the Confederates would have had to cross through this small depression. This would have given the Federal troops a height advantage over the approaching Confederates. The Union soldiers put up a good fight here, but were mostly new recruits, coming from around the Louisville area. Eventually though, they became no match for the more experienced troops of the Confederate army. So, the Federals eventually gave way and retreated back to Richmond, five miles to the north.

Station 5 is the Mt. Zion Christian Church, situated just behind the Union line, on the west side of the highway. It became a Federal hospital during the battle, but was eventually overrun by the advancing Confederates.

Station 6 is about half way between the initial fighting to the south, around Mt. Zion Church, and where the Federals took their next stand in Richmond. This is high ground, and should have been where the Union troops set up their next defensive position. But by the time that the retreating troops arrived here, it was too late to try to set up a line. So, they continued back to Richmond. Since nothing occurred here of importance, I don't understand why it has become a stopping point on the tour.

Arriving back in Richmond, Station 7 is located in the cemetery, on the south side of town, and on the west side of the highway. Here, General William Nelson arrived on the scene as the Union troops entered the town from the south. He quickly set up a defensive position in the cemetery. I find it interesting that during my trips, I have discovered that it was not an uncommon occurrence for part of a battle to be fought in a cemetery. This had been the case on my travels in Missouri, and other states. It is now happening again in Kentucky. My first thought is that I would have expected a cemetery to be considered hallowed and respected, and that fighting amongst the dead would not have been thought of. However, on the other hand, I suppose that in the middle of a battle, these pleasantries are probably of least concern for the commanders. But in the 1800s, rules and guidelines were more respected. I wonder what was considered proper, if anything, when dealing with cemeteries. I guess this is something that I should explore in the future, for I have not yet found an answer to this question.

Entering the cemetery, the Union was positioned near the north end of the grounds. A gravestone-type marker memorializes the battle that took place here. After the fight, the dead from both sides were buried here. The Federal troops were eventually moved to Camp Nelson, south of Nicholasville. The cemetery is flat, with a scattering of tall pine trees.

I look out across, and over, the tops of the gravestones that abound in the cemetery. They are not in rows, but seem to be placed in groupings, separated by small open areas. Each grouping consists of variable sizes and shapes of grave markers; no uniformity exists at all. Over and around these small obstacles, the Confederate army would have advanced. As I stand here at the Union defensive position, I can picture the Confederates advancing towards me; the gray line walking in step, grim faced, with their rifles protruding to their front, with bayonets attached.

I look now to my left, and picture the blue line of men extending off into the distance, preparing their rifles for the fight that is about to commence, concentrating on what they are about to do. In order to rally his troops, General Nelson, all 300 pounds of him, sat on a horse, riding up and down the line. As a confidence booster, he remarked that if the Confederates could not hit something as big as him, there was nothing for them to be afraid of. Of course, as usually happens with comments like that, he was almost immediately hit in the thigh with a bullet, and had to be removed from the field.

Station 8 is the Madison County Courthouse, situated on Main Street, and north of the cemetery. The Confederates sent the cavalry to the east, and around to the rear of the retreating Union army, in an attempt to cut off their withdrawal. The prisoners were taken to the Courthouse, and eventually paroled, which was the custom during the early stages of the war.

This concludes the tour of the Battle of Richmond. It also concludes my activities for the day, since it is now late in the afternoon. I am surprised that there is no station posted on the north side of town, where the Confederate cavalry had set up to stop the Federal retreat, or a drive along a road that follows the route that the cavalry had taken in order to get into the rear of the Federals. As I leave Richmond, on US Highway 25/421, to return to Lexington, I watch for any markers along the side of the road, which may indicate where the Confederate cavalry was positioned. I believe that I know where the area is, but as I pass by it, I do not see anything. Reaching the intersection with Interstate 75, I veer onto it, for a quick trip back to Lexington.

Wednesday, August 7

On this hot sunny day, my excursions will take me to the southwest of Lexington again, but this time beyond the Perryville and Lebanon region. The first stop is to be Munfordville. So, off I set early in the morning, first traveling west on US Highway 60, as I leave Lexington, then turning southwest onto the Blue Grass Parkway, 10 miles from the city. After about an hour, I reach the end of the Parkway, at Elizabethtown, and veer south onto Interstate 65. Munfordville is located 30 miles south of Elizabethtown. I exit the interstate, onto US Highway 31W, and head southeast towards the town, arriving in it from the north.

Driving along Main Street, I notice a small building on the right, with a sign that reads Hart County Historical Society. I figure that this is probably a good place to start, since I don't know where exactly the fighting took place in this town.

A couple of elderly ladies are inside this old structure, which I will come to find out was built in the 1890s. I tell them that I am interested in the Civil War battle that had occurred around here, and I wonder if they can direct me to its whereabouts. They respond affirmatively, that they are familiar with the battle. The remains of the old earthen fort, Fort Craig, are located about a mile south of the Green River, on Woodsonville Road. The fort is located behind a cemetery.

They then add that they have created a historical walking tour of their small town, and hand me the brochure. They talk briefly about what I would see if I went on the tour, and they appear to be very proud of the history of their little community. I commend them for enthusiasm.

I believe that more towns and villages should take an interest in what trials and tribulations their communities went through in order to reach the 1990s. Too many people grow up and live in a town all of their lives, but know nothing of the history of their surroundings. I have come to see that firsthand. Many of the places that I have visited, during my search for Civil War battlefields, have been tiny, where probably not much else has happened. Yet when I inquire about a skirmish that took place in the area, I, a stranger to those parts, have, in a lot of instances, end up knowing more about the battle, and history of the place, than do the local people. This is unfortunate. I think of the person in a small town in Missouri, who knew everything about what happened in his county, from a historical perspective. There should be more people like that. I believe that it is necessary to know the small, and some may think, unimportant details, as well as the major events. One should know the history that shaped their country or state, but one should also know their own local history. For this local history has probably had as much, or more, impact in shaping who they are today than has the broader history. In the case of the Civil War, although the major battles are what shaped the final outcome, the smaller skirmishes did have an impact. Thus, they need to be included, and understood, in order to get a full picture of how and why things turned out as they did. So, my hat is off to these ladies, and their attempt to preserve the history of their community.

Thanking them for their time and help, I step outside. Reviewing the walking tour brochure, I do not see anything in it that is directly related to the battle. So, I head on over to the battle site.

Munfordville is nestled right against the north shore of the Green River. The town is on a high hill, which rises sharply from the river, on the west side of Main Street. A cliff, at about the same elevation as the town, juts from the river on the south bank, and a bridge straddles the river at this height. The road, which is still US Highway 31W, curves to the right on the south side of the water. It has been slightly carved out of the cliff, so that the rock rises above it, and rounds off. Growing on top of this stone is the darkest green leafy vegetation that I have ever seen. It looks like some kind of large ivy that has gotten out of hand. It completely covers the ground, and is a nice pleasant change from just seeing rock. I think that this is a good idea, to have some nice looking vegetation, instead of just rock to view. I will find out later on, that this has been my first experience with kudzu.

Almost immediately after rounding the curve in the road, I come to Woodsonville Road, on the right. I turn onto it, and rise up a small knoll. There before me is the cemetery. I stop the car and get out. There are a few small grave markers scattered amongst this very unkempt spot. This is rather disappointing, to find a cemetery in such a disheveled way: the grass has not been mown for quite some time; weeds are growing where lawn should be; and some of the gravestones are not set upright.

Walking a few yards through the dew-covered grass, to the back of the cemetery, at the top of the knoll, a fenced-off section, and a marker, indicate that this spot was Fort Craig. It is not possible to enter the earthen fort. I would hope that there are future plans to possibly allow that to happen; perhaps after the area is cleaned up and the structure protected to prevent its destruction.

From where I stand, I can make out the earthen walls, which are about 3-4 feet in height; the remains of a ditch are still visible in front of the walls. The ditch and sides of the fort are completely covered in long grass. A number of trees are growing from the walls, and within the fort, completely shading the bastion. I cannot make out what the formation of the fort had been; it is obstructed from my view by the walls. A small flag, which appears to be a Confederate flag, is sitting atop a long thin pole, which is leaning to one side. The flag is drooped down, since there is no wind today.

The marker indicates that the battle took place here from September 14-17, 1862. The battle came about because of the movement of Confederate General Braxton Bragg into Kentucky, as part of the invasion of 1862. While General Kirby Smith advanced into the state to the east, through Richmond, Lexington, and Frankfort, Bragg commenced his advance through the western part of the state, headed for Louisville.

The first engagement for the western troops, here on September 14, was unplanned. Confederate troops, sent to destroy the railroad to the south, continued northward, and attacked the Union troops who occupied the fort. The attack was repulsed. Bragg then sent two larger forces, which surrounded the fort on September 16.

Land of the Pioneers

After realizing the size of the enemy force aligned against them, the Federals surrendered on September 17.

Looking south from the fort, the land is an open pasture of small ripples and folds, which become more prominent as the land continues into the distance. In the background is a line of forested hills, protecting this small valley. Across these fields, the Confederate soldiers would have marched, advancing towards their objective, and for some of them, their death. As I walk back through the cemetery towards the car, I notice some of the names and dates on the gravestones. It appears that some of the soldiers who died during the battle are buried here.

The ladies at the historical society had mentioned that part of the battle had taken place near the railway bridge, as well as at the fort. As I had crossed the highway bridge to this side of the river, I had peered off to my right, and saw large stone pillars, the only remains of a previous bridge. This, I take to be where the railroad had crossed. I makes sense to me that the fort here, on the southern side of the bridge, would have been built to guard the railroad, on its approach to Munfordville. An old road leads north from the cemetery, towards the river. So, I drive the short distance in that direction, trying to get to the bridge at the south side of the river. But I am not able to. The land here is all grown up with thick vegetation, and the old road ends before it reaches the river.

So, I drive back across the river to Munfordville. Just past the bridge, I can see a road, on my left, that goes down the hill, to a park next to the river. I drive down to the park, in order to examine the remains of the old bridge.

The supports tower over the grounds. They are about 30 feet in height. I stare up at the remains of the bridge, going over in my mind how this site would have looked during the time of the battle, and fighting taking place on the other side of the river. At this point, a train whistle goes off in the distance, adding an eerie effect to the scene that I am playing in my mind. It is as if the whistle was from a train out of the past, adding real sound effects to the images that are going through my head. A railroad bridge must still be here, but farther to the west.

In fact, I will find out later on, by reviewing the walking tour brochure that the ladies have given me, that the remains of the bridge, was part of the old highway that crossed here, and it was not the railroad bridge. On further investigation, I will discover that the railroad, and bridge over the river, are where they have always been, to the west of the town. So, I am not viewing where some of the fighting had taken place along the railroad. That had taken place on the south side of the river, and to the southwest of Fort Craig. But I do not know that while I am here.

The next stop is about three miles south, on US 31W. I have it listed as Rowlett's Station. The name on the map though, is Rowletts. I assume that this is the same place, but that the name has been modified over the years. As I drive south, my assumption seems to be verified, for the railroad is running parallel to the road. I am deducing that Rowlett's Station had been so named because it was a stop on the railway.

Arriving at this small hamlet, I find a marker on the east side of the road. The battle took place about 400 yards west of the road, on December 17, 1861. Federal troops crossed a pontoon bridge at Munfordville, and scouted southward. The advance was met here at Rowlett's Station by Confederates, who attacked. The Federals withdrew to a stronger position to await reinforcements. The Confederates then withdrew upon approach of these reinforcements.

The land here is mainly flat, for it sits atop a long low hill, which descends slightly in the north and south directions. On the west side of the road, a grassy field extends to a distance of about 100 yards, at which point a number of large deciduous trees block my ability to see beyond them. I look around to see if there are any roads or paths that I might be able to drive over, in an attempt to get back to the area where the skirmish had actually occurred. But I cannot see anything that will allow me a closer look.

While I was at the Visitors Center in Lexington yesterday, I had picked up a booklet entitled *Kentucky Heritage Tours*. It lists different driving tours that can be taken within Kentucky, and is based on various themes. There is a Daniel Boone tour, a Lincoln tour, and a number of others. One of the tours included is a Civil War Heritage. This tour indicates 25 stops around the state that are related to the Civil War. All of the sites listed in the book, I already have on my itinerary, or are not of interest to me, except one. This is the Battle at Tebb's Bend. I had noticed information on this battle in the *Kentucky Vacation Guide* that I have, but it does not describe where it is. Now I do have the directions that I need, and it turns out to be in the vicinity of Campbellsville, the area that I am concentrating on today. I had actually already been through the town on Sunday past, as I headed back to Lexington from my expedition to the southern part of the state. I now start back towards Campbellsville, in order to visit my next site, Tebb's Bend.

From Rowletts, I return towards Munfordville. Just before the bridge though, I turn east, onto State Highway 88. After a cross-country trek of just over 25 miles, I come to State Highway 61, just north of Greensburg, and turn south onto it. At Greensburg, I connect with US Highway 68, which takes me northeast to Campbellsville, about 10 miles away.

From the information that I have, I know that a guided-tour brochure is available at the Jacob Hiestand Stone House, on the western outskirts of the town. The battle site is about 10 miles south of Campbellsville, on State Highway 55, where it crosses the Green River. State 55 passes by Campbellsville on the west end of town, and I connect with it to reach the battlefield.

Just before the river, a road called the Romine Loop Road, which was part of the old Columbia Turnpike Road, turns off to the southwest. The battle occurred along this road. As I stated earlier, I have found that things are not always marked as well as they should be along the highways of Kentucky, and I miss the turnoff, because it is not identified. When I reach the Green River, I realize that I have gone too far, and backtrack. Of course, the road is marked coming from the southerly direction, and I am now ready to start my tour.

The battle took place on July 4, 1863, and was part of the raid through Kentucky and Ohio that cavalry Confederate General John H. Morgan undertook in July 1863. I had already visited some of his skirmishing sites in Tompkinsville and Lebanon. Morgan had camped just to the south on July 3. He planned on attacking the Federal garrison stationed here, which guarded the Green River bridge, on July 4. This he did. But after numerous assaults during the day, he failed in his efforts. He then crossed his men farther downstream, at Johnson Ford, and headed on to Campbellsville, bypassing the Federals here at Tebbs Bend.

The first stop is high on a hill, on the north side of the river. The hill drops off quickly to the right, and another hill ascends just as steeply beyond it, forming a ravine between the two. The two hills are open fields, but trees grow within the ravine, hiding it from view. The high open ground to the west was where the Union troops had set up their campsite, overlooking the Green River to the south, and the road leading up from it. A spring in the ravine was used by the men for gathering water, both for themselves and their horses.

The next stop is down at the bottom of the hill, near where the bridge crosses the river. A stage coach stop was located here, which was used as a hospital during the battle. The building still exists, but not in its original form.

The bridge at the river is the following point of interest. A narrow one-lane structure, the bridge is now built using steel beams of a rust color. During the battle, a small Federal force defended the bridge from a cavalry attack by the Confederates, while the main battle took place on a plateau above them, on the other side of the river, to the southeast. The Union soldiers were aligned along the north bank, as well as by the bridge. The river is a muddy piece of water, and it doesn't appear to have any current at all. The defensive effort by the Federals prevented the Confederates from taking the bridge.

Crossing to the south side of the river, the road immediately makes a 90° turn to the west, ascending up the side of a cliff. It is difficult to see how a cavalry unit, descending this road, would have been able to get close enough to attack the bridge. Going down the side of the rock face, the Confederates would have been completely vulnerable to fire from the Federals, and would not have had any maneuverability with their horses on this narrow ledge. Springs run down the side of the rock. The water was gathered by the soldiers for their use.

Near the apex of the cliff, the road turns south, and I complete my climb to the top of the precipice, through a forest that completely enshrouds the road from the sun. The road then turns to the east, and I come back into the sunlight. I notice that am atop a large plateau. Not very far along, after exiting the woods, I stop at the site of the stockade. This had been burned during a previous Confederate raid. Since the Federals felt that this site could not be defended, they moved their line farther to the east.

The road angles to the southeast, and I come to the next stop, the Union defensive line. The line ran north from the road, down the hill to the river. The river does a 180° loop just to the west of the bridge, and comes back to the south of this position. A steep ravine runs near the river on the south side of the road. The Union line also ran south from the road, through the ravine to the river. Thus, the flanks of the Federals were protected by the river on both sides, making this spot very difficult to overrun, as it could not be flanked. The line was fortified with felled trees to the front.

I cannot see the ravine, or the river, to the south, because of the thickness of the vegetation that has grown up there. A house has been built on the north side of the road, where the land is above that of the road. Behind the house is a line of trees, which probably now extends all the way down to the river. This heavy forest would have existed during the time of the battle, making movement through it by the Confederates, during the attack, very difficult.

Looking up the road about ¼ mile, to where it bends to the left, that is where the Federals positioned a sharpshooter pit. The remains of it are no longer visible, since a house and lawn now reside on the site. After a number of attacks by the Confederates, the pit was eventually overrun, and the Federal sharpshooters retreated back to the main line. But the Confederates, after eight attempts over a three-hour period, were unable break through and hold the Union defensive line.

A flanking maneuver was tried by the Confederates, up the bluff on the south side. Looking down in the direction of that steep obstacle, I cannot comprehend how men were able to climb up through the entanglement of vegetation, and then have had energy left to attack a defended position. I am amazed by the audacity of these men.

Moving up to where the rifle pit had been located, the land here opens up in front of the position, which would have given the sharpshooters a direct line at the approaching Confederate force. The only thing that allowed the Confederates to take this trench was their numerical superiority.

Further up the road, to the southeast, is where the Confederate artillery was set up. This is high open ground, which would have allowed the guns to fire down towards the Union rifle pit. On the south side of the road, the thick woods continues its growth. But the rifle pit, on the north side, was in clear view of the artillery. A downside for the artillerymen here, was that they were close enough for the Federal sharpshooters to be able to pick them off, which is what happened, eventually silencing the guns.

The last two stops consist of the Confederate cemetery, which was created on land donated by a James Griffin, and the original site of the Griffin House, which has now been moved across the road to the Interpretive Center of the Green River State Park. The house was used as a hospital by the Confederates during the engagement.

This completes the list of sites that I want to visit today. It is still only early afternoon though, and since I am in the vicinity, I decide to visit Abraham Lincoln's birthplace. I feel that I have gotten to know him some, through the reading of his writings and speeches. This was one very remarkable man, and he came along at the right time in history in order to lead the country through a very difficult ordeal. I am not sure if anyone else could have done it, for he seems to have seen beyond the trials and tribulations of the day, and been able to focus on what really mattered. It is unfortunate that he died so quickly after the ending of the war, for I believe that that delayed the healing process of the country, some may argue for over 100 years, or maybe not even yet. Certainly, the history of the United States would have turned out different if he had remained alive. But I have come to have quite a bit of respect for the man, and what he did in order to preserve the country. His thoughts and decisions were always geared towards the betterment of it. So although I am mainly interested in the battlefields of the war, where the decisiveness of these fights ended up determining the outcome, I want to visit the birthplace of a man that I have come to know through his writings.

I return to Campbellsville, and get on State Highway 210. This takes me northwest, to Hodgenville, about 30 miles away. Lincoln's birthplace is located three miles south of Hodgenville, on US Highway 31E.

Pulling up to the Visitor Center, I go inside to pick up a brochure, and view the exhibits. One of the interesting things here is the genealogy of Lincoln. After two generations, Lincoln's direct line of descendants is gone. His son married, but only had daughters. These daughters either did not marry, or married but had no children who survived. So now, there is no lineage left from this great man. I find that interesting.

The site consists of the grounds on which sat the farm where Lincoln was born, located on the west side of the highway, and an Environmental Study Area and trail, on the east side of the road. The farm contains a cabin, similar in structure to the one in which Lincoln was born. It is set atop a small hill, and enclosed in a marble and granite neo-classic memorial building. I believe that the cabin sits where the original one was built. A large granite staircase leads up to the building.

Entering the air-conditioned tomb, I immediately encounter the doorway into the small log home. Standing at the entranceway, I am surprisingly overcome with emotion. I am standing in the presence of the spirit of Abraham Lincoln, who inhabited this residence as a small child. I have goose bumps running up and down my arms. My mind goes back to that time around 1810, when Lincoln would have been a toddler running around the yard, and in and out of the cabin. I had not expected these emotions. I had only decided to visit this site since I had extra time from my travels. Now, I am standing where he had trodden so many years before, adding another dimension to my understanding of him, and coming to know the man even more.

I look inside this minute lodging, and see one room that served as kitchen, living room, bedroom, and all other types of rooms that now make up a present-day house. Here in this room, without privacy, the lives of the Lincoln family unfolded. I cannot comprehend daily life back in the days of the pioneers; what would have comprised living and working on a day-to-day basis for these people. I know that survival, in general, would have been quite high on the list of priorities. But why one would try to raise a family in this wilderness, I cannot understand without more study on the matter.

My bubble of being in the presence of Lincoln is burst by one of the park rangers, who is answering questions within the memorial building. I overhear her say that it is believed that this is not the cabin in which Lincoln was born, and lived for the first two years of his life. The structure located here is similar to the one in which Lincoln had resided, but it is not the original. Up until this point, I had believed that this was the cabin that the Lincolns had occupied. Although this somewhat disappoints me, and at first I feel that my emotions have been falsely aroused by a relic, pretending to be the real thing, I decide that overall, this doesn't make a difference. This is still the spot on which Lincoln spent some of his life, and I am now standing on these hallowed grounds.

Stepping out of the memorial building, I walk the grounds that made up the homestead. In front of the cabin site, at the bottom of the hill, is Sinking Spring. I'm not sure of its significance, except that it is probably where the Lincolns got their water. Glancing around, I am disappointed that the homestead is not in a similar condition to what it would have been during the time that the Lincolns resided here. The cabin is entombed in a memorial; the grounds are made up of lawn and large shade trees. I can't even imagine what the landscape would have been like during that time: whether it would have been open fields, or a small plot of land cut out of the forest.

Other than the cabin here, nothing else interests me. So I stroll over to the east side of the road, and the walking tour that has been set up here. The walk is about a mile in length, through the woods of Kentucky. What I will observe within this greenery are the resources that were available to the pioneers, which helped them survive from year to year.

At the entrance to the woods, a patch of small plants is growing. These are greens, such as sassafras and mint, that would have been used to make tea. Other plants identified here would have been used for medicinal purposes. Just inside the woods is a demonstration of corn, which would have been grown by the settlers, and the multiple uses that crop was used for, employing both the edible and non-edible parts of the plant for various purposes.

Further into the forest, I come across the old road that would have run by the Lincoln homestead. This was the only road through this area, and many a wagon would have rolled along its path during those early days. Now it is enclosed by the woodland; its purpose of no more need. Just beyond the old road is a large depression that contained a spring, up until the 1930s. This is something that the settlers would have looked for before deciding on where to select a site: a good natural spring.

The next stop is where a number of apple trees are growing. The apples are known as May apples, and the pioneers would have eaten these as part of the diet. Farther along the trail, it is noted that about 30 feet up a large oak tree, is a knot. The hardness of the tree, and the knot, presented a good piece of wood for making bowls and utensils. The next presentation is a display of the types of animals that would have been a source of food for the settlers. These include small animals, such as opossum and raccoon, and larger animals, such as deer and bison.

The second last stop discusses the white oak tree of the area, and its usefulness as a resource for cabin logs, fence rails, and fuel.

This stop puts me at the farthest point from the beginning of the trail. Continuing on in a kind of elongated circle, I start back towards my starting point. However, there are no other exhibits on the circuit back. I don't understand why almost all of the displays are at the far end of the trail. It is unnecessary to walk through the woods for a mile in order to get an idea of the type of terrain that the pioneers would have had to track through on a daily basis.

Having tread through quite a few pieces of woodland during my trips, I also have come to recognize when a trail has not been used much by the number of spider webs that I end up walking through. It doesn't take long for spiders to spin a web between two trees on either side of a path when there is not much traffic along it. I can tell that I have been the first one to follow this route in quite a while, for I end up walking along with one of my arms stretched in front of me, in order to notify me when I have encounter a web on the trail. This saves me from walking into it face first, or getting it all over my body and legs. The webs though, certainly come off easily, and are only a bit of an inconvenience. But this bother is not worth missing out on experiencing history. The last display, near the exit from the woods, shows the shagbark hickory tree, which was also prized by the settlers, and used for wagon parts and tool handles.

Finishing up here, and still having a bit of time left in the afternoon, I decide to drive over to the east side of Hodgenville, and visit Lincoln's Boyhood Home. Located about 10 miles from where Lincoln was born, this site was known by him as Knob Creek. So, I return to Hodgenville, then head northeast, continuing on US Highway 31E, to arrive at the site.

Another cabin, similar to the one located at the Lincoln Birthplace, is set up here. Of course, I would assume that this was the common sort of dwelling built by the settlers of the time, and Thomas Lincoln, Abraham's father, would have constructed a lodging of what he knew. Therefore, that would make this structure identical to the previous one. Lincoln had memories of the home here. I remember reading about his descriptions of helping his father plant crops on the seven acres located behind the homestead. The land here is flat, but is surrounded by a number of hills that shoot up out of the level ground. These high mounds obscure my ability to see very far into the distance in any direction.

Standing back a bit from the cottage, I am able to get a better view of the type of structure that it is. The outside walls are made of rough logs, which have been cut lengthwise, in order to give a flatness to them. In the middle of the front of the house is a small doorway. One small square window has been cut out of the right side of the wall; not quite centered between the doorway and the end of the cabin. Since the chimney is built on the right side of the house, this window would be located in the kitchen area. There are no other windows cut into the walls, front nor back. The walls reach a height of about seven feet, and the roof extends up for about another three or four feet. The roof is covered by wooden shingles. The chimney is an odd curiosity. It is made out of wooden logs, and has a large square base of about three feet. From a height of about three feet, each successive row of logs is shorter than the previous one, eventually becoming a small chimney top, which extends from just below the top of the roof to a height of about ½ foot above the roof.

Walking behind the cabin, the land that Lincoln would have toiled over with his father is laid out in front of me. Today, it contains a meadow that has been recently mown; the rolled hay still lies scattered in the field. The land is hemmed in on both sides by high steep tree-covered hills, which angle in towards each other at the back of the field, creating kind of a triangular-shaped field. Knob Creek, hidden by a forest that continues on up and over the hill, runs along the east side of the property. I can picture the young boy, walking along with his father as he tries to plow the land, falling back once in a while as he stops to remove rocks from where the plow has turned the soil. Even though the farm consisted of 228 acres, the seven acres here that were cultivated, would have been what the Lincolns subsisted off of. They remained at this site for about five years. Thomas Lincoln then again moved his family, this time to Indiana.

Returning to the front of the cottage, I take in the view of what young Lincoln would have seen every day of his life here. The house is on the north side of the road, and the front faces southeast, as the highway here runs northeast-southwest. On the far side of the road, a medium-sized hill protrudes upward out of the level ground; another one is located to the south of the first. A small creek runs along the bottom of the hill. I wonder how many times the young boy fished the creek, or rambunctiously climbed the rock monuments, which were just waiting to be challenged by a lad of Lincoln's age.

Getting in my car and starting eastward, back towards Lexington, I stop about a mile from the homestead, get out, and look back from where I have just come. The road skirts the south side of a hill. To the south, another hill rises, creating a pass that travelers must move through. To the rear of this pass, another distant hill closes off the opening created by the two nearer mounds, eliminating my ability to see very far into the distance. Here at this location, the sun would have risen late and set early, caused by the hills towering over the small cabin.

I now continue northeast towards Bardstown, about 20 miles, where I get back on the Blue Grass Parkway, heading east. This will take me the rest of the way to Lexington. This has turned out to be a more interesting day than I had anticipated, with the Lincoln sites adding extra effect to the battle sites that I visited earlier in the day.

Thursday, August 8

This day is planned for an excursion to the mountainous terrain of the eastern part of the state. My first stop is to be the battle at Middle Creek, just west of Prestonsburg. I leave Lexington, driving eastward on Interstate 64, until I reach the Combs Mountain Parkway, 16 miles distant. Getting onto this road, which runs mainly in a southeast direction, I continue on until it ends, 77 miles later. I am not very far out of Lexington before the terrain starts getting hilly, then becomes mountainous. The parkway cuts through the rock, thus allowing the vehicles to maintain a high speed. This is good for me, because the trip to Prestonsburg is going to take about two hours. The parkway ends at its meeting with US Highway 460, and I move onto this road, continuing to move to the southeast. After two miles though, the highway turns to the northeast. But State Highway 114 heads towards Prestonsburg, and I veer off onto this road, heading towards the town, 15 miles away.

As I near Prestonburg, I notice a marker on the south side of the road, in a small flat field. It is related to the Battle of Middle Creek. This tiny piece of land is the only level terrain in the vicinity. Large rocky hills, overgrown with vegetation, erupt upwards all around. The roadway continues onwards as a twisting snake, maneuvering between these uprisings. Middle Creek runs along the back edge of the field, at the bottom of one of the hills, creating another obstacle for the two armies that met here. So, on this small flat piece of open space is where the battle had been fought. By my deduction, it was the only place where the two armies could have met. Everything else appears to be an obstacle to advancement, by either army.

The battle was fought here on January 10, 1862. The Confederates had occupied Kentucky starting in September 1861, even though the state had claimed neutrality. Union troops then moved in to displace them. The eastern mountain region of Kentucky wasn't controlled by the Confederates until December, and the Federals also attempted to counter this movement.

The Confederates set up a defensive line in the hills that I am standing amongst, especially on the south side of the road. Even though it would have been more pleasant to fight on this flat piece of soil, the Union forces had to climb up into the wooded hills in order to dislodge the defenders. The Federals came from the east, through Prestonsburg. I look eastward, from where the Federals would have approached. How they were able to accomplish the removal of the Confederate soldiers from these rises, I cannot understand. How they were even able to maneuver amongst these hillsides, I cannot comprehend either. It would appear to me that the Confederates, defending these steep hillsides, would have had the advantage, and there would have been no way to dislodge those troops. But somehow, with a lot of tenacity, it was accomplished.

The next site that I want to visit, I only have a rough idea of where it is. The place is called Ivy Mountain. I know that it is somewhere to the south of Prestonsburg, and in Floyd County. So I drive into the town, and search for a Visitor Center, or such. What I find is the Floyd County Chamber of Commerce.

Going inside, I inquire to two ladies who are present, if they know where Ivy Mountain is located. They respond that they do not, but then ask a gentleman in the back room if he is familiar with the site of Ivy Mountain. He says that he knows of it, because a Civil War battle had taken place there. I tell him that that is the reason that I am looking for it, and wonder if he can direct me there. He says that he can, but first he thinks that he may have some information related to the battle that I can have, since I have no facts about the fight.

In a book entitled *Floyd County Sesquicentennial*, he finds a chapter describing the battle at Ivy Mountain. He says that Ivy Mountain is about 13 miles south of here. One of the pages that he has photocopied for me shows a picture of the mountain in the 1930s. He continues that the picture is not a good indicator of how the mountain looks today, because in recent years, the side of it has been excavated in order to widen the highway. He tells me that there is no marker there, but to watch for a service station and restaurant. Thanking him for the information, I set out to find the mountain.

The site is located towards Pikeville, to the southeast, and I depart Prestonsburg on US Highway 23. Counting off 12 miles, I start looking for signs that will indicate to me which mountain is Ivy Mountain, for as I drive along, the highway skirts one mountain after another. From the picture that I've seen, I know that the mountain will be on the left. Since the photo was taken from the south, I will have to look behind me to ascertain if I have found the correct summit. After a false discovery, because there isn't a service station and restaurant here, the next mountain seems to have all of the indicators that it is Ivy Mountain. Turning left onto a side road, I get out of the car to wander around and try to ascertain if this is in fact the correct site or not. Running next to the side road is a small creek, which continues under the main highway and into the Big Sandy River, on the west side of it. The name of the creek is Ivy Creek. I have found the mountain.

I then pull out the description of the battle that had been given me, and read it. The fight had occurred here on November 8, 1861. A Confederate force had been operating in the Prestonsburg area, trying to recruit the local population into joining the army. A Federal force was sent from Louisa, situated to the north, along the Kentucky-West Virginia border, with the purpose of chasing the Confederates out of Kentucky. Leaving Prestonsburg as the Union troops approached, the Confederates set up a defensive position at the narrows of Ivy Mountain, by the mouth of Ivy Creek, and on the north side of it. A bridge over the creek was to be their escape route. After a little more than an hour, the Confederates were beaten by the larger Federal force, and fell back, eventually retreating into Virginia. They returned to the area in January, to continue their recruiting efforts, and were chased out again, after the battle at Middle Creek.

The Confederates had selected a good position to set up their defenses. Running along the west side of the main road is the Big Sandy River; this region known as Big Sandy. The river, flowing northward, runs up to the south side of Ivy Mountain and skirts it to the west, creating a 90° elbow as it starts its course around the mountain. The road follows next to the river, around the rocky obstacle, but at a higher elevation, so it is cut more out of the side of the mountain. The battle description says the road was at a height of 25 feet above the river. As the road comes out of the elbow curve at the base of the mountain, and continues its route southward, it immediately must cross Ivy Creek, which flows west into Big Sandy River. The creek runs in the valley between Ivy Mountain and the next mountain to the south. A bridge would have crossed the creek then. Now, it flows within a culvert that goes beneath the highway. If I hadn't stopped at this point, I never would have known that a creek was present here, since it is enshrouded by bushes and shrubs. Except for the highway, and some residences that line it, the rest of the landscape consists of rock and forest. To the west of Big Sandy, mountains immediately rise from the edge of the water. About 1/3 of Ivy Mountain has been excavated to widen the highway. The south side of the hill is now a cliff, rising about 2/3 of the way up.

The Union troops, having to march down the narrow road that existed then, would have been hemmed in by the river and the mountain, and would not have been aware in advance that the Confederates were located here, until they rounded the bend in the road. By then, it was too late; the Confederates would have started shooting. The Federals did regroup though. With the help of cannon, which were eventually hauled to the top of the mountain and fired down into the ranks of the defenders, they did prevail.

This finishes with the sites that I have planned to visit today. However, as part of the description of the battle at Ivy Mountain, it mentions that a preliminary skirmish had been fought at West Liberty. It is now only late in the morning. So, I decide to stop by the town of West Liberty on my way back to Lexington, and see if anything is there. It will also give me an excuse to take a different route back, and see some of the rest of the eastern part of the state.

I usually like to take circuitous routes when possible, instead of just driving over the same ground twice.

I retrace my route to the outskirts of Prestonsburg, and turn west back onto State Highway 114. As I climb up the side of a mountain, with the town off to the east, I notice a marker on the side of the highway, and pull over to read it. It indicates that General Morgan had visited this area during his raid through Kentucky in 1864, and that he had also come through here during his retreat after the battle at Mount Sterling. Since I am not aware that fighting had taken place at Mount Sterling, I now have another site to visit. Looking on my map, I find that after visiting West Liberty, I can continue on to Mount Sterling, on my way back to Lexington. This will work out pretty well.

I continue my trek west on State 114, which merges into US Highway 460 just before the Combs Mountain Parkway. But instead of turning back onto the parkway, I continue in my northwest direction on US 460. The two highways mostly run parallel to each other, 20 miles apart.

Arriving at West Liberty after about 25 miles, I enter it from the east. At the center of town, the highway turns south onto Main Street, and I follow this path. On this street, I find a marker that describes the skirmish that took place here. The battle occurred on October 23, 1861, as Federal forces routed the Confederates, who were operating in the area. The Confederates moved back to the Prestonsburg area, from where they again had to depart after the Battle of Ivy Mountain.

Continuing generally westward on US Highway 460, first southwest, then turning to the northwest, I head for Mount Sterling through the mountains and hills, 50 miles away. Coming into the town from the south, I head for the downtown area, to see if I can find any markers.

Arriving at the Courthouse, a marker here indicates that Morgan had taken the town during his raid in 1863. But there isn't any marker pertaining to the fight that had taken place in 1864. Knowing that the Confederate forces had left the town heading south, I think that maybe they had entered the town from the west. So, I drive in that direction along Main Street, US Highway 60.

At the intersection of US 60 and State Highway 686, which circles the town on the west side, I find a marker. The marker states that US troops had found the Confederates camped by Camargo, which is about six miles south of Mount Sterling, and along US Highway 460. Thus, I had passed through it on my way to Mount Sterling. They then pushed the Confederates northward, and through Mount Sterling. The Confederates had turned eastward and retreated. This was on June 9, 1864. But the marker does not imply that any skirmish had actually taken place here; it seems to be describing the fight in general. I had not seen any marker at Camargo.

So, having found no evidence of where fighting had actually taken place around Mount Sterling, and not having any more sites to visit today, it is time to return to Lexington. I take State 686 north, until it meets US Highway 460, where I turn north onto it. Within a short distance, I intersect with Interstate 64 and get on it, heading west, for a quick trip back to Lexington.

As I drive along, the sun becomes blocked by dark clouds, and a quick, but heavy, shower pours down on me. Fifteen miles along, I pass the beginning of the Combs Mountain Parkway. I have come full circle within 15 miles of Lexington, after a full day of discovering Civil War battlefields. Nearing the city, the sun breaks out again, and begins to dry the wet roads.

Friday, August 9

I have finished visiting all of the sites that I had set out to find over the past week, partially because the weather had cooperated fully, with each day bringing sunshine and warmth. So, I now have a day in which to relax, and do a bit of driving around locally. Since Mary Todd Lincoln had been born and raised in Lexington, one of the things that I decide to do is visit the house where she grew up, and perhaps get more insight into my knowledge of Lincoln and his family. This stop will turn out to be more informative than I had expected.

The house is located on the southeast corner of Main and Jefferson Streets, just north of the downtown core. It is a large red-brick two-story structure, which is built right next to the street. In the center of the house, on the lower level, is a white doorway, with four steps leading up to it from the street. On each side of the door are two large windows, painted in white, with black shutters. The second story façade is identical to the first, except another window resides in the center, where the door occupies that space on the ground level. Two large trees shade the front of the house from the noises of the street. The residence is quite wide, and three windows adorn each of the two levels on the side of it, but without the shutters. Two smaller windows are built into the gable. On the outer sides of these small windows, a square brick chimney extends from the roof. An extension to the house has been built on the back, along Jefferson Street. It appears to be about 1½ stories, instead of the two stories that make up the main house. The two windows that occupy the first floor are the same size as the others, but the ones in the upper level are smaller, like the ones on the main house within the gable. The roof of this extension starts at about midpoint of the second story windows of the main house. This is topped by a roof that is not as steep as the main roof, and a rectangular chimney protrudes from it, at the far end. A brick wall of about eight feet in height continues down Jefferson Street, to the end of the block. The street has a small downward slope to it. The foundation of the house is made out of gray stone, and three small white windows are cut into the side of it, along Jefferson Street. This would have been a very large building during the mid-1800s, and the Todd family must have been well off in order to afford a place such as this.

    I find it an interesting contrast between this house and the one in which Lincoln grew up. They could not be more different. Where Mary Todd had enjoyed luxury, Abraham Lincoln had grown up in poverty. The paths taken by these two people of opposite upbringings, in order to meet and marry, must have been quite fascinating, and now I am intrigued to find out how this happening had occurred. What had happened in order for Mary to fancy someone with the upbringing of Lincoln? What had been Lincoln's course through life, for Mary to have taken an interest in him? I would like to find these things out.

    Entering the house, I am in the main hallway, bordered by dark wood. A stairway leads up to the second floor. Openings along both walls of the main floor are entrances into other rooms. I am greeted by a couple of ladies, who welcome me to the house. One of them will be my tour guide as I examine the contents of the residence. Since there are no other people present, the tour will be specifically for my benefit. This will turn out to be very advantageous, for the conversation that we will have, as we wander through the house, will be a one-on-one session. It will thus allow me to learn more about Mary, and get my specific questions answered.

Before my tour commences, I explain to the ladies that I am not interested in Mary Todd Lincoln herself. My interest is in the Civil War, and therefore Lincoln's role in it. Thus, I would like to learn about the impact, and influence, that Mary may have had on Lincoln during this time. So, I am more interested in finding out about Mary the person, than in looking at where she grew up, and the furniture of the house.

So, as my hostess moves me towards the first room of the house, she starts to describe the family, and Mary's upbringing. Mr. Todd was a lawyer and a businessman. He had moved his family into this house in 1832. This was not where Mary was born, or had spent her early years of life. She was about 14 when the family relocated here.

As a prominent member of the community, Mr. Todd often held dinner parties, which included many political guests, which included Henry Clay. I comment that in my readings on Lincoln, much of his early thinking seemed to be formulated by Henry Clay. Lincoln had often talked about the leadership of Clay in politics, and tried to emulate the man. I say that Lincoln's awareness of Mary's connections to Clay must have been very exciting to him. To which my hostess agrees.

But Lincoln had very little opportunity to visit the Todd House, and was actually here only three times. While here, Lincoln would sit for hours, reading through the many books that were in the library. She states that Mr. Todd was very open about allowing the women, and particularly Mary, to remain in the dining room after the dinner, to partake in the conversations. His stipulation was that if Mary participated in the discussions, she would have to stand on her own ground, and not become overly emotional. To this Mary agreed, and often was involved in these conversations. She also was well educated, going as far in school as was permitted for girls. Females were not able to attend college. But, her connections to some of the professors at Transylvania University allowed her to continue her pursuit of knowledge. Even though she could not attend classes, the professors would give her the books that were used for the courses, so she could study at home. She would even take the exams, although there would never be any official recognition of her marks.

The sitting room is located next to the street, on the left side of the house. Of interest to me in this chamber is the size of the furniture used for sitting; it is especially small. There is one chair in which the seat is about two feet from the floor, and looks like there is only enough room to sit a doll on it. My guide explains to me that all of this furniture was used by adults. She says that the average woman in the 1860s did not even reach five feet in height, and usually had a very small frame. Mary was not a tall person. With Lincoln raising above six feet, a height that would have been uncommon back then, they made a very odd-looking couple when standing side-by-side.

Moving on to the other rooms, we continue our conversation about Mary. Because of the discussions that she had been involved in with Clay and others, her thinking was very liberal on slavery. I ask my hostess if she believes that Mary had quite a bit of influence over Lincoln. She responds affirmatively, and continues that Mary understood the issues of the day, and would have let Lincoln know how she felt. I say that I find that interesting. For although I don't know much about Mary, which is the reason why I am here, I have never read anything that would have given me any kind of indication that Mary may have had an influence on Lincoln when it came to affairs of state. My impression of her, up to now, is that she was not a major player during the war, and had not figured much in the shaping of history. My hostess says that no, this had not been the case.

As we climb the back stairs, from the kitchen to the second floor, for there are two ways of getting upstairs from the main floor, the discussion brings me to the question about what kind of marriage the Lincoln's had. I say that from the writings that Lincoln had made, I could tell that he very much loved Mary, but that I wasn't sure if this was reciprocated. I continue that I know that Lincoln's death had devastated Mary, and that she never did fully recover from it. This gives me the impression that there was a deep love there. But it is an area that I have not gotten much information on. My hostess replies that Mary indeed loved and adored Lincoln immensely. His death did affect her, and for awhile, she was devastated by it. But she was also strong. The family did have its share of bad luck: the Lincolns had buried three sons due to illness, and then Mary lost her husband as well. So even though there had been losses of loved ones to her over the years, she was strong enough to overcome them. Later in life, Robert, the eldest son, had Mary placed in an asylum, believing that because of the grief that she had been going through, she had lost her mental capabilities. But this was not the case, and by writing letters to some prominent people, she was able to have herself released.

The upstairs of the house consists of bedrooms, as is to be expected. One thing of note, on the back side of the master bedroom is the nursery. Going down a few steps, there is a short hallway of a few feet that leads across to the back section of the house. This opens onto a large room, where the smaller children slept and played. The young ones were expected to spend most of their time up here in the room, away from the adults. There were slaves whose duty it was to ensure that the children remained out of sight, and that noise would be kept to a minimum. The children remained in the nursery until they were old enough to occupy one of the many bedrooms. This arrangement could take place because as the older children got married, they would move off, creating a vacancy in one of the bedrooms. I mention that I think that it is a bit of poor planning to have the nursery, with multiple tots occupying the premises, so close to the master bedroom. I feel that with all of the noise that could disseminate from the room, I would have preferred that it probably be on the other side of the house from me. My guide explains that by the time the Todds would retire to the bedroom, the small ones would all be asleep. As well, for nursing purposes and sickness, it was preferable to have the children nearby.

My hostess indicates that on the topic of the older children getting married and moving out, there was quite a bit of worry for some time by the younger Todd women that they would be prevented from getting married and moving on. The custom of the time was that the daughters had to marry in order of age; the eldest having to wed first before the next eldest one was permitted to, etc. For a time, it did not appear that there were any suitors for Mary that she fancied. This created a problem for her sister. She had already met someone who she wanted to marry, but was prevented from doing so by the fact that Mary was older than her, and had no intention on becoming wed. The problem was finally alleviated when Mary moved to Springfield, Illinois, to live with her sister. By moving out of the house, even though not through marriage, this allowed her sister to wed. Of course, it was while in Springfield that Mary met Lincoln.

While in one of the guest bedrooms, the guide indicates that one of Mary's younger cousins was a frequent guest at the house, and often stayed in this bedroom. She then tells the story about the cousin, who had never met Mary, or her husband. While coming back on the train from a trip out of town, he arrived here at the Todd residence, and commenced to tell about this couple that had been in the same car as he was. He was quite upset. These two parents had done nothing to discipline their two unruly children, who had complete freedom to roam around the passenger car, creating as much noise and havoc as was humanly possible. As he was going on about how this family was so unruly, and he hoped that he never had to see them again, he happened to peer out of the window onto the street, and saw a carriage pull up with the Lincolns in it. For they were coming to visit. He pointed in shock that that was the family of whom he had been speaking. Upon seeing them getting out of the carriage, he said he refused to stay in the same house with such an disorderly bunch, and rushed out of the back door, remaining away from the house during the entire Lincoln visit.

I mention, while smiling at this story, that I had heard about the Lincoln children having complete control of the White House during the Lincoln term. My guide says that yes, it was not uncommon for the door to fly open during a meeting, and one of the boys to come rushing in, interrupting the conference. Lincoln would do nothing about this interruption but chuckle, and go on with the business at hand, usually to the consternation of the other members. She continues that neither Lincoln nor Mary believed in punishment, or in reeling in the enthusiasm of the boys. I find this interesting, since I think of those times as one in which society expected a heavy emphasis on strictness and discipline. There was an expectation of how people should behave, and certainly this thinking on chastisement by the Lincolns would have been quite an anomaly. I wonder how the Lincolns had arrived at this decision. But I know from what I have read, and heard, that I probably would not have had much patience for these small hellions. If I had been a friend of the Lincolns, I am sure that I probably would have dreaded seeing them coming for a visit accompanied by their children, as I know was the case with many of their friends.

My guide and I have arrived back at our starting point. Although she has given me details of the furniture in every room that we have visited, it is not the rooms themselves that have interested me. Except for a few oddities, there is not much here that I have not already seen in other houses from the era. My objective here has been to try to get to know more about Mary Todd Lincoln. Certainly, my hostess, who is very knowledgeable on this subject, has helped me to attain this goal. The conversations that we have had, as we wandered around the house, were very enjoyable. They have allowed me to form a picture of Mary as a person; someone whom I had not had much information on before this. I certainly come away from the tour with a much-improved picture of who Mary Todd Lincoln was, and have more respect for what she had achieved, even though she was a woman. I thank my guide for the enjoyable, and enlightening, time that I have had, and I am a little disappointed that this interesting conversation has come to an end.

At the door, she passes me a paper, which lists a number of books pertaining to Mary, and I thank her for it. But for now, my interest in finding out about Mary has been satisfied. My hostess mentions that the books listed on the page show Mary in a positive and, in her opinion, realistic light. She says that there are quite a few books that have been written about Mary that tend to accuse her of all of the wrong things that went on during the Lincoln administration. Some of the people who have written books about her, do not like her, and therefore have cast her as the reason for some of the misdeeds that occurred. I thank her again for the information. As I leave, I wonder if maybe the books on this list are biased towards ensuring that Mary is still not seen in a true light, only show the good side of her. The bottom line though, is that I will have to read some of them myself, and form my own opinion.

This now leaves me with the rest of the day to explore the environs of Lexington. Since the city is noted mainly for the horse farms that surround it, I decide to take a drive along one of the scenic routes, and enjoy the beauty of the area. I had picked up a map of Lexington during the week, and now study it, to decide in which direction to journey.

The map denotes what is called the Bluegrass Drive, which does a circuitous route around the northern part of the city. It also lists all of the locations of the major horse farms in the region. Having already been along part of the route, when I had returned from

Cynthiana on the Paris Pike, which runs northeast to Paris, I am not really interested in following the Bluegrass Drive. I notice that the Old Frankfort Pike is also lined with many horse farms. So I decide to go in that direction. The old pike is State Highway 1681, and it heads northwest out of Lexington, towards Frankfort.

The drive turns out to meet all of my expectations. I am having a pleasant afternoon in the country, following a road that traverses the rolling hills of the area. In quite a few places, the road is enshrouded by large shade trees, which grow along both sides of the road, creating almost a tunnel effect. The sun though, is able to penetrate through the large branches in spots, so that the route is not too dark. As well, it is not uncommon to have stone fences follow the path of the road, separating the highway and trees from the open grasslands, over which the horses move. At other spots, the land opens up into a vista of rolling hills, on which are built large estates, nestled off in the distance. All-in-all, it is a very spectacular view, and a very pleasant way to spend a leisurely afternoon. At times, I just stop the car along the side of the road, and take in the view for a few moments. But, because of the lay of the land, and the shadows that are created by the sun and trees, it is also necessary to remain alert to oncoming traffic, for it is not always easy to identify vehicles moving from the opposite direction.

The Old Frankfort Pike ends at the intersection with US Highway 60, just south of where US 60 meets Interstate 64, southeast of Frankfort. After a quick break, I decide to head back to Lexington along US Highway 60. It runs southeast from Frankfort to Versailles, then east to Lexington. I had already traveled along part of the highway, Lexington to Versailles, for just east of Versailles is where the Blue Grass Parkway starts. I had used the parkway during my exploration of the area around Abraham Lincoln's homes. But I had not yet driven along the stretch between Frankfort and Versailles.

Just east of where the Blue Grass Parkway connects to US 60, I happen to glance on the north side of the road, and am amazed to see a castle. I turn the car around, to go back and have a closer look at this structure. It is set atop a grassy knoll, about ¼ mile from the highway, and surrounded by a rail fence. It does not appear to be some type of tourist attraction, but actually someone's house.

The structure consists of an outer walled fortress, which protects an inner complex, built in the middle. The outer walls look to be about 10-12 feet high, and possibly made out of cement. The fortress is square, and about 150 feet in length on each side. I drive up a side road, to see if I can get a better view of the castle, or to try to find out if it is indeed someone's residence. There are no signs to indicate what it is, nor is there any activity inside or outside of this fortress. So even though my curiosity is not satisfied, I depart, and continue on back to Lexington. I never do find out any more information on this odd-looking structure, which is so out of place amongst the rolling hills and farms of Central Kentucky.

Saturday, August 10

Thus ends another vacation of exploration with continuous days of sunshine. It is now time to drive back to Louisville, to catch the plane to Ottawa. Kentucky is certainly a land of various landscapes: rolling hills in the central region, which is what I had expected that the majority of the state would be; a mountainous region in the east; and a hilly area in the south and southwest. Earlier in the summer, I had also experienced the flatland to the west, along the Mississippi River. This is certainly a very diverse landscape.

The concentration of history in this state appears to be on the settlement of Kentucky by the early pioneers. From my findings of the remains of the Wilderness Trail, in the southeast, to the old road that ran by the Lincoln homestead, in the southwest, the history centers on the settlers, led by Daniel Boone, and the people who followed in his footsteps shortly thereafter. So, when my thoughts during the week were not concentrated on the Civil War, they were on the early pioneer days, and how Kentucky came to be. It was information that I found to be of interest, and in the future, it will help me to understand the settling of Kentucky through time, as I continue my readings and research into the Civil War, and the paths that were taken to get there.

Looking east from atop Starkweather Hill towards the Cornfield at Perryville

Looking south from the Federal position at Fort Craig, near Munfordville

Looking east at Middle Creek, fighting took place amongst the wooded hills

Looking northwest at Ivy Mountain from the Confederate position along Ivy Creek

Tennessee: Virginia of the West

September 7-19, 1996

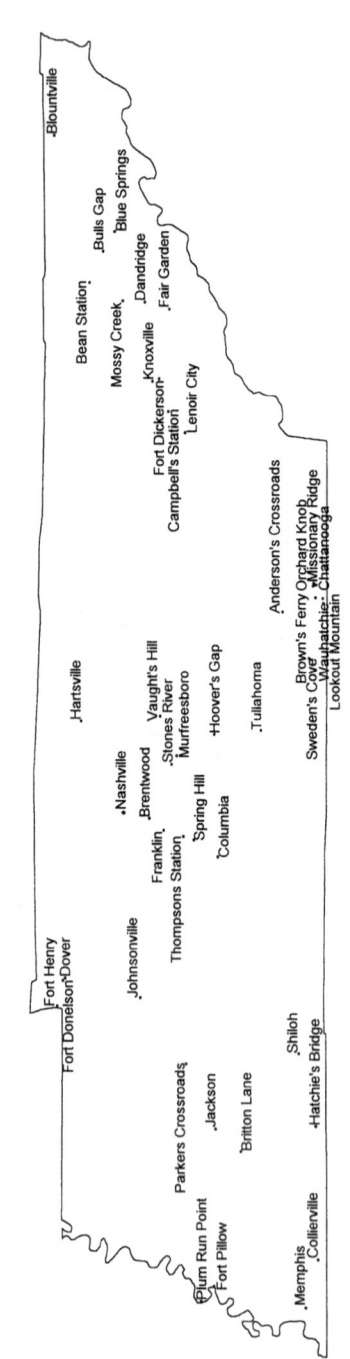

September has rolled around again. Thus, it is again time to be off to explore more Civil War sites in another state. The state of selection this time is Tennessee. After Virginia, the most battles had taken place in this state. So I am anticipating visiting quite a few sites, both big and small. It was where the battle for control of the western part of the country was mainly fought.

Never having visited the state before, I don't know what to expect, geographically speaking. But, I am expecting that the terrain is similar to what I had encountered in Kentucky, since Tennessee is directly south of it. I know that the Appalachian Mountains border the state in the east, and the lowlands of the Mississippi River occupy the west. In the center, I suspect that there are rolling hills, as I had found in the central part of Kentucky. But since I have never heard of, or read about this, unlike the Bluegrass Region of Kentucky, I am not quite sure what I will find there.

From my reference sources, I map out 39 sites where battles or skirmishes had occurred. I am able to categorize the sites into four areas of interest, centered around the four major cities of the state: Knoxville, Nashville, Memphis, and Chattanooga. With this categorization, I will spend a few days situated in each city, using it as my base of exploration, before moving on to the next one.

This will be a modification of the two types of trips that I had been on up to this point. The first type was to go to one city or town, and remain there for my entire stay, departing each day in different directions to find and explore the various battle sites. The other type was to travel from location to location; each day ending up in a different city or town after visiting the sites along the way. I have found that I prefer the first type of trip. With this kind of travel, I am able to set up in one location, and become familiar with that locale. At the end of each day, I know exactly where I am going, what restaurants and other amenities are in the area for me to choose from, and I can just go back to the hotel and relax. The other type of trip requires me to have to search out a motel for the night, after arriving in each new town, getting settled in, but not able to fully unpack, having to find all of the amenities before I can do anything, then repacking the next morning, checking out of the motel, and doing the same thing again the next night. Although this sort of trip is not totally unpleasant, for all of my trips have been very pleasurable, I prefer the first type of travel. The journey to Tennessee will be a modification of these two kinds of trips: spending between two and four days in a city before moving on.

The next part of my preliminary scheduling is to decide on whether to drive from Ottawa by car, or to travel by plane to one of my selected cities, rent a car, then explore the state in that fashion. The eastern part of Tennessee is within my guidelines of being able to reach my destination by car over a two-day period, or less than 1000 miles distant. However, from Knoxville, in the eastern part of the state, to Memphis, in the west, the distance is almost 400 miles, a full day drive in itself. So, if I drive down, I will not only have to be able to reach my starting point within two days, but I will also have to be able to reach home again within two days of driving. I finally determine that I can use my own car, traveling from Ottawa to Knoxville on the outward journey, and from Chattanooga back to Ottawa on the homeward part of the journey. So, my trip will consist of a counterclockwise loop through the state: stopping first at Knoxville; continuing on to Nashville; going further to Memphis; moving cross-country along the southern part of the state to Chattanooga; then back through Knoxville and home again.

Lastly, I select motels to stay in each city that I will be visiting. Although I am not sure if some of these locations will be suitable to my needs when I book them, they will all turn out to be ideally situated.

Another difference on this trip is the fact that I will not be traveling alone. My girlfriend Sue, will be accompanying me. We had met the previous fall, and over time she had become familiar with the Civil War, and now also finds this period of time very fascinating. But she views this era in slightly different terms than I do. Whereas my main interests lie with the armies, the battles, and the strategies that produced the outcome of the war, Sue is more intrigued by the people: who they were; how events changed their lives; the hardships that they endured; and what became of them. As my interest in the Civil War has been passed on to her, her interest in the people of that time has been passed on to me. Although what had always made this period interesting to me was the people who produced the events, Sue helped me to become more aware of the characteristics of the men and women of these times. The topic that is starting to come to the forefront for her is the contrast between the slaves and their masters. This area will be developed for her over the course of the trip.

I had not traveled with anyone in the past, because I prefer to explore the battle sites on my own. This allows me to investigate the scenes of fighting at my own pace, without having to take into account whether the other person is bored, or isn't interested in driving through the countryside all day. If I had found someone as fascinated with the Civil War as I am, and I was able to do everything that I wanted to, I would have traveled with them. But I did not know anyone with as much of an interest in this period as I have. I also have no problem traveling alone, and usually ended up meeting people during my trips.

Even though Sue's interest is slightly different than mine, I have invited her along. She had not gone with me on my Missouri or Kentucky trips, but I feel that she will enjoy herself in Tennessee. The battlefields do not particularly interest her; as I stated, she is more interested in the people. She certainly will not want to spend six hours walking through a battlefield; she doesn't have that kind of patience. But she is also independent enough to find things to do on her own. So while I am away during the day, driving through the countryside, she will play golf or explore the city in which we happen to be staying. Then in the evenings, we will be together to do things, like eat out or go to a movie. Certainly, she feels that she will want to visit some battlefields, but definitely not 39 of them. As part of the itinerary includes visiting sites during the days when I will be moving from one of the four cities to the next, Sue will have to visit those sites with me, as she will be traveling with me.

So all-in-all, there are new twists to this upcoming trip. I will also have someone to pass the time with during the many hours of travel in just getting to the state, and getting back home again.

Saturday, September 7

The first leg of our trip will take us from Ottawa to somewhere around West Virginia. Having traveled this part of the route before, on my trip through the Shenandoah Valley, I know that I will be able to get to the vicinity of West Virginia in about eight hours. Entering into New York state from Canada, the entire drive to Knoxville will be on Interstate 81. It is a nice sunny day, and we pass the time by talking and listening to music.

As it turns out, we make it to Winchester, Virginia. During the evening, I show Sue around this small town, which changed hands 73 times during the war. Our motel is on the eastern outskirts of town, beside the interstate. The Third Battle of Winchester had taken place through the fields and woods that now include the location of our motel. I show Sue a bit of how the battle had unfolded, and explain to her my disappointment that this area is now commercial, instead of there having been attempts made to preserve it.

Sunday, September 8

Another sunny day is upon us. This part of the trip will take us through the Shenandoah Valley, southwestern Virginia, and finally, our destination of Knoxville. As we journey southward, I point out to Sue some of the sites that had become part of the fight for the Valley. Of course, the most obvious physical monument to the battles is Massanutten Mountain, at the northern end of the Valley. Used as a signal and observation post by both sides, it towers above the surrounding landscape, splitting the Valley in half. It was used as an obstacle very effectively by Stonewall Jackson, during his Valley Campaign of 1862.

Farther to the south, as we are passing by New Market, she suddenly notices some cannon sitting in a field. She points out what she has found, and that there must be a Civil War site nearby. She suggests that we should stop, so that I can view this spot. I respond that I had already been here; this was the Battle of New Market. I tell her about the story of the cadets from VMI who had fought here. As we travel on, she is amazed by the beauty of the surroundings: the Valley nestled between the Blue Ridge Mountains, to the east, and the Allegheny Mountains, to the west.

One of the topics of conversation between us, as we move southward, is the amount of water in the cultivated fields, and the flooding that has taken place within the streams and rivers. Yesterday, the remnants of Hurricane Fran passed through this region, dumping a large amount of rain, and today, the fields have not yet dried, or the rivers returned to normal. We agree that the rainfall and winds must have been plentiful, and that we have lucked out by missing it by one day. I had been aware of the hurricane coming inland, and had watched it closely as time for the vacation approached. The storm cut northwestward, through the middle of Virginia. Even though the day before we left, I felt that it would go through the Valley before we got there, I still had a concern that it would eventually turn eastward before it released all of its rain, giving us problems during the first stages of our trip. But this is not the case, and although we view the remnants of Fran as we drive along, it has not impacted us.

By early afternoon, we have crossed into Tennessee, heading towards Knoxville. The agenda that I have for tomorrow consists of visiting sites that are to the east of Knoxville. I will start at the farthest eastern point, and move westward, finishing in Knoxville. The furthest site is about an hour east of Knoxville. But there is one site that is about 100 miles to the east of the city, and it seems a bit ridiculous to travel almost two hours back just to visit one site. So, I will stop and explore this site today, as we pass by it, instead of coming back so far tomorrow. This will also give Sue a taste of what I do on my excursions, and how I go about finding sites.

The name of the town is Blountville, about 10 miles southwest of Bristol and the Tennessee-Virginia border. A skirmish had occurred there on September 22, 1863. The Union forces had decided to clear the roads and gaps in East Tennessee to the Virginia border of any Confederates. As part of this action, a cavalry force, with artillery, was sent forward to burn railroad bridges near Bristol. Returning by way of Blountville, as they attempted to leave the town to the south, they ran into Confederates. The two sides shelled each other across the town and, by a flanking maneuver, the Federals forced the Confederates to eventually withdraw.

We exit the interstate onto State Highway 37, and drive the short distance south into the town. We come to the intersection with the main street, Bristol Avenue, which runs in an east-west direction. The intersection is in a valley, between two hills that rise at each end of the main street from this low point. Even though we have been driving in the mountains most of the afternoon, this region is not mountainous, although there are numerous high hills around that seem to push right up out of the earth.

The very small community consists almost exclusively of the main street. Just to the east of the intersection is the Courthouse. Not knowing where the battle would have taken place here, I figure that that building is a good place to start. A marker has been placed outside of it, commemorating the fallen of the skirmish in 1863. What the marker does not indicate though, is whether the fight had actually taken place right here on the street or not.

So, we decide to walk up the street to the east, to see if we can find any more indicators of where the battle had occurred, or possibly talk to someone that might have more information. Since it is Sunday, the town is completely deserted in this area. There are a few old-looking buildings just up the street. I think that they may be open to the public, and someone there can help us. Walking up to these structures, we find that many of them are from the early 1800s, and late 1700s. All of these are marked as being on the National Historic Register. We both find it very interesting, and odd, that a town so small could still have so many very old houses and inns. Unfortunately, none of them are open today. Most of the houses are situated right beside the road. One of the buildings, set back from the street, is called the Cannonball Inn. From this name, I deduce that the skirmish must have taken place right here along the main street, and that somehow this inn was renamed in recognition of the fight.

Still having a bit of time, and since I am not completely convinced yet that the battle had actually taken place on the main street, we decide to drive around for a short time, to see if we can discover anything more. First, we head east.

At the top of the hill, the land levels out, but remains elevated above the terrain to the north and south. If I find any marker, I believe that it will be along this road, County Road 126, since it would have been the main thoroughfare at the time of the fight. Finding nothing after a couple of miles, we turn around and head west, passing our starting point on the main street, Bristol Avenue.

Near the top of the hill on the western side of downtown, the main road veers off to the left, while another road on the right goes up and over the crest. Not sure which road would have been the main road during the war, I veer to the left, following the main highway. I have a suspicion though, that the other road may have been part of the old highway. I feel that during those times, the roads tended to follow the lay of the land, instead of skirting hills. So, I will explore that possibility if I don't find anything along this route. But for now, I drive westward on County Road 126.

Going up the road a short distance, and not finding anything, we turn around. Coming back to the hill on the western end of town, I see a road that goes up the western slope, and decide to explore in that direction. This road, County Hill Road, runs east up the side of the hill. This route turns out to be the old part of the road, as I have suspected, and now I cross the crest of the hill, from the west.

At the top of the hill is the town cemetery. Still having found nothing more to indicate where specifically the battle had taken place, Sue suggests that we stop in the cemetery. Perhaps some of the soldiers are buried there. I ask her if it would bother her to walk through the cemetery, and she replies that she enjoys it, reading the names and dates on the gravestones, and wondering who exactly those people had been.

Getting out of the car, we start walking in separate directions amongst the gravestones. The cemetery is situated on flat land, and is bordered to the north and west by woods. The east side looks out over the small town below. Most of the markers are old, and it does not appear that this cemetery is still in use. Many of the people buried here predate the Civil War. There are sections where the gravestones are laid out in rows, while other areas have large gaps where there are no markers at all.

There happens to be two men in the cemetery, who are taking pictures. In her wanderings, Sue approaches them, and starts talking with them. She indicates that I am interested in the Civil War, and that we are looking for where the battle had taken place here in Blountville. As it turns out, one of the men is a professor from a local university, and teaches history. So, he unfolds the events of the skirmish here for me, while Sue continues on her exploration through the cemetery.

The gentleman states that there had not been much of a fight here. The Federals had set up their guns right in the cemetery, and shelled the town below. The Cannonball Inn had gotten its name because one of the cannonballs from the bombardment had lodged in the western wall, and remains there to this day. The inn had been a hostel at the time of the battle.

He then describes for me some of the local history pertaining to the war. He says that Bristol was a very important town, and the Union troops were set on trying to capture it. During the 1800s, the tracks that the trains ran on were not necessarily of the same gauge. So, trains from one railroad may not be able to run on the tracks of another railroad. This was the case between the railroad that ran to Bristol on the Virginia side and railroad that ran to the same town on the Tennessee side. So, a great junction had been built at Bristol, in order to transfer the goods from the Tennessee side to the Virginia side. This became very important during the Civil War, as it was essential that food destined for the Confederate army in Virginia reached its destination. He continues that during the time that the town was in Confederate hands, a very large hospital had been built beside the train tracks. Large ramps had been constructed that extended from the second floor of the hospital to the edge of the trains. The Confederate wounded would be rolled off of the trains and into the hospital.

He also mentions that there was quite a bit of sympathy for the Union in East Tennessee. There was a lot of guerrilla warfare and ambushes on both sides. There were a large number of nighttime sabotages that took place during the war. Neighbors tended to stay together in groups, in order to avoid being attacked by the other group. He says that even though there were not any major battles that took place in the region, the warfare here was quite nasty. I thank him for his time, and information, and go to see if Sue is ready to leave.

So as it turns out, the fight here had taken place along the main street. I have also gathered up some additional information concerning the local history that would probably not be found in very many books. The guerrilla warfare, and how it affected the families, is something that I will have to pursue. But now, it is time to get to Knoxville.

We return to the interstate, and continue our westward journey. As we start out, I comment to Sue that she now has an idea of what my days consist of on these trips. Except for the major battlefields, many of the sites are now unmarked, or contain only a marker. So in order to find out any information on a specific fight, I have to do some investigating around the area. Sometimes I find something, and sometimes I don't.

I then ask her what she had discovered in the cemetery. She says that most of the grave markers are quite old and, as I have mentioned, predate the Civil War. She asks me if it was a common practice for slaves to be buried next to their master. I reply that not only did I think that it was uncommon, I believe that slaves would not even have been buried in the same cemetery. If there was a cemetery at all for slaves, it no doubt would have been beyond the limits of the town, especially in the Southern states. Sue says that if that was the case, then she had found an oddity at the cemetery. She continues that in a row of gravestones, she had found the markers for a husband and wife, and extending out on one side from this plot were the gravesites of the children. However, extending out from the other side, were the plots of the slaves who belonged to the family as well. The main marker had said something to the effect of here lay the remains of Mr. and Mrs. So-and-So, and their children, and their slaves. I comment that as far as I know, that was a very strange occurrence. It would not have been a common incident at all. This intrigues Sue, and she becomes really interested in trying to find out why this person had done this. It probably would not have made him very popular amongst the townsfolk.

Because of our discussion, I think that this becomes the start of Sue's real interest in the slaves, how they existed, how they were treated, and what type of masters they had. A little while later, as we continue towards Knoxville, I guess after she has had a bit of time to ponder our discussion, and roll over these events in her mind, she asks me if we will be going by Blountville again. I reply that yes, on our way home, we will have to travel over this same stretch of highway, and that we will be passing by the town.

She asks if we can stop again at the cemetery. She wants to see if she can find out any more information on the family, and wants to take a few pictures of the marker, which indicates that the site contains the slaves, as well as the family. I respond affirmatively to her request.

Arriving in Knoxville after our excursion, the motel where we are to stay ends up being about 10 miles west of downtown. At first, I think that I am not real keen on this, because I will have to backtrack through the city tomorrow in order to get to the sites that lay beyond the eastern edge of Knoxville. But as it will turn out, this becomes a very good selection.

Monday, September 9

The day starts off very foggy. But my first site is about an hour east of the city. So, I figure that by that time, the fog will have been burnt off by the sun. Thus, I am not too concerned. Sue has found a golf course nearby; she will spend the day golfing.

I head east on Interstate 40, which will change to Interstate 81 just to the east of Knoxville. As expected, I hit rush hour traffic, heading into the city from the west. It is stop and go for awhile, but I soon make it to the city center, and things clear out for me as I continue eastward. Driving back through the countryside over which we had passed yesterday, it consists mainly of high hills, with mountains off in the distance, on either side. Not much farming is done in this region; the land is mainly forested, with some small open fields mixed in.

About 60 miles east of Knoxville, I turn north off of Interstate 81, onto US Highway 11E. The sun is now out, although it is still cloudy, and the fog remains in the near distances. My first stop is to be Bulls Gap, about three miles north of the interstate.

Actually, I am hoping that my first stop will be Blue Springs. But I do not have enough information to identify where I should be looking for it. All I know is that this battle took place in Greene County. Where in Greene County though, is the question that I do not have an answer for, and without more details on where it occurred, I could spend an entire day driving around the county looking for it. I have reviewed the county in the road atlas, and have seen that there are quite a few roads that I would need to traverse. So, my attempt to find the spot will consist of hoping that Blue Springs is on the way to Bulls Gap.

Exiting the interstate, I am in Greene County. During my drive north towards Bulls Gap, I watch for signs that would indicate that I am passing by Blue Springs, or a marker identifying where it might be. My deduction is that since there was no fighting, that I know of, that took place farther east than Bulls Gap, except for Blountville, and hence my reason for starting with Bulls Gap and working my way westward, then perhaps Blue Springs is in this area as well. But as I near the community of Bulls Gap, I cross into Hamblen County, and my hope of finding Blue Springs disappears.

The Battle of Blue Springs took place on October 10, 1863. In early September, the Federals had taken Knoxville, and the Confederates had withdrawn to this region. The Union commander wanted the roads and gaps in East Tennessee cleared of all Confederates, to the Virginia border. This movement included the battle that would take place at Blountville. But in early October, a Confederate cavalry force set out to disrupt the Federal communications lines. After skirmishing in the vicinity of Bulls Gap for a few days, the Confederates positioned themselves around Blue Springs.

On October 10, the Federals approached the town from Bulls Gap, with the intention of attacking the Confederate cavalry there. After the Federal cavalry had fought for most of the day with the Confederates, the Federal infantry pitched in at 5:00, overwhelming the Confederate defenders. After dark, the Confederates withdrew to Virginia.

Not very long after crossing the county line, I arrive at the community of Bulls Gap. In November 1864, the Confederates had undertaken to advance from Virginia into East Tennessee, drive out the Federals, and pick up Confederate sympathizers for the cause. Between November 11 and 13, the opposing forces met at Bulls Gap. The Federals had entrenched at the gap. The Confederates attacked early in the day on November 11, but were repulsed. An artillery duel between the two sides continued throughout the rest of the day. The next day, the Confederates attacked along the ridge to the east, and also from the rear, getting through at Taylor's Gap, to the west. But the Federals held of these assaults, and remained in their position. Only skirmishing took place on November 13, for the Confederates were moving to the east, in preparation for a flank attack. But through the night, with the Federals low on ammunition, they withdrew. The Confederates pursued them, until bad roads and weather forced them to give this up.

The highway bypasses this small village, to the east of it. I turn off of the highway, to the west, onto Sycamore Drive, and follow a narrow twisting road that curves to the south, and brings me to the center of the town. The compact core is on an S-curve, and consists of a few rundown buildings. It looks completely deserted, and reminds me of one of those ghost towns that I had seen in movies. The place is set atop a rocky outcrop, on the top of a hill. Because the highway bypasses it, the town appears to have been left behind by time. Turning left, and driving past these old buildings, the road curves to the right, and reconnects back with Sycamore Drive. A bridge crosses a gap in the rock. In this cut, the railroad has been dug out of the stone; so the railway is actually underneath the town. The railway was probably the main reason that there were troops in the vicinity to begin with. Reaching the highway, southeast of the community, I have not seen any markers indicating the battle that had taken place here. So, I backtrack to the few buildings that make up the town, and find an office that has something to do with the town, or county.

Entering the office, I find an elderly lady, who gives me the impression that she does not get too many visitors, and she prefers it that way. Even though she doesn't appear to be doing anything, I get the impression that I am interrupting her non-activity. I inquire if she knows of any Civil War battle that had occurred around the town, to which she replies that she does not. That is the end of the conversation. There is no interest from her in trying to help me, or with suggesting some other place, or person, that may know about the fight. So, this concludes my search for the battle site.

Returning to the highway, I turn left, to continue northwest on US Highway 11E. Within a short distance, the highway turns towards the southwest. After about 12 miles, I reach the intersection with State Highway 32, and turn north. My next stop is to be Bean Station, located at the intersection with US Highway 11W, about 10 miles away.

Along State 32, I have to cross Cherokee Lake, which by the number of boats and trucks in the area, I take to be a popular camping spot. I assume that the lake has become the size that it is because of the impact of the Tennessee Valley Authority. I remember learning about this in history class, in high school, and that it included the building of many dams within the state during the 1930s, in order to bring electricity here. However, that is all that I remember about it. Probably in the long run, it has been for the betterment of the state. But from my point of view, I know that during my travels throughout Tennessee, I will run into instances where terrain has been modified, or sites are now underwater, because of damming of the rivers. This will not allow me to see the landscape as it had been during the time of the war. I know of one instance already, where the site is now underwater, Fort Henry, and there may be others. But that is not going to stop me from at least getting to the vicinity of those sites.

Arriving at Bean Station, which is nothing more than a crossroads, I search around for any indications that a battle had taken place here. After their loss at Knoxville in late November 1863, the Confederates retreated eastward, along what is now US Highway 11W, to Rogersville. On December 14, 1863, they returned here to confront the pursuing Federals. The Federals deployed their force at Bean Station, and throughout the day, the Confederates assaulted their lines. Holding off these attacks, the Union troops retired at nightfall. Finding no markers, I move on to my next site.

The problem with my next site is similar to my situation with Blue Springs: I am not quite sure where it is located. The name of the place is Mossy Creek. From a map that I have, it gives a rough approximation of where it is, or was, which is in Jefferson County, and in the vicinity of Bean Station. But where exactly in the county, I do not know, although I think that it may be along the Holston River. So, I decide to travel on County Road 375, which runs along the north shore of Cherokee Lake. I suspect that if it is beside the river, that the site may have disappeared by the enlargement of the lake. Part of the reason for me taking this route is that it will also lead me towards my next site, to the southwest, which is Dandridge. If I don't find anything along County 375, I will end up in the vicinity of Jefferson City, and from there, I will continue on to Dandridge.

The Battle of Mossy Creek took place on December 29, 1863. After their loss at the Battle of Knoxville, in November, the Confederates had withdrawn to the area around Dandridge to go into winter quarters. On December 28, hearing that the Confederate cavalry was near Dandridge, the Federal commander at Mossy Creek ordered the cavalry to move in that direction, to attack it. The next day, after the majority of the Federal cavalry had departed, the Confederate cavalry attacked those units left behind at Mossy Creek. During the day, the Confederates were driving the Federals in front of them. But then the Federal cavalry units returned from Dandridge, and arrived on the battlefield. The momentum then switched to the Federal side, and they drove the Confederates back to their starting point. During the night, the Confederates withdrew.

I return south from Bean Station on State Highway 32, until I reach the north shore of Cherokee Lake. I then turn west, onto County Road 375, and follow the outline of the lake. Driving over the hills, and through the forests that line the north side of the water, this turns out to be a pleasant and scenic drive. But I do not find Mossy Creek. I do though, see quite a few offices of the TVA, verifying my assumption that Cherokee Lake was created by the damming of the Holston River. At the western end of the lake, I connect with State Highway 92, and turn south. I drive through Jefferson City and continue on to Dandridge.

Arriving in Dandridge, State 92 runs east along the northern edge of downtown, then turns south to cross Douglas Lake. The main street of the town runs perpendicular to highway, just to the west of where the highway turns to the south. The town is built along the side of a hill. So the main street descends to the south, from the intersection with State 92, to level out in the central part of the town.

I find a marker at the Courthouse, indicating that the battle occurred here. The marker states that the fight occurred on December 24, 1863, while the information that I have refers to a battle occurring on January 17, 1864. Even thought the dates are different, the descriptions of the fight are similar, so it may or may not be the same engagement. Both references though, refer to the battle as taking place during the time after the Battle of Knoxville, when the Confederates had retreated to this area for the winter.

The marker denotes that the Union cavalry had moved through the town, from the west, and were stopped by the Confederates about four miles to the northeast, at Hays' Ferry. The Federals were then pushed back through the town, and they eventually retreated. The information that I have indicates a similar type of engagement, where the Federals were moving through Dandridge towards Kimbrough's Crossroads, again to the northeast, and met the Confederates within four miles of their objective. Retreating back to Dandridge, the Federals formed a line to receive the attack of the pursuing Confederates. Holding off this assault, after dark the Union troops retreated back to New Market, to the northwest. Whether fighting actually took place around the Courthouse is not indicated.

So I drive around the few blocks of the central part of the village, in order to see if I can find any more markers. Not finding anything, I then decide to see if I can locate Hays' Ferry. All I know is that is was four miles to the northeast, which doesn't make sense to me. I am assuming that water had to have been involved, since the name of the place that I am looking for has the word ferry in it, indicating proximity to water. But Dandridge is on the north side of the French Broad River, and so the river runs south of the town, in an east-west direction. Thus, my deduction has it that a ferry should be to the southeast of Dandridge, not the northeast. Perhaps though, a smaller stream is to the northeast, and the ferry crossed it, instead of the French Broad.

I drive east along US Highway 25W, and then northeast on County Road 66, which meanders through some rolling hills. Finding no markers, or references to Hay's Ferry, I decide to move on to my next site. This is Fair Garden, another place like Blue Springs and Mossy Creek, which I have not found on the map.

I know that it is to the southwest of Dandridge, in Sevier County, and somewhere in the vicinity of Sevierville. Returning to Dandridge, I drive southwest along the north side of the river, on County Road 139, until it connects with State Highway 66. I turn south on State 66 for a short distance, until it crosses the French Broad River, then west onto County Road 338. The landscape along this stretch of road consists mainly of rolling hills, populated with forest. There are very few houses or farms. Not finding Fair Garden, and reaching US Highway 441, I head west back towards Knoxville. It is now raining.

The Battle of Fair Garden took place on January 27, 1864. After the Battle of Dandridge, the Federal cavalry moved to the south side of the French Broad River, to patrol the roads and disrupt Confederate foraging details. The Confederates, in an attempt to remove these patrols, had concentrated a force near Fair Garden. The Federals moved from Sevierville to attack the Confederates there, and did so on the morning of January 27. By the afternoon, the Confederates had been routed.

This concludes my list of sites for the day. But since I have not found a few of the places that I was looking for, it is now only early afternoon. The first site that is on my itinerary for tomorrow is Knoxville. But I believe that I have enough time to visit it today. So, if by the time that I reach Knoxville, it has stopped raining, then I will explore the city. As I move towards Knoxville, it is now only raining intermittently, and not heavy. So the chances of it continuing are minimal. I am approaching Knoxville on from the southeast.

Upon arriving in Knoxville, the clouds are breaking up, and the sun is coming through them. I had decided that even if it was still raining when I got to the city, I would go to get information on the battle that occurred here. Then tomorrow, I would be ready to go exactly to the places of interest, without having to get the preliminary information first. But now with the sum coming out, and the area drying, I am going to explore Knoxville today. So I head for the Visitor Center, located on Henley Street. Crossing the bridge on US 441, the highway becomes Henley Street. A few blocks north of the river, I spot the Visitor Center.

At the Center, I receive a Knoxville Civil War tour sites page, which has a map of the city on one side, and a small description of each stop on the other. I also pick up a small booklet entitled *A Path Divided: Tennessee's Civil War Years*. It lists all of the major civil war locations within the state, and the exact address of each. This will save me time throughout the trip, as I now know where to go to get appropriate information and maps when I arrive at each site.

Equipped with the necessary information for Knoxville, I start out to find the noted points of interest concerning the Battle of Knoxville. The battle had taken place on November 29, 1863. The Confederates had approached the city from Chattanooga, with the objective of removing the Federals from East Tennessee, and their occupation of Knoxville. After some delaying tactics by a portion of the Union army, which had gone out to meet the advancing Confederates to the southwest of the city, the Federals withdrew into the defenses of Knoxville.

The defenses created a rectangle, bounded on the south side by the Holston River. The lines were dug about ½ mile west of the city, and about one mile east of the city. On the north side, the defenses were built along the edge of the city line. A redoubt named Fort Sanders, at the northwest corner of the lines, was thought to be the weak point to the defenses. A small basin, in which a creek flows, was not visible from the fort. So the Confederates decided that they could form up there to attack the fort, out of sight of the Federals.

Thus, that is where the Confederates struck, on that cold and rainy morning, attacking from the northwest. Their forward motion was initially stopped by telegraph wire, which had been strung amongst tree trunks, left from the felled trees that fronted the redoubt. As the Confederates stumbled through this area, it gave the Federals in the fort opportunity to fire into the ranks of the Confederates, who were in the open and temporarily halted. Soon, the wires were cut though, and the attack continued.

A ditch dug in front of the fort, was about eight feet deep. The Confederates had thought that the ditch was much shallower. But as they approached the fort, and entered the trench, they found that the wall in front of them was steep, and ice covered, giving them little opportunity to advance any further up it. The Federals rained down excruciating fire, and tossed down lit cannonballs into this Confederate fiasco. The Confederates could not move forward, and most of them did not dare to retrace their steps across the open ground to the rear, because of the heavy Federal fire that occupied that zone. After 20 minutes, the fight was over, without the Confederates having had any impact on the defenses of Knoxville, and hardly any losses to the Federal troops. The Confederates had over 800 casualties, to a few more than 10 for the Federals.

The tour starts on the west end of the city. From downtown, I take Cumberland Avenue, which changes into Kingston Pike, for a distance of about two miles. Here, the Holston River, which dips to the south just west of the downtown area, cuts back to the north, and meets the Kingston Pike. It is invisible from the road though, because of the large growth of vegetation that lines the area between the road and the river.

My first stop is the Bleak House, on the south side of the road. Confederate General James Longstreet set up his headquarters here during the time that the Confederates were positioned outside of Knoxville. The house was built in 1858, and sits back from the road. It is an odd-shaped two-story structure of brick. It has been painted white, including the sills around the windows, and the chimney. There is a section on the right side of the house that juts forward, and a section to the right rear that extends to the right. A large stately tree shades the left side of the house from the road, and a circular driveway is set in front of the structure.

Scanning around, I can tell that the road and house are set on high ground, but my ability to see very far into the distance in any direction is limited, because of the many large trees that grow here. On the north side of the road is a wooded area, which occupies the side of the heights. Any woods in this area would have been cut down during the time of the war. The tour guide brochure indicates that Longstreet had sharpshooters positioned in the windows, who regularly picked off Federal soldiers in the distance, to the east. This certainly could not be attempted today because of the trees.

As I am standing here, and getting my bearings, an older lady has come out of the house to get the mail, and inquires about my interest. I explain my reason for stopping here, and she invites me inside, describing the history of the house as we proceed towards it. It was sold to the United Daughters of the Confederacy in 1959, and they now look after the care and upkeep of the building. It has been restored to the time of the Civil War, and is open for visiting. I thank her for her invitation to view the house, but I am not interested. I have already seen the interiors of many old houses on my travels, and they do not especially interest me enough to view them in detail. She hands me a small brochure that describes the house and its history.

Stepping back outside, I look through this brochure on my way to the car. A letter written by the wife of the owner of the house describes that cannon were placed on the front lawn, and pickets surrounded the home. After the death of Union General Sanders, who was killed by a sharpshooter from the tower of the house, the Federals fired cannon and bullets at the structure, creating a gaping hole on the northeast side, smashing many windows, and marking every wall with bullet holes.

Moving eastward on the Kingston Pike, the next stop is just around the bend from the Bleak House. A hill on the north side of the road rises up to the Second Presbyterian Church. A marker by the road indicates that this is where Union General William Sanders was mortally wounded, on November 18, 1863. In charge of the cavalry, Sanders was responsible for the delaying tactics in front of the advancing Confederates, while the rest of the troops returned to the defenses of the city. Earlier in the month, part of the Union army had gone out beyond Knoxville, in an attempt to slow the Confederate advance towards Knoxville from Chattanooga. This certainly would have been a good spot to set up a defensive line. With the hill to the north, and the steep ground that descends to the river to the south, the only easy access to Knoxville would have been along this road, creating a bottleneck at this position.

Not very far to the east is another house, set in from the south side of the road. This residence, known as Crescent Bend, was used by Confederate General Joseph Kershaw during the time that the Confederates were on the outskirts of the city. This is a two-story rectangular building of white masonry, with a portico covering the front doorway. There are two windows on both sides of the door, and above these on the second story. A window of the same size as the others has also been built on the second floor, above the doorway. On the side of the house, a single window occupies each story on the front half of it; there are none on the back half. As at the Bleak House, all of the windows are painted white, as is the chimney, which protrudes above the roof from the end of the house. A large extension has been built on to the back side of the house, but I suspect that this was not part of the original structure. Large shade trees are growing at both ends of the structure.

Crescent Bend sits at the corner of Neyland Drive and Kingston Pike. To continue the tour, I turn south onto Neyland Drive. This street travels along the north bank of the Holston River, first bending to the southeast, then turning to the northeast. Just to the east of the apex of the bend, and on the south bank of the river, is Cherokee Heights. The heights are formed by cliffs that rise straight up from the south bank of the river, and tower over the land on the north side, which is not much above the height of the river. The layered rock that forms the precipice is mostly hidden by trees, which are growing out of the sides, and along the top.

The Confederates seized this high ground on November 23, 1863, for the purpose of shelling Fort Sanders. But this attempt failed because of the distance that the fort was from the guns. Looking up at the heights from below, if there were any guns that were positioned there, I would not be able to see them; the woods would conceal them from my view. I cannot be sure if the trees that occupy the high ground today would have grown there at the time of the fighting, or if this ground would have been cleared.

A bit further east on Neyland Drive, a marker indicates where the Union defenses began on the western side of the city, next to the river. The trench line ran northwest from the water here, which would have been perpendicular to the edge of the river. After some distance, it turned north, ending at Fort Sanders, on Cumberland Avenue/Kingston Pike. The land between the river and Cumberland Avenue is now occupied by the University of Tennessee. During the 1860s, these trenches would have been more than ½ mile beyond the western edge of the city. The terrain rises quickly from Neyland Avenue, but since there are a number of university buildings here now, I cannot be sure how close the land resembles that of the time of the war. Certainly in general, the landscape ascends towards the heights at Cumberland Avenue, but whether the terrain rose across straight level land, or as a series of hills and valleys, I cannot be sure.

Looking southwest from this point, Cherokee Heights, and the position of the Confederate artillery, can be viewed in the near distance. But apparently, the guns there were not interested in this position, and the men who manned the trenches here, but in Fort Sanders, farther to the north. From this spot, the Federal troops would have been able to watch the cannonballs shoot off into the distance, smoke spewing forth from the guns as they fired at their target. The marker indicates that the Confederate pickets were only 1200 yards to the west of this position, once the Confederate army had approached the city.

Continuing eastward to where Neyland Drive ends, at the eastern edge of the downtown core, a marker shows the position of a pontoon bridge, which had crossed the river here. Central Avenue, running northward, used to begin at this point. So the bridge would have been an extension of it, to the south side of the river. The bridge was used to bring in supplies collected on the other side, and as a line of communication with the cavalry, which during the siege, still held the high ground overlooking Knoxville, on the south side of the river.

Looking across the water, the land near the river remains flat, or rises slightly. But in the distance, a set of high distinctive hills loom. Today, they are covered in green by forests. However, during the time of the war, probably all vegetation had been cut down, to give a better view of the area. Knowing that those heights were controlled by their own troops would have given the men in the city relief, for it appears that the hills protect the city from some unknown force that may be approaching from the other side of them. The hills, from east to west, were known as Sevierville Hill, Fort Stanley, which is directly across from here, and Forts Dickerson and Higley.

Finishing along the river, the next stop is Fort Hill, located to the east, on Dandridge Avenue. Neyland Drive turns north from the river here, and I follow it a short distance to Hill Avenue. I turn east onto it, and drive along it as it veers to the northeast. I reach Dandridge Avenue, and turn east. This area is a series of hills that rise above the city on the east side. Now a residential district, it was beyond the city limits at the time of the battle, and was occupied by Union troops. The apex of Fort Hill is on the north side of Dandridge Avenue, and just west of Surrey Street.

I turn around and start back to the west, still on Dandridge Avenue. According to the tour brochure, on the north side of the road, near the intersection with Rosedale Avenue, is the Mabry-Hazen House. Built in 1858, the house served as headquarters for various generals on both sides during the course of the war. To the northeast of Dandridge Avenue, on Bethel Avenue, is the Confederate Cemetery. Most of the men buried there died of disease. Neither site interests me enough to stop for a few moments.

This finishes with the points of interest at the eastern end of the city. The next area to tour is to the south of the city, and across the river. Located there are the forts on the heights that overlook the city, and the approaches from the south. I retrace my path west to Hill Avenue, then south along it and Neyland Drive, to the Henley Street Bridge. Here, I turn south, traveling on Chapman Highway, US Highway 441. Just on the south side of the river, the highway runs between two large hills. On the south side of the western hill is the entrance to Fort Dickerson, and I turn right, into the park. Following the roadway through a forest, north to the apex, I come to the entrance to the fort, which is located in Fort Dickerson Park.

Overgrown now by the infringing forest, these heights would have been cleared of all vegetation during the time of the war. This earthen fort is similar to ones that I had seen before. The remains of the ditch surrounds the outside fort walls, which slant inwards, and rise to a height of about 10 feet. Because of the plant growth, it is impossible to get any view of the terrain that the fort would have towered above, giving the inhabitants the advantage of spying approaching troops well before they arrived before this obstacle.

The fort was attacked on November 15-16, 1863, by the Confederate cavalry. They were advancing from the south, ahead of the main Confederate army, in an attempt to secure the heights on the south side of the river. The main army continued its movement from the southwest, along the primary road from Chattanooga, to arrive in front of Knoxville from the west. The assaults by the Confederate cavalry were repulsed. The guns of the fort participated in the fighting that took place around Fort Sanders during that battle on November 29.

On the east side of Chapman Highway, and built on the next hill over, was Fort Stanley. Apparently, there are no remains to that fort, or any that are indicated in the brochure. But I want to see if I can find anything over there anyway. So leaving Fort Dickerson Park, I turn north onto US Highway 441, then quickly northeast onto Martin Mill Pike. At Lippencott Street, I turn east, and drive along this road. I move through a residential area, looking for any markers, or remains of the fort, but don't find any. Thus, I return to the main highway.

It is now about 5:00. The question is whether I should continue on, and try to finish touring Knoxville, or wait until tomorrow to complete visiting the sites of the battle. I decide that if I finish touring the sites today, then that will only give me one more spot to visit tomorrow. That location, Campbell's Station, is situated in the vicinity of where we are staying, on the west side of the city. I then will not have to return back into the city. By finishing in Knoxville today, and visiting Campbell's Station tomorrow, then the only other thing that needs to be done is to drive to Nashville, which should not take very long. Thus, I will have some free time, and perhaps can spend part of the day golfing with Sue. Since the sun is shining brightly, I decide to continue on, to complete the tour of Knoxville.

I turn north onto US 441, and cross back into the city. The last part of the tour deals with the sites in the downtown core, and the battle at Fort Sanders. I turn east onto Cumberland Avenue, and then north onto Gay Street. On the right side of the road, at Clinch Street, is the site of the Crozier home. The land is now occupied by an eight-story building, which was originally the Farragut Hotel. The Crozier home was the headquarters of Union General Ambrose Burnside during November 1863.

Continuing north on Gay Street, I then turn west onto Vine Street. Vine Street appears to be the northern border for downtown, and most of the streets running north from the river end at it. Vine Street runs along the top of a ridge, which drops off quickly on both sides. At the center of this short street, Battery Wiltsie was located. The battery was part of the earthworks that circled the city. The defenses on the north side of the city ran along connecting ridges, from Fort Sanders in the west, to Fort Hill in the east. The street is now occupied with two- and three-story houses and small apartment buildings. So it is difficult to view the region to the north, now also residential. It is hard for me to formulate in my mind how this spot would have appeared during the war, since it is now all pavement and bricks. But looking to the east, I can make out the ridges that the defenses would have ran along, now also occupied by houses.

I turn south onto Walnut Street, and at Cumberland Avenue, I head west, leaving downtown again, as I had done to start the tour, earlier in the afternoon. Just past the railroad tracks, I turn north into Tyson Park, and descend from the streets above to the floor of Third Creek. The entrance is very difficult to see, and is surrounded by multiple highways.

The park, and the creek, are situated below the streets and bridges that surround it, and a haven from all of the noise and traffic that I have just driven through during rush-hour. The quietness of the park is a complete contrast to its surroundings, and many people have taken refuge here, to just sit in this greenery, or to walk along its path.

For me though, this is more than just a pleasant pause from my tour of the city. It was along this shallow, but fast-flowing creek that the Confederates assembled on the morning of November 29, 1863, before their assault on Fort Sanders. The creek runs between two large hills. Beyond the hill to the east, would have been the Union troops, occupying their fortified earthworks. Here in this quiet refuge, the Confederate soldiers would have had the opportunity to assemble without interruption, out of the view of the Federal defenses. There is no marker here indicating what had taken place in this area. As I walk back to my car, I wonder how many of the people here, jogging by or just relaxing on the grass, are aware of the significance of this park: that men in gray had stepped up into line in silence, knowing that in a few moments they would be marching up the hill in front of them to do a formidable task, many of them never to return to this quiet and secluded spot.

Getting back onto Cumberland Avenue and heading east, not a very easy feat, I start looking for 16th Street. Finding it, I turn north, and search for a parking spot along the street. This area was the location of Fort Sanders. The land now contains buildings of the University of Tennessee.

A marker at the next street corner to the north, Laurel Avenue, marks this spot as part of Fort Sanders. This is the only indication that the fort once stood here. That is unfortunate. For all of the importance of the fort, nothing remains but a marker. Many of the students pass it by each day, probably never stopping to read it, or trying to comprehend what went on over this ground, that members of both armies had tread upon over one hundred years ago, definitely under different circumstances than the young people who walk by here today.

The National Cemetery is located next to Old Gray Cemetery, on Tyson Street, north of here, but I am not interested in visiting that site. Thus ends my tour of the Battle of Knoxville. As a consequence of this tour, I have gotten to explore the downtown part of the city, as well as some of the surrounding residential area and landscape. I now have a better understanding of what had taken place here. I had expected the city to be built amongst mountains, which I knew existed in the eastern part of Tennessee. But Knoxville, although surrounded by multiple hills, is not within a mountainous region. It lies in a valley between two sets of mountains.

Tuesday, September 10

Not knowing how long it would take to do all of the sites in the Knoxville area, I had set aside two days. However, I have already completed all of my itinerary, except for one site, on the first day. This was partially because of my failure to find a few of the places. So, only having one battlefield left to visit today, which I feel won't take me very long, I suggest to Sue that we go golfing, after which we will drive to Nashville. The previous day, as I wandered through the countryside, she had gone to a golf course near the motel. As difficult as the course was, she wanted to try it again. So, she will go with me to visit the battlefield, then we will go golfing.

The site that I want to find is Campbell's Station. A battle had occurred there on November 16, 1863. As the Confederates had approached Knoxville, a small Federal force had been sent out to delay the movement of the Confederates. As the Confederates neared the Federals, they retreated, without a fight. The Confederates, moving along a line parallel to the Federals, hoped to reach the intersection at Campbell's Station first, thereby blocking the Union withdrawal to Knoxville, and forcing the Federals to have to fight on open ground, rather than protected by the defenses of the city. The Union troops arrived first, and set up a defensive line, just 15 minutes before the Confederates started to get there. The Confederates attacked, and included a flanking movement. But the assault was unsuccessful, and the Union line held. The Federals then continued their withdrawal back to Knoxville through the night. The Confederates did not give chase.

Our motel is on Campbell Station Road, so I know that we are in the vicinity. We drive south to the main intersection, which is with Kingston Pike. Campbell's Station must have been right here. But this area is now part of Farragut. Driving around for a bit, we look for any markers that might indicate where the battle had been. But we find nothing.

So now we debate on whether to go golfing or not. The golf course is just down the road, but it is very foggy this morning. It will be difficult to play, since the fog has reduced visibility dramatically. This is the second day that it has started out foggy first thing in the morning. Later on the trip, as I watch the weather conditions during our travel around the state, I will notice that Knoxville is usually fogged in first thing in the morning. I'm not sure whether this is a common phenomenon for this region, but it certainly seems to be a normal occurrence while we are here in Tennessee. We decide that rather than waiting around for the fog to clear, we will drive on to Nashville, and if the weather is fine there, then we will play golf.

I've been driving southwest on the Kingston Pike as we've been discussing our options for golfing. When we make our final decision, I decide that it is easier to continue southwest until we reach the interstate, which will cross this road after a few miles, instead of backtracking to the north to get onto it by the motel. Kingston Pike, US Highway 11, turns to the south after a couple of miles, but I continue to the southwest on US Highway 70. Very shortly, we reach the interstate, and getting on it, head west towards Nashville.

As we are driving along, we notice that quite a few hills and rock outcroppings have a plant growing on them, kind of like an ivy, but with very large leaves, and the color of it is a very dark green. I had noticed this plant in a few places in Kentucky, but it is very prevalent here in Tennessee. We can tell that it is something that is specifically planted, instead of being native to this area. We will find out that what we have been seeing is called kudzu, a Japanese ivy, which has been imported to create a nice vegetation cover along the highways. As often happens though, there are unforeseen consequences. This plant has started growing very quickly and taking over much of the other vegetation. As we continue with our tour around the state, we will see this. There will be telephone poles and trees completely covered with this vine. There will even be a few houses where it has started to grow up the side of the walls. The comments we will get from local people is that it was a bad idea, and to them, it is a weed that should be gotten rid of. For a visitor though, it is a nice change, seeing this vegetation growing along the sides of the roads, as opposed to just rock or cement. But we also will see the consequences of this idea, and for all its visual appeal, it is a nuisance.

Arriving in Nashville in the late morning, we find our motel, which is near the airport. I had selected this one because it was near the intersections of a number of the main routes around the city, and has a larger room and kitchen area. Since our room is not ready yet, I identify on the road atlas that there is a golf course just up the road. So, we decide to spend the afternoon relaxing with a round of golf, and then register at the motel.

By the time we have gotten to Nashville, the sun is out, and it is now very hot and humid. We are located on the east end of the city, and as we golf, we discover that on some of the holes, we can make out the tall buildings of downtown, through the haze. We also find out that we are right across the road from the Grand Ole Opry. I had not realized that it is in the vicinity of where we are staying; I had thought that it is located downtown. Finishing our round, we head back to the motel, to unpack and get settled in.

Wednesday, September 11

The first of three planned days for exploring the battle sites around Nashville is to take me to the south of the city. I get on Briley Parkway and head south, passing by the airport. At the south end of the airport, I connect with Murfreesboro Road, US Highway 40/70S, and turn southeast. I travel over the long hills of the region, through the outskirts of Nashville, and then out into more open country. After 30 miles, I come to Stones River National Battlefield Park, just to the northwest of Murfreesboro, and follow the signs to the Visitor Center, a short distance to the west of the main highway.

The battle here took place between December 31, 1862 and January 2, 1863. The Confederates had located to the area around Murfreesboro after their defeat at Perryville, Kentucky, in October, 1862. The Federals had followed them south, and positioned themselves at Nashville. By late December, the Federals were ready to attack again. Union troops left Nashville on December 26, along three separate paths, all to converge at Murfreesboro. The Confederates were aware of the Union movement, and the cavalry harassed the Federals during their trek southward. The main Confederate army formed a semi-circle along the banks of Stones River, starting about a mile to the west of Murfreesboro, and running to about a mile north of the town. This was done in an attempt to block all of the roads leading to Murfreesboro. By the night of December 30, the two armies faced each other at the river, along a southwest-northeast direction. The Federals were on the west side. However, the Confederate line was split by the water, with the southern two-thirds also on the west side. Both planned to attack the right flank of the other the next morning.

The Confederates were first off of the line in the early morning of December 31, the gray of their uniforms mixing with the fog and haze. The right flank of the Federal line was anchored at the Franklin Road, which runs east-west, and the troops faced southeast. The Confederates hit the unsuspecting Federals there, coming from the southeast and south, and extending beyond the end of the Federal defenders. As part of the attack moved against the end of the Federal line, other units, including cavalry, passed around the flank, and got into the rear of the Federals. This caused much confusion amongst the defenders, and they were overwhelmed. The rightmost Federal units then broke apart and retreated. However, the next division in line did not break, but bent the end back to face southwest, and meet the Confederate attack. Towards the center of the Federal line, to the northeast, the Confederate attack was not as coordinated, as the units were sent in one at a time. As well as being forced to withdraw in front of sustained Federal resistance there, the failure of the attack in the center also caused the assault to stall along the southern end of the line.

Regrouping, the Confederates attacked near the center. By this time, the Confederates who had been successful to the south had turned their attention on the right flank of the Federal line, which had bent back to the northwest, and faced southwest. They hit this line, as well as flanked it to the north, again getting into the rear of a Federal division. The pressure was too much for the Federals, and another division dissolved, retreating northward. With the line to the south having disintegrated by the Confederate attacks, the next Federal division north of this, under the command of General Phil Sheridan, angled his southernmost units back to face west, connecting with reinforcements coming from the north. Sheridan's line then formed a V. The Confederates continued to attack the Federal position from both sides. But instead of breaking this time under the pressure, Sheridan was able to move his units slowly back to the north, reforming them on the north side of the Wilkinson Pike.

With the withdrawal of the Federal center to the north side of the Wilkinson Pike, the Confederates pursued them and attacked again. Although initially able to hold back this onslaught on all sides, Sheridan's units were running short of ammunition. Earlier, the Confederate cavalry, which had gotten into the rear of the Federal defenses, had attacked the ammunition train, forcing it to withdraw to safety to the north, and out of reach of the Federal units that needed its supplies. Thus, Sheridan was required to withdraw back to the Nashville Pike, the next road to the north. Holding the center of the Federal defenses, Sheridan's withdrawal towards the Nashville Pike caused a gap in the line. The Confederates then focused on this hole, in an attempt to break through into the rear of the Federals. But, the units on each side of Sheridan also withdrew, pulling back to the Nashville Pike, and connecting on either side of him.

The Federals that had withdrawn to the Nashville Pike faced southwest, the pike running in a northwest-southeast direction. This new line connected with the original line at the southeast corner, the original line still running northeast, back to the river. At this intersection of the two lines, a salient was formed. The troops in the salient were positioned in a clump of woods, known as the Round Forest. Believing that this prominence was susceptible to crossfire, the Confederates then focused on this area. But the attacking units had to cross open ground in order to reach the defensive position. Heavy fire from the defenders in the Round Forest, and supporting artillery to the rear, prevented the Confederates from reaching their objective, and the remnants withdrew.

By early afternoon, the Confederate attack on the left was sputtering out. These men had pushed the Federals from the Franklin Road, where they had faced southeast, all the way back to the Nashville Pike, where the Federals then faced southwest. Having been resupplied and reorganized, the Federal position was strong. The Confederate commander, General Braxton Bragg, decided to focus on the left part of the Federal line, between the Round Forest and Stones River, to the northeast. He felt that this part of the line had been weakened in order to strengthen the Federal right flank, the units on that side of the line having had to fight all morning against the Confederate onslaught. But Bragg was out of reinforcements on the west side of the river, and had to wait for additional units to arrive from the east side before he could continue the attack. Thus, a lull settled over the battlefield for most of the afternoon, as Bragg waited for those reinforcements to arrive in position. This though, also gave the Federals time to reinforce the line anchored at the Round Forest with additional artillery support.

Late in the afternoon, the Confederates were ready. But instead of waiting for all of the reinforcements to arrive, Bragg ordered an attack with only half of the division present. Moving across the open fields, as their comrades had done earlier in the day, the results were the same. Federal artillery, massed on the high ground behind the Round Forest, fired into the ranks of the Confederates at long range. As they neared the Federal position, the defenders of the Round Forest then added to the lead already in the air. The Confederates were forced to retreat. By this time, the second group of Confederates had arrived and positioned themselves for attack. Following in the footsteps of their fellow units, the results were the same: more death, with no gains. The Round Forest would become nicknamed Hell's Half Acre by those who fought there.

With darkness approaching, this ended the fighting for the day. Bragg felt that he had won the day. Through the night, the Federals sent their wounded back to Nashville in wagons, which then picked up supplies to bring back to the front. Noticing these wagons moving to the rear, Bragg felt that the Federals were retreating, and that his army would be spending the next day chasing the Federals back to Nashville. But the Federal commander, after consulting with his subordinates, was determined to stay where he was.

During the night, the Federals reduced their lines, pulling back from the Round Forest towards the northwest. At the northeastern end of the line, a division was sent across to the east side of Stones River. As January 1 dawned, Bragg was surprised to see that the Federals were still in front of him. He moved his men into the Round Forest, closer to the Federal lines, and sent the division that had originally been on the east side of the river back over there again. But because Bragg had not expected the Federals to still be in front of him, he had not developed a plan of attack. Thus, except for some skirmishing around the Round Forest, and on the east side of the river, no attack was made.

During the day of January 2, Bragg felt that the position of the Federals on the east side of Stones River, which was on high ground near the bank, gave them the ability to enfilade the Confederate line at the Round Forest. He thus determined for his units on the east side of the river to attack the Federal position, and remove this threat. As preparations commenced for this assault, the Federal commander could see what was happening, and repositioned supporting units, including 58 artillery pieces, on the west side of the river, to the rear of those on the east bank.

In the late afternoon, in rain and sleet that had been falling all day, the attack commenced. Having to cross open ground, the Confederates pushed forward against the defenders, who held the higher ground. Finally reaching the Federal position, hand-to-hand combat ensued. After fierce fighting, the Federals began to give way. The Federals streamed down the east bank and crossed the ford to the safety of the Federal line. As the Confederates crested the hill in pursuit, they were greeted by the 58 guns of the Federal artillery, as well as rifles of the supporting infantry units. But instead of halting, as they had been ordered to do by their officers, the Confederate soldiers continued down the east slope, after the retreating Federals. The fire from the guns though, up to 100 rounds a minute, was too much for the Confederates, most of whom found themselves trapped in the river, or next to the water on either bank. At that point, the Federals counterattacked. Some Confederates raced back up the hill, pursued by the Federals, while others surrendered by the river. The Confederate officers tried to reform their men near the crest of the hill, but to no avail. When the Federals reached the top of the ridge, there was no resistance to meet them. The Confederates kept retreating, back beyond their starting point to the east. Darkness ended the Federal pursuit.

During January 3, the two armies continued to face one another along the banks of Stones River. The Federals were receiving reinforcements and ammunition from Nashville; the Confederates had nothing additional. Finally, on January 4, Bragg decided that the odds were stacked against him, and he ordered his army to withdraw to the southeast, towards Tullahoma. The Battle of Stones River was over.

The battlefield is part of the National Park Service. The park is located on the Old Nashville Highway, which runs parallel to, and west of U.S. 41/70S. It is roughly a rectangular plot of land, bounded on the north by the Old Nashville Highway, which was the Nashville Pike, and on the south by the Manson Pike, which was then the Wilkinson Pike. This is where the main part of the fighting had taken place during the afternoon of December 31, after the Confederates had pushed the Federals back from their initial positions into their defensive lines against the Stones River.

Arriving at the Visitors Center, I go inside to view the film, which gives an overview of the battle, and to pick up a brochure, which describes the stops on the tour of the park. While at the Visitors Center, I also wander through the bookstore, to see what books they have, and to find out if there is any reference material that may aid me in my travels around the state. While looking over the shelves, I come across a booklet entitled *The General's Battlefield Guide*, published by Blue & Gray Magazine. As well as describing the battle that took place here, including pictures, at the back of the publication is a driving tour of the battlefield, mainly concerned with the fighting that took place outside of the park, and finishing up with the stops within the park. This is similar to what I had found in Perryville, Kentucky, and had enjoyed so much. So, I decide to buy this issue, in order to broaden my understanding of the battle. After taking a few minutes to study it, get my bearings, and try to comprehend a bit of what I am setting out to see, I commence my tour of the Battle of Stones River.

Starting at the entrance to the park, on the Nashville Pike, I turn right, southeast, and stop at two markers on the right side of the road, about ¼ mile past the Round Forest. This is the site of the Cowan House. The house was located to the southwest of the markers, on a bit of high ground, now enveloped by a clump of trees. The house ended up burning before the battle had begun.

One of the markers here indicates that the troops of Confederate General James Chalmers marched across this open land towards the Round Forest, in the distance to the northwest. The land is still flat, and open grassland. Chalmers' troops had initially been held in reserve. They started their attack after the Federals had been forced back across the Nashville Pike, and into the vicinity of the Round Forest, which was late in the morning. This Confederate force never made it to the Round Forest, but was decimated by Union artillery before reaching it.

The second marker identifies the movement of the other Confederate brigade that was held in reserve, that of General Daniel Donelson. Positioned behind Chalmers' brigade and the Cowan House, to the southwest of here, Donelson's troops advanced after Chalmers' men were repulsed. However, the Cowan House, and Chalmers' retreating soldiers, forced Donelson's advancing men to split into two separate groups. Thus attacking as two smaller forces, they did reach the Round Forest, but were repulsed by the Union defenders there, ending up having to retire also.

Continuing southeastward on the Nashville Pike, and crossing the railway tracks, which were here during the time of the battle, I make a sharp turn to the left, onto a side road, and climb a bank to the top of some high ground located here. On the right, cut out of a clump of trees, is a bit of lawn, and a marker of stacked cannonballs, indicating the site of Confederate General Braxton Bragg's headquarters after the initial fighting of December 31.

From here, I am supposed to continue southeast on the Nashville Pike, and cross Stones River. On the eastern bank is high ground, which ascends from the riverbed. At that spot is situated Fortress Rosecrans, built after the battle to protect the Union supply base. However, the bridge that crosses the river is being rebuilt, which means that I have to backtrack to Van Cleve Lane, which is beside the National Park. The lane, on the north side of the road, connects Old Nashville Pike with the present highway. Not interested in the fortress, because it had nothing to do with the battle, and was never part of any action after its construction, I then check to see what the next stop on the tour is, and continue on to that one.

The Old Nashville Pike connects with US 41/70S, just beyond where it crosses Stones River, to the southeast. After leaving Fortress Rosecrans, I am supposed to get on the highway and continue to the southeast. I return to near the park, and turn north onto Van Cleve Lane, the road that I had used to get from the highway to the park. At the highway, I turn southeast, cross the river, and pick up the tour again as I pass by College Street, on my right. I turn right at the intersection with State Highway 96, Franklin Road, its name during the time of the battle, and drive westward until I cross Interstate 24. Just beyond the interstate, I turn left, south, onto Cason Lane.

Near this intersection, on the right, is the trace of an old road into the woods. This was the access to the Rideout House, which is no longer standing. I cannot find any significance of this house, so I continue on.

A short distance further on Cason Lane, I turn left, onto Racquet Club Drive. In the northwest quadrant of the intersection of Racquet Club Drive and River Rock Boulevard, which is now located in a residential area, is the fenced cemetery of the McCulloch family. In this cemetery are buried two Confederate officers. Across the road, on River Rock Boulevard, is the McCulloch House. I am unable to see it from here because of a growth of trees. This was the headquarters of Confederate corps commander General William Hardee. All of this residential area contains the original position of the Confederate left flank, before its attack on the morning of December 31. The line ran north-south here, and faced west before the assault commenced. The landscape in this region of battlefield is flat, containing no hilly sections at all.

River Rock Boulevard circles back and connects with Cason Lane. Returning back to Franklin Road, I turn west, and drive about ½ mile to Gresham Lane, situated on the right. I turn north onto Gresham Lane and pull over.

This was the far right flank of the Union line, the last brigade located on the west side of Gresham Lane. The Federal line angled northeast from this intersection. A few houses line the road on both sides. The land rises slightly in the distance to the north, but here where I am standing, the land is flat. The Confederate line, moving westward from the area around Cason Lane, initially was in a north-south alignment, but pivoted in a counterclockwise direction to hit the Union line from the southeast and south. Here, at the far end of the line, the Confederates attacked from the south side of Franklin Road, and pushed the Federals north, parallel to Gresham Lane.

Just to the west of the Union line, along Franklin Road, phony camps had been set up. This was a ploy by the Federals to make the Confederates think that there were more soldiers here than there actually were. This ploy forced Confederate General Bragg to move more of his troops to this area, thinking that the Federals were fortifying this side of the line in order to attack. Thus, he weakened his right wing, the side that the Federals had planned on attacking. Unfortunately for the Federals, the Confederates attacked first, and with a much stronger force than Bragg had originally intended. This ploy of making phony camps to deceive the enemy was employed by both sides during the war.

Continuing north on Gresham Lane to a rise in the road, this is where the Federals tried to reform their line after the first assault. About ½ mile to the north was a reserve brigade, which was brought up to reinforce this line. However, the onslaught continued, and the line was broken. This area is now being developed into a subdivision. The houses are being built on large lots though, which allows me to get an idea of how the landscape here would have been during the battle. It consists of open space, which continues back from the road in both directions. This would have allowed the Federal line that reformed here to see the approaching Confederates, not only directly in their front, but also on their flanks as well.

Gresham Lane angles to the northwest, and runs parallel to Interstate 24, ending at Manson Pike, called the Wilkinson Pike during the war. The original part of Gresham Lane had continued straight to the north, to connect with Wilkinson Pike. But because of the construction of the interstate across the old road, a new section was built parallel to the interstate, so that Gresham Lane still connects to Manson Pike, but farther to the west. Driving along the new section of the road, and looking northeast across the interstate, a farm comes into view. It was at that location, then the Gresham Farm, that Union corps commander General Alexander McCook had his headquarters. The body of Union General Joshua Sill was also found at that location by the Confederates, when they overran it.

The next two stops are houses that existed during the time of the battle. The first one is near the end of the new section of Gresham Lane, where it meets Wilkinson Pike. In a new subdivision on the left, sits an older house, which was the Jenkins House. Turning left onto Wilkinson Pike, and going a short distance to the west, the General Smith House is located on the left side of the road. Both of these residences would have become involved in the melee, as the Union forces retreated northward from their original positions, back towards the Nashville Pike.

Across from the General Smith House is a lane running to the north, which used to be the beginning of Ashbury Road. The entrance to Ashbury Road is now farther to the east, just past the interstate. As with Gresham Lane, the original lane has been cut by the construction of the interstate. A large Federal wagon train was parked here on Wilkinson Pike when the attack began. During the initial assault, the Confederate cavalry, operating on the left flank, headed around the right flank of the Federal line and to the north, threatening to capture the wagon train parked here. To prevent its capture, the supply train quickly turned north onto Ashbury Road, and headed to safety.

A side trip from the main tour can be taken at this point. After reading through the description, I decide that the side trip does not interest me. The side trip goes about ¼ mile further west, to where Wilkinson Pike crosses Overall Creek. There, two days preceding the battle, December 29, Union troops marching down from Nashville ran into Confederate soldiers on the west side of the creek. A small skirmish took place, with the Federals chasing the Confederates across the water. Farther to the west of the creek, at the intersection of the Wilkinson Pike with Blackman Road, in what is now the village of Blackman, the Federal troops camped on the evening of December 29.

To keep on with the main tour, I drive back to the east on Wilkinson Pike, for about a mile. On the left is the foundation of the Blanton House. A short distance beyond this, and on the right side of the road, is the entrance to the Harding House. The site was about ½ mile south of the road. Very vicious fighting took place around the house during the early stages of the battle.

I continue the tour by driving east a little further, turning right, south, onto Van Cleve Drive, and driving to the end. Facing south, the site of the Harding House is off to the right, and hidden by trees. As I look out onto a flat field of wild grass, bordered on three sides by trees, the Confederate attack would have come into the open from the left, and angled towards my right rear. The Union troops were pushed across this meadow in front of the Confederates, moving off to the right, and back out of my sight again. Somewhere in the field of my vision, Union General Joshua Sill would have been killed. His men carried his body onward to the Gresham House.

Turning around to face north, a brigade of Federal General Philip Sheridan's division was stationed on an angle, southwest-northeast, on the left side of the road. As Federal troops were pushed back across the field to my rear, the brigade stationed here held firm. The Federal line to the south of these troops was forced to pivot back on itself, and ended up to the northwest of Sheridan's brigade, facing west. This created a salient for the men that held the line here, and they found themselves being attacked from three sides. A story goes that during the height of this onslaught, a Union corporal walked up to his colonel, handed him his gun, and calmly told the officer that he was going on furlough. Before the colonel could reprimand the young soldier, he realized that the corporal's intestines were seeping out of a hole in his abdomen. After intense fighting here, the Union line eventually had to move back to the north with the rest of the troops, as they set up to make a stand along the Nashville Pike.

At this point, another side trip can be taken. Again, because the stops on this detour are not directly related to the battle, I will continue with the main tour. The side trip goes east on Wilkinson Pike about a mile, to the headquarters of Confederate General Leonidas Polk, the corps commander of the right wing. It then proceeds on to near Stones River, and the earthworks of Fortress Rosecrans, which were built after the battle, and are of no interest to me.

From Van Cleve Lane, I turn left, back onto Wilkinson Pike, and head west. At Asbury Lane, which as stated earlier, is a new part of the road and was not here during the war, I veer to the right, onto it. As it straightens out to the north after a short distance, I am now on the original part of the road. It was along this stretch that the Union wagon train made its escape from the advancing Confederate cavalry. At the end of the road, on the north side of the intersection with Asbury Road, sat Asbury Church, which no longer exists.

Turning right onto Asbury Road, I head east for ½ mile, to the Widow Burris House, a small white structure located on the north side of the road. On the south side, Union reinforcements, coming in from the northeast, set up a defensive line along the road to block the advancing Confederates, who were moving from the south. This line was set up to prevent the Confederates from flanking the army to the right, and overrunning Asbury Road, the Federals lifeline back to Nashville. The defenses here became a mass of confusion, as the men holding the line became intermingled with retreating Union troops and the oncoming Confederate army. The retreating Federal troops here were remnants of the right flank, which had been attacked along Franklin Road and Gresham Lane. This line here stopped the momentum of the Confederate onslaught.

I cannot get an idea of the landscape over which the ferocity of the battle took place along this road, for the battlefield is obscured by a field of very tall corn that grows almost to the edge of the road. In the distance to the south, I can identify the tops of trees that probably form the edge of some woods. But what the terrain actually looks like in between, and how the fight may have unfolded here, cannot be ascertained by me.

What I have to keep remembering, as I drive around and tour this battlefield, is that the battle took place at the end of December. At almost all of the other battlefields that I have visited, the fighting had taken place in the spring, summer, or fall. Thus, the vegetation that I encountered during my visits to those sites, gave me a similar viewpoint to what the soldiers would have seen, taking into account if vegetation was growing at those particular spots at the time of the battle. But here, I have to keep in mind that that is not the case. The high corn that I see growing before me now, would have been harvested by the time the fighting began. Even though forests would have been here then, and I will encounter some shortly, the leaves of the deciduous trees, and most of the undergrowth, would have fallen away by the battle, giving the soldiers more opportunity to see through the woods than I will have.

Continuing east to the end of Asbury Road, at the intersection with Nashville Pike, I turn left, and proceed about ½ mile, to Rosecrans' headquarters, the Union general in command of the army. On the west side of the road, a marker of stacked cannonballs, similar to what marks the site of Bragg's headquarters, indicates the site of the command center.

At this point, I have the option of taking another side trip. Further to the northwest, at the intersection with Hord Road, which connects to the Nashville Pike from the south, is the Hord House, on the north side of the road across from the intersection. Confederate cavalry advancing northward along Hord Road, temporarily captured a Union hospital set up at the Hord House, and a wagon train. They were eventually chased off by the Federal cavalry. I am not going to go on that side trip. So my next stop is the National Battlefield Park, where the heaviest fighting took place as the Federals started to make the Confederates fight for every inch of soil that they gained.

I drive southeast on Nashville Pike just over ½ mile, to the entrance to the park, on the right. I have completed a clockwise circle from when I left the park earlier to begin the tour. Already having a tour brochure for the park, I proceed along the road that circles the battlefield in a counterclockwise direction. The tour starts near the Nashville Pike, moves south, then loops back to the north.

Stopping at each point, it will become very difficult to keep my bearings. I usually know my directions, and always have an idea of the motion of a battle. But here at this battle, I will find it very difficult to figure out how that part of a battle was unfolding as I tour the stops. A number of times, I will expect the Confederates to be facing in one direction, and the Federals against them, only to find out that the troops were in actual fact positioned to the reverse, or facing in another completely different direction. This is because of the way that the battle unfolded. Troops who were originally positioned in one direction wound up facing in totally different directions as the fight continued, caused by the Confederates pushing the Federals back. In some instances, the line collapsed, while in other instances, the defenses merely folded back on themselves.

The first stop is the position of the Federal artillery, which supported the northwest corner of the salient, just south of the Asbury Road. The guns are facing in a southwest direction. They are lined up along the edge of some woods. This position is a knoll, which overlooks a small open field, surrounded by thick woods on all sides. Across this field of knee-high grass, the gunners would have caught the sight of retreating Federal soldiers coming towards their dug-in position. Behind these men, they would have seen Confederate soldiers pursuing them. The fire from the guns here halted the Confederate advance, and forced the enemy back into the safety of the thick woods.

As I wander amongst the guns, I hop onto a large rock to get a better view of the land that slopes away in the distance to the tree line. As I am taking in this site, I realize that the rock that I am standing on would have been here during the battle. I start to think about the commotion that would have swirled around this piece of stone, silent and still, and a contrast to the human beings who would have been scurrying around it, setting up the guns, and positioning themselves for the battle ahead. I wonder if anyone during that time would have taken any time to even notice that this rock was here, or were they oblivious to it because of their attention to their tasks. I then think that perhaps a soldier had even stood on this rock, as I am now doing, maybe to get a better view of what all the commotion was farther down in the field. Possibly blood may have even been spilled onto this stone, washed away by time. This I find very interesting: that I am standing on something, albeit inanimate, that had been involved with the battle that took place here.

The second stop, to the south, is titled The Battle for the Cedars. This includes a small walk to the west, into the thick cedar woods of the area. In this dense vegetation, Federal reinforcements set up a defensive line, facing in a southwest direction. This line was attacked by the advancing Confederates, and a fierce fight took place here.

These woods have been compared to the Wilderness area of Virginia, where a number of battles were fought. Having toured the thick woods of the Wilderness, I do not find the forest at this spot on a scale with that of Virginia. The vegetation here consists of a dense growth of small spindly trees, but the brush that grows on the forest floor is not as high, or as thick, as that of the Wilderness. Therefore, except for the number of trees themselves, I find that I can see for further distances than anywhere I had trodden in the Wilderness. The growth there had made it very difficult for me to see any more than about six feet distant, and movement through that greenery was hard. Here at Stones River, it is easier to walk through the growth. Also, the fighting in the Wilderness took place in May, when the leaves of the undergrowth would have added to the thickness of the brush. Stones River was fought in December, when most, if not all, of the leaves would have fallen away. Of course, the cedars would have still contained their growth. Having compared to two battlefields, this site still would not have been a location where I would have wanted to try to fight with the enemy. Understanding where friend or foe was positioned still would not have been an easy task.

On my walk through the woods here, I notice that outcroppings of rock are common on the forest floor. This rock turns out to be limestone. I realize now that the rock that I had stood on at the previous stop, where the Federal artillery had set up, is not the anomaly that I had thought that it was. As it turns out, outcroppings of rock are common here.

A bit farther to the south, the next stop requires another short trip into the woods. By noon hour on December 31, this area was in Confederate hands. Walking through the thick forest, I come to a Confederate artillery piece, and immediately wonder what the heck an artillery piece is doing in the middle of the forest. It certainly would not have been of any use: cannonballs would not have penetrated very far past the first row of trees, thus reducing their effectiveness; and the artillerymen would not have been able to see any Federal troops advancing on them, until they realized that they were about to be overrun. As it turns out, the gun here was being moved up to support the Confederate attack, which was by that time nearing the Nashville Pike, to the north. Unfortunately, the thick woods and many rock outcroppings made it very difficult for the artillerymen to continue through the forest, and push forward to support their fellow troops. Thus, the infantry had to attack the Federal lines without any artillery assistance.

The following stop was where Federal General Sheridan made his stand against innumerable attacks. This spot is at the southernmost end of the park, near the Wilkinson Pike. Out in front of the rest of the retreating army, he held his ground here, after being driven back from just on the south side of the pike. The right flank of the army wrapped around this position, back to the northwest, creating a bulge in the line. This stop is at the extreme southern part of the bulge.

From the road, I walk across a bit of lawn, to the edge of the woods. Just inside the forest, darkened by the shade of the numerous cedar trees that grow here, are a couple of Union artillery pieces, broken up into pieces. This display exemplifies the ferocity of the fighting that took place here; this area became known as the Slaughter Pen. Because the park road had started its loop, moving from west to east, and this stop is on the southeast part of the park, I expect the guns, and therefore Union troops, to be facing in a southeast direction. But to my surprise, the men here were in fact facing in a southwest direction.

So, before I can understand what had unfolded here, I need to get my bearings straight. This takes a couple of minutes of going over the battle during that part of the day again, turning the map upside down, standing facing north, and a few other gyrations. Finally, I have an understanding of the positioning of both sides, and proceed to try to comprehend the ferocity of the battle here.

The broken guns are laid out amongst a large outcropping of rock that barely penetrates above the surface, probably about a half foot in height. The rock is continuous in this area, although broken, and therefore makes walking very difficult. It would be very easy to turn an ankle on this rocky and uneven ground. This initially worked in the Federals favor, for it slowed the Confederate forward movement, and gave the Union soldiers more time in which to fire into the advancing mass of men. However, in time, the Federal troops realized that they had to vacate this ground. Their retreat then became as difficult as the Confederate advance had been, with these soldiers having to withdraw across the same type of rocky landscape. Many a Union soldier was killed because of the difficulty of enacting a speedy retreat from this spot. As a matter of fact, the outcroppings to the rear of here, over which the Federals had to scramble, were 2-3 feet in height, making their movement more laborious than that of the Confederates. The Federals had used these higher rocks to effect, as shelter during some of the artillery barrages that the Confederates fired between infantry attacks. But their advantage was turned to disadvantage when they had to scramble over these same rocks to safety.

I walk deeper into the woods, to see if there is anything more of interest, but I find nothing. Returning to the car, but standing beside it, I go over in my mind again the positions of the troops, and compare what I understand them to be with the map. I am still not convinced that the artillery pieces are set up and facing in the right direction, and thus that the park is correct in displaying the position of the Federal soldiers who defended this spot. As I am contemplating this, an elderly gentleman happens to jog by on the roadway. He must have noticed the Ontario license plate on the back of the car, for he calls out, to welcome me to Tennessee. I thank him as he continues on, and think that that is a very friendly thing to do. He could have just jogged on without saying a word, but had decided to show his hospitality. It was a small gesture on his part, but it made me feel good, and I appreciated it.

The next stop, about midway back to the north end of the park, was the high mark of the Confederate advance in the morning, on the central portion of the Federal line. This was accomplished by Donelson's brigade, whose marker, back at the beginning of this morning, was the first one that I had come across, on the Nashville Pike. This brigade had marched across the open area near the Cowan site, and hit the Union line here. The stop is right along the side of the road, amongst the woods. So it is difficult to ascertain the location, and understand its relevance from a more global view of the battlefield. For the Union troops stationed here in the woods though, they would not have been aware of the approaching Confederates until they were right on top of them. Even so, the Federals held off the first attempt to break the line, and a second attack was required for the line to be broken.

The following stop, located at the northeast end of the loop, shows the Union position late in the afternoon of December 31. Here, a row of guns has been placed, indicating how the defensive line was drawn up. Again, I am initially confused by the positioning of the Union line, for the guns are pointed in a southwest direction. The previous stop had indicated that the Confederates had attacked from the east, which is what I had expected. So driving directly north, from that stop to this one, I expect the guns to be pointed in the same direction, east. However, as mentioned, the guns are pointed in a southwest direction.

Now I have to pull the maps out again, to figure out what was going on. As it turns out, the original northeast-southwest Federal line, which had been set up across the Nashville Pike around the Round Forest, still existed. I have not yet been to the Round Forest, but can seen it across the field to the northeast. So as the Federal troops along this stretch pulled back to the north, they were positioned to swing around to face to the southwest, and the line ran back to the northwest, along the south side of the Nashville Pike. Now I am ready to view this stop, and get a better understanding of what had taken place here.

The guns are situated near the pike, at the edge of a field. At the time of the battle, this was a cotton field, but today it is a field of hay. Looking over the tops of one of the guns, the ground has a very slight rise to it, then it descends again at a tree line in the distance. In the late afternoon, the formation of the new Union line here had been completed, and the Confederates attacked it from the southwest, and from the east towards the Round Forest. Out of the woods at the far end of the field, to the southwest, they came, and across the wide open ground. The Union guns had a devastating effect on the approaching Confederates; the noise from the guns was so loud that some of the soldiers stopped to put cotton in their ears. The Confederates never did reach the Federal line here, but had to retreat back to the safety of the woods.

This stop finishes the loop, but there are still a few more sites to visit. I exit back onto Nashville Pike, turning right, then immediately turn left, into the area of the National Cemetery. Here on the north side of the Pike, there is a lawn, over which stands a few large cedar trees, shading thousands of small stone markers of fallen Union soldiers from the battle. Scattered amongst the neat rows are some small square brick-size markers, which rest on the ground. I do not wander up to one to see why those ones are different from the rest. My interest in this site is that during the early afternoon, this had been the location of the Federal artillery, which supported the defensive line as it formed up on the south side of the Nashville Pike. On this slightly higher ground, the guns were lined up parallel to the road.

A little farther to the southeast on the Nashville Pike is the Round Forest. Originally encompassing about four acres, today most of the Round Forest is gone, claimed by an industrial site. It had extended all the way to present-day US Highway 41/70S.

During the course of the battle on December 31, this was the only Federal position that was not pushed back by the Confederate assaults; it held all day. A number of attacks were attempted throughout the day, and all were repulsed. This area was dubbed Hell's Half Acre.

Looking southeast from the line that was formed here, a field lies just to the front. In the background is a wooded area, which may not have been there during the time of the battle. There are also a few large pine trees to the right of this line, which were not here during the fight. Back from the road, on the north side, and surrounded by about a four-foot stone wall, is a small plot, in which lie some of the men that fell here defending this ground. A square stone monument, about 10 feet in height, and about eight feet across, has been built near the entrance to the cemetery.

Although this does not complete the tour of the National Battlefield Park, there are more sites that are part of the driving tour, which I want to visit first, before continuing with the park stops. The next section deals with the battle that took place on January 2.

So, the first thing that I do is backtrack a bit on the Old Nashville Pike from the Round Forest, to connect with US 41/70S again, by turning north onto Van Cleve Lane. Turning right onto the main highway, I head towards Murfreesboro. As the road crosses Stones River, a golf course is located on the left. Upon the side of the hill, known as Wayne's Hill, which is part of the golf course, the Confederates had set up their guns for the battle of December 31, to support the troops that were attacking in the vicinity of the Round Forest.

Continuing on for about ¾ mile, I turn left onto Clark Street, and immediately left again, onto Battleground Drive. I travel north on Battleground Drive for about a mile, then turn left onto Riverview Drive. To my left is Wayne's Hill. As Riverview Drive curves around to the north, I am now close to the river, and am following the line of attack of the Confederate troops on the late afternoon of January 2. The road is ascending, and is in a residential area. Near the top of the hill, the Union line was set up parallel to the road, and facing east. There are no markers here, so I have to get an idea of where I am from the map in the tour book. The Confederates attacked over this area, coming up the hill from the southeast, my right rear, and pivoting to the west, left. What is now a pristine neighborhood of lawns and houses, was a bloody battlefield on January 2, 1863. The Federals were beaten back rather quickly from this position.

I then turn left, onto Royal Drive, and go to the end of this road, which is not very far, to where it intersects with Thompson Lane. This is the highest point of the hill, and the Federal troops reassembled here after being driven back from their previous location on Riverview Drive. But the momentum of the Confederate charge broke this line, and the Federals raced down the hill and across Stones River. The hill here is grown up with shrubs and bushes, so I cannot see beyond the edge of the road to the other side of the hill, nor to the river.

A side trip is now possible, to visit the site of the Hoover House, where a reserve Union brigade was positioned. The site of the house is reached by turning right onto Thompson Lane, left onto Riverbend Drive, and right onto Shannon Drive. The Hoover House stood at the intersection of Shannon Drive with Londonderry Drive. Again, I did not choose to visit this site because nothing of consequence happened there. So, I continue on to the next stop.

Turning left onto Thompson Lane, I follow it south, crossing Stones River. To the west of the road, along the river, is McFadden's Ford. It was in the vicinity of this ford that the retreating Union troops crossed the two-foot deep waterway, back to the west side, after the Confederate attack atop the hill. The bridge crosses from the top of the hill, so it is quite a distance above the river. Thus, it is difficult for me to see the side of the hill that the withdrawing Federals descended.

I continue southward on Thompson Lane, to where it ends at US 41/70S, just west of where the highway crosses the river. Looking to the left, towards the river, this was the scene of Harker's Crossing. During the evening of December 29, a Federal reconnaissance group crossed the river to establish a foothold on the east side. After this was done, the rest of the brigade crossed over. A short time later, they were withdrawn, when it was realized that they faced a Confederate division. I turn right, and after ½ mile, I turn right again, onto Van Cleve Lane. This takes me north to McFadden's Ford.

Leaving my car in the parking lot, which is on high ground, I walk down to the edge of the water. The river now has trees and shrubs growing along its banks, with many of the branches overhanging the water. This makes it difficult to determine the width of the river, and where the water ends on the far side. At the time of the battle, there was very little vegetation in the locality of the river, but today, I cannot see anything to the east beyond the wall of greenery. I am on the Federal, west, side of the river. The stillness of the water would have been broken first by the retreating Union soldiers as they crossed, hoping to reach safety. However, as they advanced up the slopes on this side of the river, the pursuing Confederates were continuously firing into their ranks. Next, the Confederates crossed the river, chasing after their prey.

Turning around from the river, I see what first the Union soldiers would have seen, then the pursing Confederates. The land on this side is at a height of a few feet above the edge of the water. It rises slightly as it moves back from the river, then makes an abrupt jump of about 2-3 feet, exposing a rock ledge. This bank may have been formed by the river, if it used to be at a greater width than it is now. This area is now populated with trees. Not many though, for it is easy for me to see back up to the parking lot underneath the foliage. But there are enough to cause the edge of the river to be in the shadows. Again, this growth would not have been here during the time of the battle.

As the Confederates continued forward from the river, in pursuit of the retreating Federals, nearly 60 guns at the top of the hill, a distance of about 100 feet, opened up on them, destroying their ranks. Immediately after this, a line of Union troops stood up and sent a devastating fire into the shocked Confederates. As the Federals advanced, the Confederates turned and retreated back across the river, pursued by Union soldiers. The Federals stopped as they reached the crest of the hill on the other side of the river.

Walking back up the grade to the parking lot, and a row of Union guns, I turn around to glance back at what the gunners stationed here would have seen. Unfortunately, the growth of trees now blocks any view of the river, and beyond.

This ends my extended tour of the Battle of Stones River. I have seen quite a bit of the battlefield this morning, and I now have a better appreciation of what had unfolded here. Although at times, while walking over the battlefield, I had actually become more confused than enlightened. But in the end, I have an understanding of the difficulties that took place here.

Finishing with my tour of Stones River, I am ready to move on to my next stop. It is just a few miles to the southeast: Murfreesboro. As well as the battle at Stones River, smaller battles had also taken place in and around Murfreesboro during the war. I turn southeast onto US Highway 41/70s, and drive to the main part of the town.

I now start to search for any indicators of the war within it. The brochure that I had picked up about Civil War sites in Tennessee, states that the surrender for one of the battles had taken place at a plantation home called Oaklands. Finding markers that show the direction to it, I follow them to the site. I veer left off of the highway onto Vine Street, and drive to the east. At Maney Avenue, I turn north, and travel until I reach the end of it.

Oakland sits here on the north side of town, probably having been on the outskirts of Murfreesboro during the war. It rests a few hundred yards back from the street, surrounded by a manicured lawn, and many large trees. The house is now a museum. It was built by the Maney family, one of the wealthiest in the country at that time. The mansion hosted Confederate President Jefferson Davis just a few weeks before the Battle of Stones River. At the end of a gravel driveway, which circles in front of the residence, is the large two-story red-brick structure. A verandah stretches the length of the house on the first floor, and is adorned with numerous white pillars, paired off in an ornamental fashion to form arches. I am not interested in viewing the house itself, but am interested in the grounds upon which it sits, since a battle took place on these surroundings.

A marker at the end of the driveway indicates that Confederate cavalry Colonel Nathan Bedford Forrest raided Murfreesboro on July 13, 1862. This was part of the Confederate strategy in the summer of 1862 to interrupt the supply line of the Union army, which ran from Louisville through central Tennessee. The Union army was approaching Chattanooga from the west, through northern Alabama. Colonel John Hunt Morgan left Knoxville, entered and raided Kentucky during the month of July. Colonel Forrest was to have the same strategy in central Tennessee.

Part of his plan was the raid on Murfreesboro, an important railway hub. A Federal force was stationed in the town, but was dispersed between two camps: one on the north side of town, and one farther to the west, near Stones River. Forrest's plan called for both camps to be attacked simultaneously, while separate groups raced to the center of town to capture the jail, and other key buildings. One of the skirmishes took place here at Oaklands. This was the Federal camp that was nearest to town. The other Federal camp to the west, was also attacked. Both groups of Federals though, were able to hold their assailants off. Late in the afternoon, with a stand-off between the two sides in effect, Forrest approached the commander of the troops here, and told him that his was the only group left that was still fighting, and since he was outnumbered, he should surrender. This bluff worked. Forrest next approached the other group, and told them the same thing. This group surrendered as well. Forrest then destroyed the stores in the town and broke up the railroad.

Finishing here, I drive back into the downtown core, to see if I can find any other markers. I head south on Maney Avenue until I reach Main Street, then turn west onto it. On the Courthouse lawn, at the corner of Church Street, I find another marker, which also has to do with Forrest's raid in July 1862. It states that Forrest's men arrived here, releasing a number of civilians who were being held in the jail, and took the Federal commander captive. The Courthouse is a red-brick two-story building, with two large pillars guarding the entrance of it. Two large trees on the lawn hide the front of the structure from my view.

The other battle that I know had been in the vicinity of Murfreesboro, occurred on December 5-7, 1864, during the Nashville Campaign. As the Confederates moved north from Franklin towards Nashville, Forrest was sent again to raid Murfreesboro, to destroy the railroad, and hopefully divert some of the Federal troops that were in front of Nashville. The fighting that took place during that time was around Fortress Rosecrans, and west of it, along the Wilkinson Pike. Forrest arrived in front of the fort on the evening of December 5. The next day, he demonstrated against Fortress Rosecrans, but did not attack it in earnest. On December 7, the Federals sent out part of the force from the fort. It ran into Forrest's men, and the two sides fought at what became known as the Battle of the Cedars. The Confederates were forced to retreat. Having already been along Wilkinson Pike earlier in the day, and not having seen any markers concerning the battle of 1864, I decide to move on to my next site.

This is to be at Vaught's Hill, also called the Battle of Milton. The village of Milton lies about 15 miles northeast of Murfreesboro, on State Highway 96. From the Courthouse, I circle the block, and start east on Lytle Street, until I reach Tennessee Boulevard. Here, I turn north, and drive until I see the signs for State 96, veering northeast onto Lascassas Pike. Leaving Murfreesboro, the land is similar to what I had encountered on my trip from Nashville: hills that are moderate in height, with slopes that are not steep, but very long. In some places, the distance to descend one slope and ascend the next can cover about two miles. Before reaching the village of Milton, I top a rise, and see a white marker on the right side of the road in the near distance. Pulling over, I get out of the car to read the sign, and survey my surroundings. This is where the Battle of Milton took place.

The battle here occurred on March 20, 1863, during the lull in fighting after the Battle of Stones River. A Federal brigade, heading back to Murfreesboro from the northeast, after a raid, ran into Confederate cavalry General John H. Morgan and his force. The Union troops were pushed back from east of Milton to this hilltop, and set up a defensive line here. The Confederates attacked all through the day. In the late afternoon, Morgan heard that Federal reinforcements were arriving from Murfreesboro, and decided to withdraw.

The land here is flat, but descends very slightly to the east. There are a few farms in the area, and the open fields are pastures. In the distance, about two miles away, a line of hills, one tight against the next, circle the area from the southeast to the northeast, and block my ability to see any distance beyond these obstructions. On the other hand, it makes this spot very scenic and picturesque, having the flat green fields set against the forested hills in the background, and it remains for me one of the prettier places that I encountered during my trek through Tennessee.

It seems to me that the spot where I am standing, was not a very good position from which a defense could be made. There are not any natural barriers or obstructions, around which a strong line could have been built. There is nothing here but open fields. However, the strategy did work, and the Confederates were held off.

It is now mid-afternoon, and I have two more sites that I want to find today. One is called Hoover's Gap, and the other is

Tullahoma. I have no idea where exactly Hoover's Gap is; it is not on any maps that I have. But I know that it is somewhere between Murfreesboro and Manchester, and more towards Manchester. To the southwest of Manchester is Tullahoma, my last stop of the day. I want to look for Hoover's Gap, but not spend much time in doing so, or else I will not have any time left to get to Tullahoma. I want to finish all of the sites southeast of Nashville today, because I will probably not get a chance to be back in this area again. According to the road atlas that I have, I can take a secondary road southward cross-country from Milton, and connect with County Road 64 at Readyville to continue my journey southward. This will bring me out at Beechgrove, on US Highway 41. I will then drive southeast to Manchester on US 41, looking for Hoover's Gap as I go. Since it isn't on my maps, I'm not sure whether it had been a town that no longer exists, or whether it is landmark: a gap between a set of mountains. If I have not found Hoover's Gap upon reaching Manchester, then I will head southwest along State Highway 56 to Tullahoma.

I drive eastward from Vaught's Hill to Milton. The community turns out to be about three houses along the highway, but there is no road here that goes to the south. The road atlas that I have has no highway number for the road that I am looking for, but I figure that any road heading south from the village would be the one to take. Driving past Milton for a short distance, I find no road beyond the village that may be the right one. Not wanting to guess at which road I am looking for, selecting the wrong one, and losing valuable time, I decide to backtrack to Murfreesboro, connect up with US 41 there, and drive southward to Manchester.

Returning to Murfreesboro over the same route that had taken me to Milton, I follow the signs to US Highway 41, then turn southeast towards Manchester. As I drive along, I notice that the hills turn into mountains, shorter in length than the long low hills that I had been traveling through earlier, but greater in height. The highway meanders through the mountains of the region, choosing to go around them as much as possible, instead of over the top of them.

As I start descending a hill, I continue to glance around in all directions, as I have been doing for a few miles now, in order to make sure that I don't miss a marker concerning the fight at Hoover's Gap. Just off of the road on my right, I happen to see an old abandoned and fallen down building of white, enveloped by the heavy woods of the region. A sign on the building reads Hoover's Gap Baptist Church. I quickly slow down, but continue on a bit further, because there are no other houses here to indicate that I have entered a community. Driving on for about a mile, I find no more houses.

So I have found Hoover's Gap. At some time, there had to have been a community here, but not any longer. Whether or not the community had existed during the war, I still cannot determine. I find a road that goes off to the west, called Hoover's Gap Road. Perhaps this leads to a village, so I turn onto it. The road crosses over a bridge for the interstate, comes to the eastern base of a large rocky mountain, and skirts it to the north. It seems apparent to me then, that the main highway, which runs to the east of this mountain, goes through a gap, known as Hoover's Gap. I follow the road for a distance. It descends into deep woods, darkening the road by preventing the sun from penetrating into this area. I believe that I am also heading back north, and decide that I will not find any community, nor have I found any Civil War markers.

An engagement had taken place here between June 24 and 26, 1863. The Confederates had been in this vicinity since their defeat at Stones River, the previous December. The Federal army began moving southeast from Murfreesboro in late June, with the objective of taking Chattanooga. As they advanced, they had to get through the gaps in this area, in order to continue their trek southward. The Confederates held those gaps, and were determined not to give them up.

Here, at Hoover's Gap, was one of the places that the Federals wanted to penetrate through the Confederate defenses. A Federal infantry brigade, under the command of Colonel John Wilder, had recently been mounted, and given new seven-shot Spencer repeating rifles. In the early morning of June 24, under a heavy rain, Wilder's brigade headed for Hoover's Gap, racing about 10 miles ahead of their infantry support. This quick lightning strike surprised the Confederates; Wilder's men were almost through the gap before the Confederates reacted. But setting up a defensive line at the south end of the gap, the Confederates were able to halt the Federal momentum. Wilder's men positioned themselves on the high ground above the head of the gap. The Confederates then counterattacked, but the outnumbered Federals were able to beat back this assault with the aid of their quick-loading rifles. Holding out against continued resistance, the Federal infantry started to arrive in the early evening. All the next day, the Confederates continued their attempts to retake the gap, but to no avail. On June 26, the Federals finally broke through, forcing the Confederates to begin their withdrawal towards Chattanooga.

Returning to the main highway, the time is approaching 5:00. I decide that it is too late now to continue on to Tullahoma. Upon getting there, I would have to find the site, then view it, and I do not know how long it would take me to do that. Then, I would have to return to Nashville, more than an hour away. I figure that this would put me back in Nashville well beyond 7:00, and Sue has made plans for her and myself to meet up with a cousin of hers who lives in the city. So, with that get-together in the back of my mind, and the fact that it is getting too late in the day to explore a battlefield, I settle on this as my stopping point for today.

I see on the road atlas that there is an interchange with Interstate 24 a few miles to the south, at Beechgrove. Connecting with the interstate will give me a quicker return to Nashville, since I am about 50 miles from there. A quick look at the map, and my itinerary list before embarking on my return trip, allows me to determine that perhaps Tullahoma can be visited tomorrow, if I am done with the sites on my agenda early. Tomorrow, I will head off in a southwest direction from Nashville, planning to finish at Columbia. If I am able to complete my visits early, then I can drive east to Tullahoma, and view that site afterwards.

Driving south on US Highway 41, I near the junction with the interstate at Beechgrove. Rounding a corner, I start to ascend a short, but steep hill. On my right is a marker, and I quickly pull over and stop. The marker is entitled Beech Grove Engagement, and states that the battle that took place here, consisted of Confederate troops defending Hoover's Gap. So, even though the gap through the mountains was almost four miles to the north, the quick strike by Wilder's mounted Federal brigade had caused the battle to actually take place south of the gap, here at Beechgrove. The marker does not indicate whether this was the Federal or Confederate position. It is at the top of a hill, and could have been where the Confederates set up to halt Wilder's advance, or could be the high ground that Wilder held and the Confederates had to attack from the south.

Descending the hill from where the marker is located, I come to the intersection with State Highway 64. Turning west onto it, I quickly arrive at the interstate. I realize that State 64, which comes in from the north, is the one that I had wanted to get onto after leaving Milton. If I had done so, I would have come out at this intersection, and turned south towards Manchester. I would have ended up missing Hoover's Gap, and the marker just to the north of the junction, because of the hill that it is hidden behind.

Arriving back at the hotel in Nashville, Sue gives me a run down of what she did during the day. She had decided that she would take a break from golfing and explore Nashville. She started by catching a ride downtown on the shuttle bus. The driver told her that it would be difficult to get around downtown today, because a country music singer had passed away, and his funeral was in progress. The singer is Bill Monroe, known as the Father of Bluegrass Music. Apparently, he had been an inspiration to quite a few country singers over the years, and many of the stars of the industry were expected to be there. It was held in the Auditorium. Sue decided to start her day there, and ended up attending the funeral. She says that as part of the ceremony, some of the singers came forward to sing.

In the afternoon, she got on a bus tour, which took her out to some of the mansions where the singers live. She passes on to me information that was told to her while she was on the tour; things concerning the state of Tennessee, and Nashville, which I did not know. Tennessee was originally known as West Carolina. Thus, the three stars on the state flag represent the original three Carolina states. I had wondered if there was a region that had called itself West Carolina. While I was in North Carolina, I had toured the eastern part of the state, and it was called East Carolina, even though it was part of the state of North Carolina. I had also been to South Carolina, my first excursion into the Civil War. Now I have added West Carolina to the other three Carolinas that I had visited.

Sue continues that the largest industry in Nashville is publishing, not, as most people think, including myself, country music. She says that country music is actually fifth on the list, as far as generating money for the city. She also tells me that the Grand Ole Opry was originally downtown, centered around the Auditorium, which had hosted the funeral of Bill Monroe today. But in recent times, it has moved out to its present location, just north of our motel on the east end of the city. So, she had ended up having a full day, as had I, and is quite happy with her explorations, and what she had accomplished.

We head out now to meet Sue's cousin for supper. Sue has not seen her for a few years, but had called her before we left Ottawa, to see if she was going to be around. She said that she was, and the last evening, Sue had called and arranged to meet her. Her name is Merna. Her husband is David, and they have two children, Christine and Steven. They are living in Nashville because David is managing the Cumberland Museum and Science Center. They have lived here for about two years. Sue had told them that the reason that we were coming to Tennessee was because of my interest in the Civil War.

During the course of conversion over dinner, David asks me if I had toured Nashville yet. I tell him that I have not, but that that is what I am going to do tomorrow. He says that the Science Center is just behind one of the Civil War forts that had defended Nashville during the war. It was Fort Negley. Although it is closed to the public, he tells me that he wanders the grounds sometimes during lunch hours, to get out and get some fresh air. He says that the ruins of the fort still exist, but are falling down. He has heard that the city is going to repair them and open them up again. He offers to take me up there if I want to go. I thank him for the offer, but say that there is a lot of things that I am going to have to see during my stay here in Nashville, not only in the city, but in the outlying areas as well. I know that the time needed to do all of the sites on my list will be tight, but if I end up with extra time near the end of our stay here, then I will take him up on his offer. After a pleasant evening of conversation, in which everyone gets acquainted, it is time to head back to the motel, and prepare for another day of full itineraries for both of us.

Thursday, September 12

As I had mentioned to David last night, the day for me is to consist of viewing sites starting in Nashville itself, and then moving southwest. Sue has plans to go golfing.

The Tennessee brochure that I have, indicates that a Battle of Nashville Driving Tour booklet is available at the Nashville Visitors Center. The center is right downtown. So I head west on

Interstate 40 in order to get there. Reaching the city center, I exit onto Lafayette Street, and start to the northwest. At the confluence with 8th Avenue, I veer onto it, and head north. I turn east onto Commerce Street, and follow the signs to the Visitor Center. Finding a parking place, I proceed inside to pick up a booklet on the driving tour.

Examining it to find out where the points of interest are around the town, and where I need to start, I set off on my trek. All of the defenses, and the battle, which were in open fields and wooded areas beyond the population of the city at that time, are now completely engulfed by the much-expanded city. The three main routes out of the city to the south that were involved in the battle, are Franklin Road, then called the Franklin and Columbia Turnpike, Granny White Pike, and Hillsboro Road, then known as the Hillsboro Pike.

The Battle of Nashville occurred on December 15-16, 1864. It was the goal of the Confederates to invade Tennessee and capture Nashville. Initially, the movement into Tennessee had started out as a diversion. The Confederate army had been stationed in Atlanta, and after its fall, the Confederates had started northwest, with hopes of having the Federal troops around Atlanta give chase. At the beginning, this worked. But after pursuing the Confederates into northwest Georgia, the Federals then let them go, concentrating their efforts elsewhere. This effort was a move from Atlanta to the east coast, around Savannah. When the Federal army departed Atlanta in November, this was seen as an opportunity by the Confederates to invade Tennessee. After some preliminary fighting, the Confederates arrived in front of Nashville on December 1. Having been reduced in number because of the fighting that they had undergone before reaching here, their tactic was to dig in and fortify themselves to the south of Nashville, in an attempt to force the Federals to attack them.

Nashville is located on the south side of the Cumberland River, at a place where the river bows to the north. The Federals had built an V-shaped defensive line south of the city limits, from the beginning of the bow in the east, to near the end of the bow in the west. Inside this line, they had constructed another ring of defenses. The smaller Confederate force, numbering about half that of the Federals, built their defenses in a concave line, facing the eastern side of the Federal position, from the railroad that ran east out of the city, to the Hillsboro Pike on the western end. At the Hillsboro Pike, the Confederate line angled along it to the south. This was to prevent the Federal army, which stretched to the west beyond the Confederate line, from flanking the Confederate defenses during an attack. Whereas the Federal defenses covered a line of 10 miles, the Confederates could only produce one of four miles, and that was very thinly defended.

All through the early part of the month of December, both President Lincoln and General Ulysses Grant urged the commander at Nashville, General George Thomas, to attack the Confederate army. But before preparations could be completed, a nasty sleet storm struck, covering everything with ice, and preventing any kind of movement. Finally, on December 15, Thomas was ready.

In an early morning fog, the Federals left their defenses and formed up in front of them. At the far northeast corner of the line, a Federal division moved out and attacked the right flank of the Confederates, at the railroad. Capturing the rifle pits, they could not break the main Confederate defenses. But this assault was a feint by Thomas. It forced the Confederates on the right to remain in place, while the main Federal attack came on the Confederate left. The Confederates on the right would not be able to reinforce their brethren during the battle.

To the west, the Federals concentrated on the weakness of the Confederate left flank. All of the units had been shifted to the west side of the Hillsboro Pike. The lines spread southwestward from the pike and faced southeast, parallel to the road. The Federals then advanced over the landscape of hills, and up towards the road. The first Confederate section to be hit by this tidal wave, was the rifle pits on Montgomery Hill, just north of the angle where the Confederate line shifted from southwest-northeast, along the Hillsboro Pike, to west-east. Quickly overwhelmed, these Confederates moved south to the main line. The Federals followed them, and attacked to the east of Hillsboro Road.

Five redoubts had been, or were in the process of being, constructed by the Confederates on high ground along Hillsboro Pike. Redoubt No. 1 formed a salient right at the angle of the Confederate defenses, at the northwestern corner. Redoubt No. 2 was just south of that, on the east side of the road. Redoubt No. 3 was a short distance south of No. 2, but on the west side of the pike. All three of these salients were completed, and connected to the main line by earthworks. Farther to the south, on the west side of Hillsboro Pike, were Redoubts No. 4 and 5. These forts had not yet been finished, and were not connected to the Confederate defenses to the north. A stone wall ran along the east side of the Hillsboro Pike, and the Confederate defenders positioned themselves behind it, from the earthworks between Redoubts No. 2 and 3 to its end, south and east of Redoubt No. 5.

The first area to be hit by the Federal onslaught along Hillsboro Pike was Redoubt No. 5. Quickly taken, Redoubt No. 4 was the next objective to be concentrated on by the Federals. The Confederates behind the stone wall could only watch as those isolated positions were swallowed up. Then, the Federals turned their focus to the stone wall.

In the meantime, Redoubt No. 3, farther to the north, came under attack. Not able to depress their guns, the Confederates had to withdraw to Redoubt No. 2, before they were overwhelmed. Redoubt No. 2 then was assaulted. The Federals in that area continued their attack eastward, towards the troops behind the stone wall. Redoubt No. 1 held out the longest, and had some of the heaviest fighting there. But assaulted from the north and west, it eventually succumbed to the Federal attack.

By afternoon, most Confederate resistance was eliminated, and the Confederates commenced to withdraw to the south. Fighting continued through the afternoon, and by evening, the tired Federals stopped pursuit of the Confederates.

Through the night, the Confederates set up another defensive line, about two miles south of their original one. This one would not need to be as large, because of the reduction in the size of the army; it was only two miles in length. The line covered two roads that lead southward: Granny White Pike, on the west side; and Franklin Pike, on the east. This time, the defenses were more solidly anchored on the flanks. Beyond the Granny White Pike, to the west, the left flank wrapped around the base of what would become known as Shy's Hill, named for Confederate Colonel William Shy, who would command there. To the east, the Confederate line extended beyond the Franklin Pike and folded around the base of Overton Hill. But in order to follow the contour of the knoll, the line encircled it to the northeast of the main line, creating a salient.

During the morning of December 16, the Federals moved up into position, to the north of the Confederate line, imitating the shape of the Confederate defenses. The Federal artillery then fired a barrage throughout the rest of the morning. The Confederate guns only replied weakly. The Federal attack would commence in a similar fashion to that of the previous day. The assault would begin on the Confederate right flank, at Overton Hill. Holding those Confederate troops in place, the main attack would then follow on the Confederate left. At mid-afternoon, the plan commenced.

The Federals moved over open ground and started up Overton Hill. But the Confederate fire was too strong, and the Federals had to retreat. To the west, the Federal cavalry got into the rear of the Confederate line, behind Shy's Hill. Requesting an attack by the infantry from the north, for support, the assault finally commenced just before dark. The Federals positioned on the north side of the hill moved first, followed by those to the northwest and west. The Federal breakthrough of the Confederate lines came on the east side of Shy's Hill. Then, focusing on the hill, they started to climb upwards. The Federals to the west and northwest clambered up the slopes as well. The Confederate defenses had been built too far back from the sides and thus, the Confederates could not rain projectiles down on the Federals as they proceeded up the slopes. When the Federals reached the top though, they were met with a heavy fire. Fierce fighting then ensued for possession of the crown of the hill. But surrounded on three sides, Confederate resistance finally began to give way. The Confederates started to flee southward, all along the western part of the line.

With the breakthrough on the line to the west, the Federals in front of Overton Hill attacked again. After initial solid opposition by the Confederates, they began to give way as well, making their way southward along the Franklin Pike. As Confederates straggled towards Franklin, the Federal cavalry took off in pursuit, capturing many. But after going only a short distance, they ran into the Confederate cavalry, stationed as the rearguard. A fierce fight commenced in the dark. Eventually, the Confederate horsemen had to withdraw. The battle was over.

The tour starts at one of the forts that had been constructed along the northeast end of the Union line of defenses, Fort Negley. This is located on Chestnut Street, just east of Franklin Road. I depart southward from the central part of the city on 8th Avenue, which Franklin Road is known as downtown. Just south of Interstate 40, I find Chestnut Street, and turn east onto it. On my left is Fort Negley Park.

So after having a discussion with David the night before on Fort Negley, here I am before it the next morning, just around the corner from where he works. The fort sits on a hill that overlooks the surrounding area, and the site was chosen for that reason. As David had said, the grounds are closed to the public. The perimeter of the fort nearest the road is lawn. About 50 yards behind that is a wooded area, which contains the remains of the fort. The fort itself is not visible from where I am standing.

But I will get to see it in more detail in the near future. After we return home from our trip, Sue will receive a letter from Merna, which contains a picture that David had taken for me. One day, he was required to be flying in a helicopter, in order to survey something, and as part of his flight, he happened to pass over Fort Negley. So, he took a picture of it, and passed it on to me. The fort is star-shaped in appearance, and made of stone. Another inner wall appears to be built inside of the outer defenses. There are very few trees within the confines of the fort itself; the woods surround the fort, but do not grow within it. From the air, it seems to still be intact. However, I guess that is deceiving. I have seen forts that have less of its remains than this one does, so it would be great if the city would work on renovating it. It is the only fort, of all the ones that were built by the Federals to strengthen the defenses around the city, that still remains. The people of the city, as well as history enthusiasts, should have the opportunity to view this remnant.

Walking up the sloped lawn a short distance, and turning around to face to the south, I try to get a view of what the soldiers would have been able to see from the fort. The guns of the fort were used to support the Federal troops advancing southward towards the Confederates. The foreground is now an industrial area, and behind that is a forest, which cuts my ability to see any distance. Certainly, those woods would not have existed during the time of the battle, as the area around the fort would have been cleared of all obstacles.

I have completed my investigation of the fort, and am ready to move on. But, I am not done with getting information about this structure. As well as receiving the photograph from David in the future, tomorrow Sue will be at the Science Center with him, and she will decide to go for a walk. On the north side of the fort, she will find a marker. This evening, I will describe my events of the day to her. Since my summary will not include information about this marker, she will surmise, correctly, that I have not seen it, and will take a picture of it for me. The sign indicates that black laborers had helped to build the fort, over the period of October-December 1862. During the battle, nearly 13,000 black troops were included as part of the Federal army.

So, I will get assistance from others in my attempt to find and understand what had happened here during the Civil War. Knowing that this subject is important to me, my friends are helping me in my pursuit, and are going out of their way for something that may not interest them as much. This I very much appreciate. It also allows me to share with them something that means a great deal to me, a small area of the war that we have in common.

From Chestnut Street, I return to 8th Avenue, and turn south. Another marker soon appears on the right side of the road. It is at the base of a different grassy hill, which rises off into the distance. Large shade trees are planted over the lawn. This is the site of another fort, Fort Casino. The Union defensive line ran in a northeast-southwest direction here. Fort Negley is to the northeast. This site is now the city reservoir; there are no remains of the fort left.

At the next corner, I turn west onto Wedgewood Avenue, then south at 12th Avenue, which will become Granny White Pike. Just south of a crest, after I turn the corner, is an additional marker, on the right side of the road. It is farther to the southwest than the last stop, and I am still continuing to follow the outer line of Union defenses. This was a jump-off point for the Federals, during the first day of their attack. The defensive line here is in a dense residential area.

I continue south to Linden Avenue, and turn west. At Belmont Boulevard, I turn south, then quickly west again, to remain on Linden Avenue. At the corner of Linden and 18th Avenues, there is a hill that rises to the north. This hill was the southernmost point of the V-shaped Union defenses. Trees line the street in this neighborhood, and prevent me from getting a good view of the hill.

Moving westward to 21st Avenue, I find a marker that is not included in the tour guide. This marker indicates that the Union forces left the salient here, and moved off in a southwest direction.

They then turned to face southeast, becoming an extension of the right side of the V-shaped earthworks. The plan was for the Federal line to attack into the flank of the Confederate defenses. This start-off point is on a long plateau. I cannot see for any distance because of houses and high-rise buildings.

I turn south onto 21st Avenue, which will become Hillsboro Road farther to the south. I then turn east on Lombardy Avenue, and north onto Brightwood Avenue. I climb a steep hill, and at the crest of the hill, is Cedar Lane. This hilltop, called Montgomery Hill because the plantation house of a Colonel Montgomery stood here, was the advance skirmish line of the Confederates. It was set out about ½ mile in front of the main defenses, to the south, and about ½ mile south of the Union defenses. This skirmish line would have been facing north, the direction of the Federal earthworks. But it was hit from the northwest and west, because the Federals had shifted their troops to the southwest, outside of their defensive perimeter. Again, I am in a residential area, and even though I am on the top of a hill, the trees that line the streets tower above me, preventing me from seeing out any distance at all.

I turn east onto Cedar Lane and descend the hill, where I arrive at 12th Avenue. On the east side of the street is Sevier Park. During the war, a house named Sunnyside stood here, and was used as a hospital after the fighting.

I turn south onto 12th Avenue, then after crossing the interstate, west onto Woodmont Boulevard. A marker is located on the right side of the road, at Hopkins Avenue. A trench line ran about 20 feet north of this spot, just south of the crest of a hill. This was the main defensive position of the Confederates. Redoubt No. 1, the strongest of a line of artillery points along the works, was about 200 yards northwest of here, at the far left of the main trench line. I drive north on Hopkins Avenue, to see if I can see any remains of the trenches, but I do not find any. I am still in a residential area.

I return to Woodmont, and continue west on it, until I reach Hillsboro Road. On the southeast corner of this intersection, stood Redoubt No. 2. At this point, the Confederate defenses have turned in a southwest direction from Redoubt No. 1.

Turning south onto Hillsboro Road, I immediately find a marker for the location of Redoubt No. 3. This small stronghold would have been located on a hill on the west side of the road. This was also the end of the Confederate trenches that had been dug. The

Federals hit this spot from the west, the other side of the hill, which is lined with a number of large trees. A church now resides here, and I drive into the parking lot, to get to the top of the hill. I am hoping to be able to see more of the landscape on the western side of if. That is where most of the fighting would have taken place. But the trees at the edge of the property block my view in that direction.

Continuing south, just past Hobbs Road, which is on the right, I start to climb a large steep hill. Near the top of it, on the west side of the road, was the location of Redoubt No. 5, now holding condominiums. This artillery position, and Redoubt No. 4, which was to the northwest of it, were not linked to the main Confederate defensive line. There had not been time for that to be done. These strongholds were quickly overrun by the Federals, attacking from the northwest.

On the east side of the road is the entrance to an industrial park. The land drops down from the hill into a valley. The Confederate defensive line ran northeast from here, along the east side of the road. It was attacked by the Federals, after they had successfully taken Redoubts No. 4 and 5. The drop in the land here to the east, allows me to see two large hills in the distance, which tower above the valley below, about a mile away. The higher one to the south, with steeper sides, is Shy's Hill, around which the Confederates formed their new defensive line late on the first day. This was because they had been pushed back extensively from this area by the onslaught of the Federal attack.

This completes the part of the tour that covers the fighting on the first day. The next part of the tour follows the battle as it unfolded on the second day. Where I am, at Redoubt No. 5, was the southwestern flank of the Confederate line. At the end of the first day, the Confederates had been pushed back to a second line of defense. As I mentioned, the western edge of the second line was formed just to the east of my present position. But for the troops that had met the onslaught near Redoubt No. 1, the new line was about two miles south of that position. The new line ran mainly in an east-west position. On the western flank, it made a hook, circling back to the south around the perimeter of Shy's Hill. On the eastern flank, the line made a semi-circle around the northern side of Overton Hill.

To get to this second line, I drive south on Hillsboro Road to Harding Place and turn east. After about a mile, I then turn south, onto Benton Smith Road. Climbing up a small grade, I find a marker on the right side of the road. It is jammed between the edge of the pavement and a hill, which is overgrown with trees and shrubs, and ascends quite steeply. This is the east side of Shy's Hill.

The top of the hill is owned by the Tennessee Historical Society. The surrounding land is now part of a subdivision. A narrow path leads through the dense growth up to the peak. Wooden steps have been placed every few feet, to aid in the climb. I start my trek up to the top. This hill is fairly high, and there are rest benches along the way. Unfortunately, some of the brush is starting to grow across the path in places, making the ascent more difficult than it needs to be. Along the way, there are supposed to be trenches that can be seen, but I find none, perhaps because of the dense underbrush. As I am climbing upwards, I am thinking of the difficulty that the Union soldiers would have had in making their ascent up this hill. Although it wouldn't have been as hot then as it is today, they still would have had to make their way up this slope, certainly without the aid of a path, and more than likely with a hail of gunfire causing them concern as well.

I can tell when I reach to top, because the ground levels out. There is a small clearing cut out of the vegetation, but I know that the hilltop is larger than this. The growth is so thick here though, that it is difficult for me to wander around outside of the cleared area. Also, because of the dense brush, I can't see anything outside of the clearing, nor can I try to comprehend what had taken place here. There are no markers indicating how the battle had unfolded at this spot. This is unfortunate. This hill should be cleared of the undergrowth, so that people who take the time to climb up here can have a chance to comprehend the battle that took place atop this hill. Thus, the ascent of this knoll, for me, turns out to be a waste of time. The brochure states that when the leaves are off of the trees, the view from here is excellent. But I am here in September, not January. I would have liked to get an idea of what the Confederates holding this hill would have seen, as the Union troops approached, and to get more of an understanding of how and why things turned out the way that they did as a result of the battle here. Yet, this is unattainable for me. So, I make the climb back down the hill, in the heat of the day, not having found, nor seen, much of anything.

Before continuing on to the next point, I find that I am able to circle the hill by driving south, then turning north onto Shy's Hill Road. I am looking for any more markers, or paths, that may lead me up to something of interest. But, I find nothing, and move on.

The tour brochure describes how to get to the next stop. However, the map shows a few historical markers that I will pass before reaching it. Coming back out to Harding Place, on Shy's Hill Road, I continue north, instead of turning east onto Harding Place. A marker here in the neighborhood describes this point as the start-off position for the attack on Shy's Hill. Looking back to the south, I can make out the tree-covered peak, just a short distance away. During the time of the battle, this area would have been forested, so the troops here may not have been able to see their objective as clearly as I can today.

Returning to Harding Place, I turn east onto it, and drive to Granny White Pike. As I drive along, I notice that the houses in this area are set amongst a number of hills that rise on the south side of the road. This is probably why the Confederates had set up their defensive line here. At the corner of Harding Place and Granny White Pike, there is another marker, which is not one of the main tour stops. It states that the fighting that took place here, was part of the advance by the Federals towards Shy's Hill.

Going south on Granny White Pike, and turning east onto Sewanee Road, another marker is located at the corner of this intersection. This one indicates that this position was the center of the defensive line held by the Confederates on the second day. Looking east along the roadway, the land is a series of small humps as it moves off into the distance.

Following Sewanee Road to the east, I turn left onto Stonewall Drive, where Sewannee Road curves to the south. I am moving eastward, just behind the Confederate line that awaited the Federal attack to come on the second day. At the intersection with Leland Lane, I turn north, and arrive at the next stop on the tour.

The land here is flat. In the back yards of the houses, and running east-west, is an old stone wall, about three feet in height. It is cut by Leland Lane, but continues on the east side of the road, and out of site. The Confederates held this wall, stopping stopped repeated attacks by the Federals here. It was only after the defenses at Shy's Hill were broken that this line was abandoned. I find it amazing that this wall exists today, especially the length of it. It goes a great distance to the east and west, and is used as a dividing line between backyards. The place is so quiet and serene, no doubt a complete contrast to what happened over the course of a few days in that December of times past.

Continuing north on Leland Lane, I come to Battery Lane, which is Harding Place on the west side of Granny White Pike, and turn east. Reaching Franklin Road, I cross it, and come to a marker situated on the north side. This was known as Peach Orchard Hill, or Overton Hill, the east flank of the Confederate line.

This area is mostly forested, and I believe that I am on the high ground of the hill, which is a large flat plateau. Because of the vegetation, I cannot make out the landscape to the north. From this position, I do not appear to be on a hill, so I have to assume that the land to the north is lower than here, or this place would not be named Peach Orchard Hill. Because my view is inhibited, I cannot comprehend the Confederate and Union positions, or the occurrences that took place at this spot. The units holding this part of the Confederate line were the last ones to depart from Nashville. They had held out against numerous attacks during the second day of fighting.

This ends the tour. But the brochure suggests that two historic houses be visited as well: Traveller's Rest, and Belle Meade. Traveller's Rest is just to the south of where I am, so I proceed to that place. I return to Franklin Road, and turn south. After about a mile, I come to Farrell Parkway, on the east side of the road, and turn onto it. Following the signs for Traveller's Rest, I arrive at the house. It appears to now be a museum. Although it was around during the time of the battle, it doesn't have much significance to the fight, except that it was Confederate commander General John Hood's headquarters during December 15, the first day of battle. So I do not go in.

Belle Meade is on the southwest side of the city, near Harding Road, which was Hardin Pike during the war. Checking the tour brochure for the significance of this place, I find that there is none, except that some skirmishing took place there on December 15. I expect that it will be the same as Traveller's Rest, a house that has been changed into a museum, and therefore, decide not to go all that distance for nothing.

All in all, I am a bit disappointed with the tour of the Battle of Nashville. Although there are 12 points of interest, and a number of other markers, the brochure describes how to get these stations, but not what occurred at each one: what was the significance there; and how did things unfold. So, I have visited numerous sites, but have had to use my reference books in order to understand what I am seeing at each stop. The tour is not overly explanatory. But on the other hand, it is good that the history of the battle here is being preserved.

I now start towards my next battlefield. All of the battles that I want to visit today are to the south, along US Highway 31. As it turns out, I end my tour of the Battle of Nashville at US 31. It is the Franklin Road. Thus, I turn south from Traveller's Rest to begin my drive to my next stop.

As I drive towards Brentwood, about 10 miles away, and my next point of interest, I find a postscript to the Battle of Nashville. I guess this is not to be unexpected, since this was the main route south for the retreating Confederates, the Franklin Pike. Just north of Brentwood, a marker describes this spot as the place where the Confederates reorganized their army for the trek south. This occurred in the late evening after the fight of the second day, December 16.

The land here is flat, with a large hill to the north, overgrown with trees. The highway skirts it to the east. The Confederate cavalry was stationed here while the rest of the army withdrew. It would have been a good position to defend, since the hill would have forced the Federals to stay to the road, preventing them from flanking this defensive position. The cavalry fought a running battle during December 17, all the way from here to Spring Hill, 21 miles to the south.

I continue south to Brentwood. Arriving in the town, I find a marker on the west side of the Franklin Road, US Highway 31, at the intersection with Old Hickory Pike, State Highway 254. I pull over into a parking lot, since the traffic is very heavy.

On March 24, 1863, Confederate cavalry General Nathan Bedford Forrest raided the Union garrison that was stationed here, and forced their surrender. Located on this busy thoroughfare, that no doubt has changed over time, it is difficult to get an idea of what the place would have been like during the time of the raid.

On to the south I go, on US 31. But before I get to my next stop, Franklin, I come across a second marker concerning the retreat of Hood's army, after its defeat at Nashville. At a spot where the highway curves to the east, to skirt a steep hill in its path, the marker indicates that the Confederate cavalry, aided by infantry, set up a defensive line here to halt the pursuing Federals. This was late on the day of December 17, the day after the battle had concluded at Nashville. At first, the Confederates were able to stop the advance. But after their flanks were turned, they had to retreat, and caught up to the rest of the withdrawing army.

Continuing southward, I arrive in the town of Franklin, 10 miles from Brentwood. I am basically following in reverse order the battles that had taken place in November and December of 1864, as the Confederates moved into Tennessee with hopes of taking Nashville. Nashville had been the last, and climactic fight of this invasion. But by the time that the Confederates had reached the city, their numbers had been so decimated by the preliminary battles, that there were not enough troops to force an attack. Thus, their plan became one of waiting for the Federals to attack their strengthened earthworks, and hope for success. Of course, as I had found out earlier in the day, that success had never come.

The Battle of Franklin had occurred on November 30, 1864. As well as a large Federal force in Nashville, which was kept busy with the building of defenses for the expected attack, knowing that the Confederates were drawing nearer, another force had been stationed to the south, around Columbia. The Confederate plan was to move between the two Union armies by a flanking maneuver, attacking first the exposed one, then the other in Nashville, before the Federals could combine. The Federal force at Columbia was there with the idea of stopping, or slowing the northward movement of the Confederates. But the Confederate army had started to flank this force at Columbia.

Realizing this, the Federals raced northward in order not to be trapped. The Federal vanguard won the race to Spring Hill, 12 miles north of Columbia, holding the crossroads open for the rest of the army, but not without a fight. The Confederates, coming in from the southeast, attacked the guard holding the village, in an attempt to gain possession of the crossroads, and block the movement northward of the main Union army. That would pin the Federals between those at Spring Hill, and the rest of the

Confederate army, following the Federals from Columbia. But the Federal force at Spring Hill held off the attack. The Federals marched through the night, passing by the sleeping Confederates, who were in the fields to the east of the main turnpike. The next morning, realizing what had happened, the Confederates gave chase.

Arriving at Franklin on November 30, 15 miles north of Spring Hill, the Federals were forced to halt and dig in, until bridges could be built for the supply trains to get across the Harpeth River. Similar to Nashville, the river forms a bend here, and Franklin rests in the bow of it, on the south side. The Union troops built a defensive line, which formed a semi-circle to the south and west of the town. The line focused on the Franklin and Columbia Turnpike, the road leading into town from the south. This was where the largest concentration of men was placed, as it was expected that any Confederate attack would come from the south.

A weakness in the placement of the troops though, was that ½ mile in front of the main line, where the rearguard set up a defensive position, straddling the pike. Having skirmished with the Confederates two miles to the south, at Winstead Hill, they had withdrawn to the new line, and were ordered to wait until the Confederates advanced in full force before pulling back to the main defenses.

On the north side of the river, and to the east of Franklin, Fort Granger had been built the year before. Artillery pieces were placed there to support the defenses on the south side. Southeast of the fort, the cavalry was positioned, in order to prevent the Confederate cavalry from crossing to the north side and getting into the rear of the Federals, to attack the wagon train.

In late afternoon, the Confederates formed up to attack the Federal position. This was to be a frontal assault. They crossed two miles of open ground, straddling the Franklin and Columbia Pike. As they neared the forward position of the rearguard, spread out beyond it on both sides, the Federal defenders fired. But the Confederates came on, easily outnumbering their foe. The small Federal force then raced to the rear, in an attempt to reach the main line before overwhelmed.

But this created a problem for the defenders holding that line. They could not fire at the Confederates without hitting their own men. So they waited. The Confederates became aware of the predicament, and rushed on, on the heels of the fleeing Federals. They wanted to reach the defenses at the same time, and concentrated their efforts on the opening where the road ran through the line. With the remainder of the rearguard, those who had not been captured, finally reaching the earthworks, the Federals fired into the advancing Confederate line. But it was too late. The Confederates began to overwhelm the defenses. On top of this, the momentum of the retreating Federals, who passed through the earthworks, pulled some of the units along the line off of the defenses, leaving them unmanned. They soon became manned by Confederates.

Just to the rear of the Federal earthworks, was the brigade of Colonel Emerson Opdycke. His unit had been part of the division that was rearguard. But he had refused to remain outside of the main defensive line when the rest of the division had stopped to set up to the south. As his men rested, he realized by the commotion to his front, that the Confederates had broken through the earthworks. He immediately ordered his men forward to plug the gap, picking up remnants of the scattered rearguard as he moved. Ferocious hand-to-hand fighting ensued. The counterattack by Opdycke eventually forced the Confederates back out of the defenses. But the Confederates only moved to the outside of the trench line; the two sides continuing to fight across the earth that had been heaped up between them.

To the east, near the river, the Confederates came under fire from the Federal earthworks, and also from the guns on the opposite side of the river. An enfilading fire was created by the artillery positioned with the cavalry, and the guns in Fort Granger. Thus, most of the Confederate troops were pinned down before reaching the Federal lines. To the west of the pike, the Confederate line was thin compared to the position held by the defenders. Therefore, numerous attacks by the Confederates on that end of the line were unsuccessful. On the north side of the river, the two cavalry forces collided. As expected, the Confederate cavalry, under General Nathan Forrest, had crossed to the north side of the river, to attack the flank and rear of the Federals. But his force was met by the Federal cavalry, which initially pushed Forrest's men back to the river, then necessitated a withdrawal by them, back to the south side.

Throughout the evening, the two sides continued to shoot at each other. The Confederates in the center held on in the trench, at the foot of the Federal defenses, unable to retreat. The two sides would climb to the top of the earthworks and fire down on the other. Men were pulled over the defenses and killed. Some Confederates surrendered, but others did not.

The plan of the Federal commander, General John Schofield, still stood, though. Once the bridges had been rebuilt, and the wagons were safely across the river, the Federal troops were ordered to pull out. Even though the attack had been stopped, and the Confederates had immensely more casualties than the Federals, including six generals lost, the Union troops began to withdraw near midnight. By early morning, this had been accomplished, leaving the blood-soaked ground to the Confederates. The disaster here for the Confederates was the main reason why an attack on Nashville could not be attempted, once Hood's men reached there.

I stop at the Visitor Center, situated on Main Street, to pick up a brochure for the tour of the battlefield. The tour starts at the Carter House, located in the southern part of the town, on Columbia Avenue, previously known as the Franklin & Columbia Turnpike. So, I drive southwest on Main Street until I reach Columbia Avenue, turning south onto it. After a short distance, I arrive at the Carter house.

The structure is on the west side of the street, and now within the central part of the town. At the time of the battle, it was just beyond the edge of the community. All of this area was open fields and farmland. But it is difficult now to understand the terrain at that time; the vicinity is all pavement and housing.

The main Federal line crossed the road here, on the south side of the Carter House, running from the east, and moving to the northwest. The small one-story red-brick structure is still standing. A tour of the house is available, but I am not interested in the house itself, only what had taken place across the land that surrounds it. It is difficult for me to get an understanding of the significance of this stop. All of the descriptions here discuss the house, but not the battle. There are no remains of the trenches that were dug in this area, or any details of what unfolded at this farmhouse.

Not finding anything of significance here, I continue on. Across Columbia Avenue from the Carter House is the Lotz Home. This is a large white two-story house, with green shutters on the windows.

Two big square pillars at the entrance support a second floor verandah, which is protected from the elements by a roof that overhangs it. The house is almost as wide as it is long. There is no significance to the house itself, as it pertains to the battle. This is the area where Opdycke's troops were stationed before rushing forward to plug the hole created in the line, after the Confederates had smashed through it. There are also no details here that describe how the battle had unfolded.

Driving south on Columbia Avenue, to Everbright Avenue, I pull over and stop. Here is the Battle Ground Academy, founded in 1889. The brochure says that it sits on part of the original battlefield, but does not say what action took place here, or how it fits into the overall events of the battle. I can tell by the map that this area is between the main Federal lines to the north, around the Carter House, and where the Federal rearguard had built their exposed defenses, which is to the south.

So, not having found much of significance yet, I continue on. Getting back on Columbia Avenue, and continuing south, I turn west onto Battle Avenue. I follow that until I reach Carter's Creek Pike, and turn right. This is taking me northeast, back towards the center of town. The road curves and becomes Main Street. At 11th Avenue North is the next stop. Here, the Union line crossed the road, running parallel to the avenue. This is on the southwest side of town.

The next stop is just a bit farther northeast on Main Street, at the Boxmere Home. Here, a young lad climbed one of the trees, which are still standing, to watch the battle that was going on around him.

At 9th Avenue North, I turn left. I follow this to State Highway 96, and turn right. At 5th Avenue North, I turn left, heading northwest. I pull over where 4th Avenue meets 5th Avenue, at a small park. Here, a small monument, next to the river, indicates that this was the right flank of the Union line, where it connected to the river. This is on the northwest side of town.

Turning onto 4th Avenue, I almost immediately come to the Old City Cemetery. But I do not stop here, since there is nothing of importance related to the battle. I continue onward, until I reach Main Street. Turning right, I go a couple of blocks to 6th Avenue, where St. Paul's Episcopal Church is located. It was used as a hospital after the battle. I then turn left onto 7th Avenue, and at Columbia Avenue, turn left again. This brings me back to 5th

Avenue. Here is the First Presbyterian Church, which was also used as a hospital after the fight.

Turning right onto Main Street, I come to the Courthouse, at 3rd Avenue. The big red-brick two-story building was the headquarters for the Union troops during the battle. Two large white pillars on each side of the doorway hold up a roof, which shelters the entrance from the elements. A small verandah on the second story allows people to step out onto it, through a large glassed door. A big shade tree on each side of the building hides most of the walls and windows.

The next couple of sites are all along Main Street, so I get out of the car to walk along the promenade. In the square in front of the Courthouse, a statue is dedicated to the Confederate soldiers who fought here. Just to the east of the square, on the south side of the street, is Dr. McPhail's Office. This site served as Federal General John Schofield's headquarters, prior to the battle. I cross 2nd Avenue. On the avenue, next to a church, is the Hiram Masonic Lodge. This very large two-story building has a cupola, which was used during the battle as an observation point. It seems to me that the building is a newer structure, and could not have been around during the time of the battle. But perhaps, the cupola on top remains from a building that once stood here. On the north side of Main Street, close to 1st Avenue, is the Old Factory Store, which also served as a hospital after the battle. At 1st Avenue, I am next to the river, and view the highway and railroad bridges. This completes my walking tour, and I return along Main Street to the car.

I drive east on Main Street, following the path that I have just walked, and turn right onto 1st Avenue South. After a couple of blocks, the street curves around to the west, near the river, to become South Margin Street. At 3rd Avenue South, I turn left. This takes me southeast, and across the river, where the road then turns east and becomes Murfreesboro Road. To my left is Pinkerton Park. I turn north onto Eddy Lane, and then west onto Fort Granger Drive. This brings me into the park, on the north end. On a hill in the distance to the left, covered in trees, is Fort Granger. This redoubt contained artillery that fired across the river into the flank of the advancing line of Confederates. A hiking path leads up to the fort.

After climbing the bluff on which it sits, I enter the remains. The earthen walls are covered in grass, and shaded by many large trees that are growing out of the walls and interior. The walls are about five feet in height, but probably have eroded over the years. The fort is very large inside, and rolls in the ground were probably once placements of some sort that are now gone. A deep ditch has been built on the outside of the walls. The fort seems to have been constructed kind of in the shape of a clothes hanger, with the flat end along the side facing the river, and the town beyond, to the west.

From the southeast corner of the fort, I peer across to the southwest, in the direction of the advancing Confederate line. But all that I can see today are treetops, which block my ability to view the ground beyond the river. In the distance is a row of hills. Certainly, this land around the fort would have been cleared at the time of the battle. But today, I cannot get any idea of what the soldiers stationed here would have seen.

Coming out of the park, I turn east onto Murfreesboro Road, and drive for about 1½ miles, to Royal Oaks Boulevard. Turning south, I follow it as it curves around to the west, and ends at Mack Hatcher Boulevard. I am near the river, southeast of the town. At this point, the river flows northwest towards Franklin. Just to the south, the boulevard has been cut through rock that forms high bluffs above the river. The Federal cavalry was posted atop these bluffs, to prevent Confederate cavalry General Nathan Bedford Forrest from fording the river and flanking the Union line.

Turning south onto Mack Hatcher Boulevard, I cross the river, and stop just beyond the bridge, in order to get a better view of the Federal position. Looking back to the north, the bluffs rise very quickly from the river, giving the Union cavalry the advantage of high ground. A ford existed here by the bridge, just to the west of the present highway. It is marked as McGavock's Ford in the brochure. Forrest used this ford, and another to the southeast, which is now part of a golf course on the south side, to cross the river to the north bank. Thus, it was in this vicinity, on the north side of the river, that the two cavalry forces clashed. A subdivision on the north bank, and east of Mack Hatcher Boulevard, now sits where much of this battle between the two forces would have taken place. The west side of the boulevard on that side of the river is still forested. Forrest did lose this fight, and had to retreat back across the waterway; the only time that he was defeated by a force inferior to his.

I continue along the highway to the southwest, until it comes to the Columbia Pike, where it ends. Here, in the flatness of the land, just to the north of a line of wooded hills, the Confederates formed up to begin their advance across two miles of open ground.

Turning south onto Columbia Pike, US Highway 31, I drive about ½ mile, up and over a line of hills, and down into a large open plain on the other side. Here on the right is a mid-sized two-story red-brick house, with a marker in front of it. This is the Harrison House. It was the headquarters of Confederate General John Bell Hood. In this house, he made his plans for the battle. The structure has four large white square pillars, which reach up to the roof around the entrance. They support a white wooden roof, which also covers a second floor verandah. A three-foot white railing borders the verandahs on both floors, each floor also containing a door into the house. It is set amongst some large shade trees, and bordered with shrubs and flowers.

I turn around, to I climb up and over the hills again. But this time, I stop at the foot of the hill that the highway bisects. This is Winstead Hill, the observation post used by Hood during the battle. The place where he stood is on the west side of the road. A parking lot and a path provide a means to get to where he watched from.

Walking up to the observation point, from this vantage I look north across the plain that lies between this hill and the town below, two miles distant. Most of this land is covered with woods now, but much of it was cleared ground during the time of the battle. Along the highway, civilization has crept out towards the hill, and can be seen in the near distance.

This is a great spot from which to watch a battle, and Hood observed his troops as they moved forward toward the Union lines. In the late afternoon sun, it is said that the rifles and bayonets of the Confederate soldiers glistened as they marched forward, creating a spectacle to behold. Today, in the late afternoon, as it was when those men marched across this land so many years ago, I stand here, blocking out the trees that now grow, and replace them with the open spaces over which the men trod. I can picture the long line of gray moving forward in silence, a drum beating, marking the march of the soldiers as they moved away from the foot of the hill. This must have been a beautiful site to observe. But at the other end of that beauty, death and destruction waited. I would have liked to see this parade unfold, but certainly not the end result. As this was a good vantage point from which to watch the battle, Hood did not move from here as the fight unfolded. But because of the smoke created by the fury of the fight to the north, he lost the ability to understand what was going on in the distance, and in the end, his ability to sway the outcome of the battle.

I drive back to town, following the path traced out by the Confederate foot soldiers, until I reach Cleburne Street. It is on the right, just north of the Battle Ground Academy. Here, along this street on the east side of the highway, the Union line was formed. On the west side of the highway, and to the south of this position, was where the Confederates broke through the line, following in behind the Federal rearguard that had been positioned out in front of the main earthworks. As more Union troops rushed forward into the gap created by the Confederate breakthrough, murderous hand-to-hand fighting developed, in some of the fiercest combat of the war. This area, where that confrontation had taken place, is now houses and stores. There are no remains of what happened here, or any markers.

I follow Cleburne Street to the east, which becomes Stewart Street as I cross Adams Street. It ends at Lewisburg Pike, and I turn southeast onto it. I drive the short distance to Carnton Lane, and turn south.

This land was the Carnton Plantation, and a very large estate house sits at the end of the lane. I do not continue to the house, but stop before that, at the Confederate Cemetery on the left. This area was the rear of the Confederate lines during the battle, and wounded soldiers made their way back to these grounds. The house became a hospital. It is located across the field, and is partially hidden from my view by trees. But I can tell that it is very big, with a two-story white wooden verandah covering the entire length of the front of the home. Wounded men would have been scattered across the entire length of the grounds. Unfortunately, some of them would never rise again. The dead were buried in shallow graves. After the war, a proper cemetery was built here. This is the only private Confederate cemetery in existence, where 1,496 bodies rest from the battle. The rows of small white granite headstones are divided by state. Large oak trees, scattered throughout the rectangular site, watch over this silent spot.

This ends the tour of the Franklin battle. Altogether, it is disappointing. The tour seems to be more interested in the houses that were around during the battle than in the battle and its events. I do not come away with much more of an understanding of the ferocity of the fight here than what I already know. It is also unfortunate that all of the trenches and such have now disappeared, except for Fort Granger, which was not directly involved in the fighting. I did like the ability to stand on Winstead Hill, and see from the same spot as Hood what he would have seen during the battle. But other than that, most of the stops were irrelevant to the main part of the fight. I had expected more to see from a battle that had produced so much ferocity, and was of such significance.

There is another smaller battle that had occurred around Franklin prior to the major battle in November 1864. That one took place on April 10, 1863. Confederate cavalry, advancing from Spring Hill, to the south, ran into Federal cavalry just outside of Franklin, southeast of town, along the Harpeth River. The Federals had crossed the river from the north side, into the rear of the Confederates, and attacked. A counterattack by Confederate General Nathan Forrest halted the Federal assault, and forced them to wade back across to the north side of the river. This action though, prevented the Confederates from continuing their foray, and they returned to Spring Hill.

During my travels around the town, and its outskirts, I have not found any markers concerning this fight. My last stop at Carnton Plantation, while touring the Battle of Franklin, had been along Lewisburg Avenue, which follows the river on the south side. The fighting in 1863 should have taken place somewhere along this road. But I had not seen any markers there, or anywhere else.

The conclusion of my tour around Franklin also concludes my itinerary for the day, for it is now close to 5:00. So, I start back towards Nashville, having slowly made my way south from there through the day. Unfortunately, I have not completed visiting all of the sites that I had planned to though. There are six sites that I wanted to explore today, but I have only done three of them. Plus, I did not get a chance to go to the site that I missed yesterday, at Tullahoma. So tonight, I need to determine how I have to change our plans. Perhaps I need to stay here for another day, or maybe, with some other form of modifications to the itinerary, I will be able to stay with the original schedule, moving to the other cities on the pre-planned dates.

From Carnton Plantation, I turn right onto Lewisburg Avenue. This takes me southeast to the intersection with Mack Hatcher Boulevard. Here, I turn north onto it, cross the Harpeth River, and come to Murfreesboro Road, State Highway 96. I turn east, and drive a couple of miles, until I reach Interstate 65, where I turn north towards Nashville. It is only 20 miles to there.

Arriving back at the motel, Sue fills me in on her day. It has turned out to be uneventful, but pleasurable. She had gotten in a round of golf, and so is content with her activities. Plans though, have been made for us to meet Sue's cousin and her family later in the evening, at the Grand Ole Opry Hotel. They had been through it before, and feel that it is something that everyone should experience. I am not real keen on seeing a hotel, but it is a night out, and we will get to be with Sue's relatives again, who we are getting along with very well.

After a quick supper, we wait across from the entrance to the motel for them to arrive. They pick us up, and we are off to the Grand Ole Opry Hotel, not too far north of where Sue and I are staying. This tour of the hotel will turn out to be very awe-inspiring and entertaining.

Friday, September 13

My itinerary today is to cover the area to the north of Nashville. First, I will visit one site to the northeast, then head west to the rest of the sites. My dilemma about visiting all of the sites still left on the list, including the ones that I have missed, has not yet been resolved. I have come up with a few potential plans, based on different scenarios. The main thing that I want to do though, is not to have to alter the schedule of when we will be going to each city, since reservations for accommodations have already made.

I have decided that we can veer up to Tullahoma while driving between Memphis and Chattanooga. The plan on that day is to visit the Shiloh battlefield, then continue on to Chattanooga. The uncertainty that I have with that idea though, is how much time it will take me to complete the tour at Shiloh; time on a battlefield is always an unknown for me. But even if we get away from there by mid-afternoon, it will still allow us to stop at Tullahoma, although this means that we will be arriving in Chattanooga late in the evening. Sue does not have a problem with that. So, that part of the trip is pretty much resolved.

For the sites that I did not complete yesterday, I surmise that if I can finish up early today, which will be at Fort Henry, about 90 miles northwest of Nashville, on the Tennessee River, then I can follow the river south to Johnsonville and visit that site. Thus tomorrow, this will allow me to start the day by completing the sites to the south of Nashville that I have not yet been to, after which I can head northwest and connect up with Interstate 40. Going southwest towards Memphis, I can stop at the sites along the way, without having to divert to the north to go to Johnsonville. But, this is all still speculative. For now though, I will focus on the sites that I want to visit today, and I start off on my journey.

Sue's plans are to meet up with her cousin's husband, David, downtown for lunch. Then, they will connect with Merna, who Sue will stay with while David goes back work at the museum. He has an exhibit opening this evening, and we have been invited. So, I need to be back for that, although everyone knows, and understands, that it is difficult for me to put timeframes on my excursions. But I know that even if I end up being late, I will still be there before the gathering finishes.

On this warm sunny morning, I head out of Nashville for Hartsville, 50 miles to the northeast. Even though it has been sunny every day that we have been in Nashville, I keep hearing on the news in the mornings that Knoxville is fogged in. So while we had been there, what we had experienced seems to be the common start of a day, perhaps because of the mountains that surround the city. I am curious though, as to whether the fog around Knoxville is a normal year-round occurrence, during this time of year, or whether what the city is experiencing now is out of the ordinary.

I drive east from Nashville on Interstate 40. After about 25 miles, I reach Lebanon, where I turn north, onto US Highway 231. I cross the Cumberland River. At the intersection with State Highway 25, 12 miles from Lebanon, I turn east. It is six more miles to the small town of Hartsville. The highway bypasses the town to the north, so I turn south onto Broadway Street to reach the center of the community.

I arrive at the few blocks that make up the core of downtown just before 9:00. According to my brochure of Civil War sites in

Tennessee, a self-guided driving tour of the battle that occurred here is available at 105 East Main Street. This turns out to be a furniture store, and I have to assume that one of the people working here looks after the pamphlets. Since the store doesn't open until 9:00, this gives me an opportunity to get out of the car and take in my environs.

Most of the buildings that I see were probably here during the time of the Civil War. This part of the town appears not to have changed much over time. The majority of people walking on the sidewalks are either merchants or farmers, who have come into town to pick up some odds and ends. A few just seem to be sitting on chairs and watching life unfold before them. The same type of activity that I am observing probably occurs here every day. It is now a little after 9:00, and the sign on the door at the store indicates that it is open, so I go in.

A gentleman asks if he can be of assistance, and I tell him that I am interested in visiting where the battle had been. He hands me the brochure. As I examine the folder, he starts to tell me about the reenactment that is going to be occurring, and gives me an insert. He seems to be quite proud of this upcoming event, and I believe that he is involved in the planning. I happen to notice that the dates for the reenactment are to be December 7 and 8. I inform him that I am only passing through this area, and definitely won't be here in December. But, I wish him luck with the endeavor. He then lets me know that there are a few things in the brochure that I should be aware of. There are a couple of signs missing that I will have to know about, including a street sign. I thank him for his information, and step back outside into the sun to start the tour.

The battle had occurred on December 7, 1862, when Confederate cavalry Colonel John Hunt Morgan attacked the Federal garrison here. Having visited Kentucky earlier in the summer, I am familiar with his exploits there. I am finding out that he was also active in Tennessee as well. While the Confederates were positioned around Murfreesboro, prior to the battle at Stones River, Morgan wanted to harass the Federal railroad line that ran from Louisville to Nashville, which was their supply link. In order to accomplish this, he first had to get rid of the Union garrison located at Hartsville. He proposed to cross the Cumberland River and do so with a group of cavalry and infantry regiments.

He started to cross the cold waters on the night of December 6, the infantry using boats at a ferry crossing, and the cavalry traversing the river at a ford farther downstream. While those troops that had made it to the north side of the Cumberland rested, and tried to warm themselves with fires, Morgan realized that not all of his troops would be across before morning. He decided to attack with the force that had made it to the other side of the river. He also found out that there were more Federals here than he had anticipated. While the cavalry moved to the rendezvous point with Morgan and the infantry, they ran into some sentries and attacked them, thereby losing the element of surprise that Morgan had hoped for.

The Federals then positioned themselves in front of their camp, and prepared for the attack. The Confederate cavalry, which was dismounted, hit the Federal right flank, while two guns on the south bank of the Cumberland River fired into the camp. The shelling brought on return fire from the Federal artillery, but this forced their focus away from the battle to their front. Morgan then flanked the Federal left, and shortly, the Federals were surrounded. Under those circumstances, they surrendered. The action had all taken place in little more than an hour. Destroying the Federal equipment and supplies, Morgan then marched his prisoners back across the chilling waters of the Cumberland to Murfreesboro.

The town sits on the north side of the Cumberland River, at the top of a loop, but about a mile north of the edge of the water. The stream then heads south for about three miles, to the southwest of Hartsville, before looping back to the north again. It takes me a couple of minutes to orient myself to the map, but the instructions about getting from point to point are very good. So the map isn't as important. But, I always like to be familiar with my directions anyway.

The tour starts to the southwest of town, near the bottom of the bend where the river loops back to the north. I leave Hartsville on County Road 141, heading south. After about a mile, I veer to the right, southwest, onto Puryears Bend Road. Following the twists and turns to stay on this road, it ends at Belcher Lane, about 3.5 miles from where it started. I turn right, south, onto this road, then after ½ mile, left, east, onto Willow Lane. This lane is basically a narrow gravel road that has been cut out of a field of wild grass. It starts out heading east, then turns south, then southwest, ending about 200 yards short of the river.

A row of trees lines the river, and prevents me from seeing it. This was the site of Puryears Ferry. Morgan arrived here, on the other side of the river, about 10:00 on the evening of December 6. Sending the cavalry farther downriver, he started crossing the men and supplies over the swollen cold river in two leaky boats. He had wanted to accomplish the crossing in five hours, but it took him seven.

I'm not sure that I can get to the river itself, because of the dense growth of trees that line it. Even if I could, I don't think that I would be able to see anything on the other side, once I got to the bank. So, instead of walking the distance to the river, across the sea of shin-high yellow flowers that appear before me, I content myself with taking in my surroundings from here. This would have been the resting-place of the soldiers after their crossing of the river. Here, they would have waited in the cold and dark of that night for the remainder of the troops to be ferried across, trying to be quiet, and not cause the arousal of the Federal troops in the town, just up the road.

Leaving this place, I start back north towards town, but this time I stay on Belcher Lane instead of turning onto Puryears Bend Road. The lane goes north about two miles, and connects up with Puryears Bend Road again at that point. The land that I drive over, just in from the river, is a series of small steep hills, populated with thick woods that consist of mostly spindly trees and brush. At the intersection of the two roads sits the home of the colonel of one of the Tennessee cavalry regiments that were under Morgan. Most of the men in that command were from the area, and were then back in familiar territory.

Turning right onto Puryears Bend Road, and going a short distance, a marker on the right indicates the next stop. This was Hager's Shop, the blacksmith shop of A.J. Hager, and the rendezvous point for the Confederate infantry and cavalry units. Morgan was familiar with the area, having spent some time in Hartsville, and had decided beforehand on this spot.

The land here is flat, and a small white single-story house is erected on this spot. It appears to be an older house, and has had additions built onto it over the years. Whether this is the original Hager house or not, I cannot determine. It sits alone here, nestled amongst the trees and tall grass, probably the same environment as when the mass of men mingled around it on that dark cold night, so many years ago. The lights from the house were more than likely the only signs of civilization along this dreary stretch of road.

Continuing north towards town, I turn right onto Lytle Drive, which loops to the north and connects back with Puryears Bend Road, Puryears Bend Road having turned to the east at this point. At the intersection at the far end of Lytle Drive sat the home of the Widow Halliburton. Here, after the battle, many of the wounded came, and were tended to by this aging lady.

I now turn west onto Puryears Bend Road, going back towards the river crossing. But where the road turns south, I turn north, onto Boat Dock Road. I am following the route of Morgan's men from Hager's Shop. I drive along across the hills and valleys for about 1½ miles, until I reach the end of the road, at Old Highway 25, the Old Gallatin Road. Turning east, the next marker is situated right before me.

Here, the road runs between two hills. All of the land is open fields, used as pasture. To the east, towards Hartsville, the road makes a sharp turn to the left, and goes around another hill situated in front of me. The top of the hill is a green meadow, but a clump of woods is nestled in the low point between where I am and the crest. It was here at this bottleneck, that Morgan set up one of his cavalry units, the one that mainly contained local boys, to block any exit that the Federals might try after the battle started. This was the Hartsville-Castalian Springs Road. With some of the men posted here, a portion of the cavalry proceeded on to Hartsville, about a mile in the distance, while Morgan and the main force headed across the fields of hills and valleys towards the southeast.

I follow the path of the cavalry eastward into town, entering it exactly as they had done early on the morning of the December 7. Coming into town earlier in the day, I had entered it off of the highway from the north. So this is a new direction from which I reenter the community. I come up and over a quick rise, and there before me lays the small town, at the bottom of the hill. No sentries were posted at the top of the hill. With the approach of the Confederate horsemen blocked from the occupants of the town by this rise, the 450 troops posted amongst the various buildings were surprised and captured.

I stop at the top of the hill, get out of the car, and survey the goings on of this small community. The brochure states that many of the buildings that were here then still stand today, and were housing quite a few of the Federals when the Confederate cavalry rode in. A couple of the structures were already over 20 years old at the time of the battle. The brochure suggests that I take a few minutes and wander through the town, examining the old buildings that existed back then. But I believe that I've seen enough of these structures already, and head to the next stop.

Going through the downtown section, I have done a complete loop, and turn south again, onto County Road 141. This time though, about ½ mile from the intersection, I turn right onto Rom's Lane. Climbing the steep hill, it appears to be someone's driveway, since a house sits atop this knoll. But slowly crawling up this hill, and rounding the side on the right, I see that another road goes off to the right, and back down the hill. Within a short distance, I have found myself outside of the town, and in the middle of a pasture. Thus, this path seems to be a road, and not just a driveway, although at any time, I expect to come upon a herd of cows, since this hill appears to be more of a pasture than anything else. Just beyond where the road forks from the driveway, there is the next marker.

Looking to the northwest, there are two other hills directly in front of me, north and south of each other. My view is straight along the narrow valley created by those two knolls. The pasture flows from here to the top of the hill to the north. A small clump of woods occupies the crest of that height. The mound to the south is completely covered by a forest. Morgan approached with his men through the small valley, from where he had left the cavalry sentries at the Hartsville-Castalian Springs Road. That place is just beyond the hills to my front. As he sent his men from here to the north and west of the Federal camp, sentries saw this, and sounded the alarm. The Federal camp was to the southeast, along the river. This spot is situated to the southwest of the town, but northwest of the campsite.

The brochure indicates that I am to continue on this road in order to get to the next stop, which means going up to the crest of the hill, where the house sits. I had assumed that the road probably ended at the house, but as I pass next to it, I see that indeed this is supposed to be a road and not a driveway. I now descend on the south side of the hill, and come out on Puryears Bend Road, southwest of where I had left it earlier. Turning left, I go back to where it meets County 141.

This area is high ground, which descends down to the river, to the south. As Morgan reached this point, he spread his troops along the ridge, which runs in a north-south direction. This high land overlooked the Federals camp, situated east of here. He sent his dismounted cavalry to the northeast, to flank the Federal line on the next hill, while his infantry moved directly east, towards the front of the Federal defenses. The land here is now wooded, and contains some commercial sites along the highway. So, I am not able to see over to the next hill, and the campsite.

Turning south onto the highway, I descend the hill to the bridge that crosses the river, and pull over before traversing it. Looking to the west, and on the north side of the river, the land is a thick growth of underbrush. A hill rises quickly from a ravine at the edge of the river, but I cannot distinguish it because of the vegetation that enshrouds it. Atop this bluff, the Confederates set up their artillery to fire into the Union camp. For this to occur, the thick woods that now occupy the hill would have had to be nonexistent then. For it is inconceivable to me that: first of all, any artillery could have been set up amongst that growth; and secondly, if this had been accomplished, that any target could have been spotted. I recognize that the battle had taken place in December, and therefore, there would not have been any leaves on the trees or undergrowth. But the forest still appears to me to be too dense for artillery to have functioned well from that spot.

I cross the river to the south side. On elevated ground on my right, directly across from the Confederate battery to the north, two small guns were set up here by the Confederates as well. Even though these guns could not reach the Federal camp, the idea was to keep the Union unsure of that possibility.

Turning around, I head back towards town. Passing by Puryears Bend Road, I make a sharp turn to the right onto the next road, Cemetery Lane. This points me in a southerly direction. About ½ mile down the lane, and on the left, sat the Union camp.

A meadow of tall grass ascends a shallow hill, which crests about 100 yards from the road. It is hemmed in by woods that probably did not exist at the time of the battle. Certainly, any wood near the campsite would more than likely have been used as firewood. Across this terrain would have sat the tents and possessions of the soldiers of the garrison. Much of the fighting occurred here, as did the surrender.

I continue from here down to the Cumberland River, at the end of the road. Before me lies the still green waters, glistening in the sun of the day. After the surrender, the troops, both Northern and Southern, came down to the edge of the river here, and commenced to cross. At that time, the water was chest high, and freezing, and there were four inches of snow on the ground. Morgan placed two to three men on each horse, in order to traverse the river. He wanted to hurry his men and prisoners across to the south side before the arrival of Federal reinforcements from Castalian Springs, about nine miles away. I think of the captured Union soldiers, dejected after their loss, and then forced to cross the chilling waters. Becoming wet as well as cold, they then had to move on, heading towards an unknown future.

Turning around and starting back up from the river, I turn right onto Herod Road. Stopping about half way down the road, on top of a hill, I look to the west, across to the next ridge. This gives me a clearer picture of the campsite and the battlefield. Most of the land in the dale below me, and on up the next hill, where the camp was located, is now overgrown with clumps of trees, although it is not a thick woods. But I still get a better picture of the landscape from here.

Down the road a bit farther, on the left, sits the Averitt-Herod House. Confederate soldiers came here for aid after the battle. Just beyond the house, to the south, I come to the camp of the Federal cavalry, positioned here to guard Hart's Ferry. They participated very little in the battle, and escaped capture. The land here has now been taken over by a forest.

I now reach the end of the road. About 400 yards south of here, at the river, was Hart's Ferry, started in 1798. I am situated on the back side of a hill, so I cannot see over the crest and down to the river. There is also no path that leads down to it. Morgan used the ferry to cross the wagons, artillery, and supplies after the battle, while the men crossed a bit farther downstream. As the last wagons were crossing, Federal troops arrived here from Castalian Springs, and fired into the fleeing Confederates, destroying three wagons in the river. But they did not pursue their adversaries to the south side.

Turning around and starting back up this sandy road, I reach Cemetery Lane, and turn right, heading back towards town. On the right, near the end of the road, is the Hartsville Cemetery. On a knoll at the rear of the cemetery, both Union and Confederate soldiers were buried. The Union soldiers were later moved.

This completes the tour of the Hartsville battlefield. I am very impressed with the detail, which displays the events leading up to, during, and after the battle. There could have been more description of the battle itself, as it had unfolded around the campsite. But since that spot is still private land, I can understand that this would be difficult. For a small battle though, I have found out more about this fight than I had at Nashville. The people who put this tour together have to be congratulated.

My next site is Fort Donelson, to the northwest of Nashville. Looking on the map for cross-country routes, there does not seem to be any easy way to get from the northeast side of Nashville to the northwest side. All of the roads go into and out of the city. So, I start back towards Nashville on State Highway 25. While on this road, I pass through Castalian Springs, the town that housed the other Federal garrison, which arrived too late for the battle at Hartsville.

At Gallatin, I get on US Highway 31E, heading southwest to Nashville. After seven miles, I veer west onto State Highway 386, which takes me to Interstate 65. Going south on the interstate until I reach the north end of Nashville, I switch over to Interstate 24, and head to the northwest. Driving along this road for about 35 miles, I exit at Clarksville, and start west towards the city, on State Highway 76. At County Road 112, I turn right. This brings me right downtown, and I drive through the core of the city, following the signs to get on US Highway 79.

An interesting side note for me is that as part of the PBS series, *The Civil War*, two towns had been chosen to represent typical communities, one from the North, and the other from the South. As the series progressed, these towns were revisited, to see the effects that the war had had on them. The town from the North was Deer Isle, Maine, and the one from the South was Clarksville, Tennessee. Although I do not stop here to get a better picture of the city, as I drive through it, I am more intent on observing the community. So, the next time that I watch the series, the happenings at Clarksville will mean a little more to me.

US 79 brings me out of Clarksville on the west side, and takes me the last part of my journey, where I arrive at the town of Dover after 30 miles, and Fort Donelson. Fort Donelson is actually on the west side of the town, and I drive through Dover to get to it.

Arriving at Fort Donelson, part of the National Park System, the first thing that I do is go to the Visitor Center. Here, I pick up a brochure of the park, and look at the displays. Then, I go back outside to start the tour.

What I had not realized before this is that Fort Donelson had consisted of a fort proper, and earthworks and trenches that surrounded the fort, which caused the town of Dover to be on the interior side of these defenses. The battle at Fort Donelson occurred along the trench line; the fort itself was never involved in the land battle. The fort lies on the south side of the Cumberland River. To the west, the river curves to the north. The outer defenses formed a semicircle around the outside of the fort. The semicircle had not been completed on the northwest side, stopping short of the river at Hickman Creek, which flows north into the Cumberland. The Visitor Center is situated at the southwest end of the trenchworks.

The battle was fought here February on 14-16, 1862. After taking Fort Henry, 12 miles to the west, on the Tennessee River, Federal General Ulysses Grant immediately decided to attack the stronger Fort Donelson, and moved to do so. The army arrived in front of the earthworks on a warm February 12. Grant did not have enough men though, to surround the fortifications. Thus, the road to the fort on the east side remained open. That night, the weather turned bitterly cold, with snow and freezing rain. It would remain this way over the next couple of days, as the battle was fought.

Grant's plan called for the navy to assist in the attack on the fort. They would bombard Fort Donelson on the river, from the northwest, while Grant attacked on the land side, from the south. On February 14, a flotilla of Federal gunboats moved upriver to attack the fort. The Confederates waited for them to get nearer before returning fire. Getting too close to the shore batteries, the boats were damaged extensively, and had to withdraw.

Before the Federal gunboat attack on February 14, the Confederates had come up with a plan for escape. They would concentrate their forces on the east side of the earthworks, break open along the road to the east, and move to Nashville, where a stronger force of Confederates was waiting. The next morning, while Grant was with the gunboats, discussing strategy, the Confederates attacked. Massing almost all of the troops on the left, they opened the way for their escape. Grant arrived on the scene in the early afternoon. Realizing what the Confederates were up to, he ordered a counterattack, to close this open route. At about that time, even though the way was clear, the Confederates were ordered back into to the fort, to await nightfall.

Grant also realized that if the Confederates forces were concentrated to the east, then the western side must have been weakened. In fact, only a single regiment held the earthworks in that sector. Grant ordered his units on the western side to attack. They quickly took the earthworks, south of the fort. The Confederates, who were moving back towards their trenches while awaiting darkness, moved to retake this part of the line, but to no avail. To the east, the Federals pushed forward to retake the ground that they had lost earlier in the day. The door to Nashville had closed.

Realizing the circumstances, the Confederate commanders decided that the only thing to do was to surrender, which they did the next day. But not before many of the troops escaped in the early morning of February 16, during a snowstorm, moving through a swamp and across Hickman Creek, on the west side of the defenses. The man leading the way was cavalry Colonel Nathan Bedford Forrest, who refused to consider surrender of his troops. Thus escaping, he would play havoc with the Federals for the rest of the struggle. The events of the war would definitely have been different if they had not included Forrest.

Leaving the Visitor Center, I start north along the park roadway, and pass through to the inside of the Confederate defenses. The first stop is a Confederate Monument, commemorating the soldiers who fought and died here.

Continuing north, I come to the entrance of Fort Donelson, the next stop. Originally built to protect the shore batteries from land attack, the walls of logs and earth were built up to 10 feet in height. The fort covered fifteen acres. Remains of the walls are still evident, but are now no more than about three feet in height. The area inside the fort is grass, and the land outside is now a forest. There are also some large trees that are growing out of the walls of the fort, but not many.

Entering the fort, I notice that the ground is not flat, but includes a number of rolling hills. Arriving along the north side of the fort, there are log cabins here. These small structures were built to house the troops, and more than 100 of them were scattered along the hillside in this area. There were more than 400 in total, inside of the fort. Similar to what I had seen in the past, these rectangular buildings are about five feet to the roofline, topped by a slanted roof. A door has been built into one of the ends, while the other end has a stone chimney attached to it. There are no windows in these cabins.

I exit the fort on the north side, for it does not extend to the edge of the river, and arrive at the banks of the Cumberland. This is where the river batteries are located. There are two batteries here: the upper battery, and the lower battery. These names refer to their relation to the river: one is upriver, and the other is downriver. The names confuse me at first, because the lower battery is actually set half way up the hill, while the upper battery is situated on the shoreline. Thus, by elevation standards, the lower battery is higher than the upper battery.

As mentioned, the lower battery is built into the side of the hill. The guns are surrounded by a wooden structure and sandbags for protection. Looking out from this battery, the guns are aimed straight down the river. The stream makes a bend to the right, about a mile distant. This would have given the gunners ample opportunity to aim and fire at the gunboats, as they rounded the corner and started their approach towards the fort. The smokestacks would have given away the approach of the boats before they rounded the bend in the distance, allowing the Confederate gunners here to prepare for battle in advance. With trees and cliffs towering above the water on both sides, it appears as though the gunboats were hemmed in, with nowhere to go to escape the deadly fire. The biggest mistake made by the Federal boats, was in getting too close to the guns, and after getting into trouble, not having the ability to maneuver around without being continuously shelled. For although the river seems to be wide here, placing four gunboats across it, as the Federals had done, would easily fill the width of the waterway.

The upper battery, today shadowed by some trees, sits nestled at the foot of the hill, next to the river, and to the right of the lower battery. The remains of this battery have not been rebuilt to the extent of that of the lower battery. A large mound of dirt is behind where the guns would have been. This was the magazine, which contained the ammunition for the guns. The upper battery also has a clear straight path down the middle of the river, but there is a different perspective here. Whereas the lower battery would have looked down on the gunboats from the side of the hill, the upper battery would have seen them at the same level. At the top of the hill, overlooking these batteries and the river, sits Fort Donelson.

I leave the batteries and fort by the same road that I used to arrive here. More than half way back to the Visitor Center is the next stop. This is a grassy knoll, on the right side of the road. The hill has been cut out of the woods, which surround it. Here, atop this high ground, the Confederates set up their defenses after being pushed back from the trenches by the Federal attack to the southwest. This was the right flank of the Confederate line, and very few men were stationed here, as the majority had been moved to the east, for the attack there, and breakout. Standing on the crest, there is nothing for me to see, because the trees block my view. Along the side of this hill, men in unmarked graves are still buried.

The next stop is along the trench line, at the far western end of the defenses. Here, the Federals attacked, and pushed the Confederates back to where they then set up at the previous stop. As at the last stop, it is hard for me to get an understanding of how the battle unfolded, because the thick forest starts just on the other side of the remains of the trench. This area of quietude would have contained tumultuous action and smoke during the time of the fighting. The contrasts are enormous.

This completes the part of the tour within the main section of the park, around the fort. The next couple of stops are along the eastern part of the earthworks, part of the outer perimeter of defenses. So, I depart by driving back to the Visitor Center, and getting on US 79, heading east. The highway runs within the outer defenses of Fort Donelson.

Turning south onto Cedar Street, I climb a hill to come to the next stop. This is the southeastern end of the trench line. A Confederate battery of artillery was positioned here, with another on the next hill over, to the west. The purpose of these two batteries was to prevent the Federals from coming up the hollow between the two hills. Again, because of the trees that have grown up here, I cannot see the side of the hill upon which I am standing, the hill beyond, nor the hollow in between. The Confederates also attacked south from this position, during the breakout attempt on February 15.

I continue east along Cedar Street, to reach the next point of interest. This is where the Confederate breakout succeeded in pushing back the Federals, and opening the way for escape. This place is also heavily forested, so I cannot comprehend how events would have unfolded here.

The following stop is in the town of Dover, which was contained within the Confederate earthworks that surrounded Fort Donelson. I turn left at the intersection with Main Street, which brings me out to the highway. I turn north onto the highway, and enter Dover from the south. At Spring Street, I turn right, east, and after a couple of blocks, turn north onto Petty Street, driving to the end of it, at the river.

Here on the left is the Dover Hotel, the place where the surrender of the fort took place. This building was rebuilt in the 1970s to resemble the original structure. It is about the size of a large house, rather than that of a hotel. The two-story building appears to have had four rooms on each floor. A verandah, covering the length of the hotel, has been built on each floor. The roof overhangs, and covers the second floor verandah. Small pillars hold up the porch, and a small wooden railing borders the one on the top floor.

The last stop is the National Cemetery, which I do not bother to observe. This ends the tour of Fort Donelson, and I am somewhat disappointed with it. Because of the growth of forest, I have not able to get a true understanding of the battle that occurred here. The river batteries are done well, but not the land battle. I can understand that it is quite difficult to keep the entire park clear of woods, but where the points of interest are, people should be able to interpret what happened there. If a site is preserved, it should also be practicable and educational. I do not find this park to be that. I had also expected to see something related to the escape path of Forrest and his Confederate cavalry, but there is nothing.

I am aware that a battle had also occurred within Dover itself. This had happened on February 3, 1863, when the Confederate cavalry attacked the garrison here. The Federals had placed rifle pits and gun emplacements throughout the town. These defenses were enough to stop the attack, and at nightfall, the Confederates withdrew. The brochure from Fort Donelson discusses the skirmish here at Dover in 1863, but does not indicate that any markers exist pertaining to this fight. So, having been through the town, and not seeing any signs related to this battle, I move on to my next site.

Twelve miles west of the Cumberland River and Fort Donelson, lies the other main river of Tennessee: the Tennessee River. On that waterway, directly west of Fort Donelson, was Fort Henry. It had been built on the east side of the river, just south of the Kentucky border. As a matter of fact, the west side of the river at that point is in Kentucky, as the border on west of the Tennessee River is farther to the south than it is east on the east side.

In January 1862, Grant made his plan to attack the fort, with the help of the Federal navy. On February 2, Grant steamed his troops up the Tennessee River on transports, and on February 3, he landed them downriver from Fort Henry. But inside the fort, the Confederate defenders had to deal with another element besides the Union troops, who had disembarked a few miles to their north: this was water. The Tennessee River was flooding, and by February 5, there was two feet of water within the walls of the fort. Because of this circumstance, the Confederate commander decided to abandon the fort, leaving only a skeleton artillery crew to hold off the Federals. By the next day, the guns in the lower level would be underwater.

It was on that day, February 6, that Grant started towards the fort. His men moved upriver on both sides: the group on the west side to seize the heights above Fort Henry, while those on the east side were to block the escape route of the Confederates. But, it was to be the navy that would force the surrender of the fort. Four gunboats steamed upriver and commenced to shell it. The Confederates returned fire, with the guns that were not flooded. But the naval shelling was too much for the Confederates. Even though they had done some damage to the gunboats, when the largest Confederate guns were wrecked by the Federal bombardment, the fort surrendered. Because Fort Henry had fallen so quickly, and easily, Grant decided to move on to Fort Donelson, where the majority of the evacuees of Fort Henry had gone.

I know that the fort is now underwater. Because of the damming of the river, as part of the Tennessee Valley Authority, the fort had been swallowed by it. But I still want to view the site where this naval attack had taken place. I leave Dover by getting back on US

Highway 79, and driving westward. At the Visitor Center of Fort Donelson, I had talked to one of the rangers about how I could get to Fort Henry. He had given me a small brochure, called *Land Between the Lakes*, which is the national recreation area that is set between the two rivers, and circled where the fort had once been.

The area that I drive through from Fort Donelson is flat, and mostly grown over with pine trees. Nearing the Tennessee River, I turn north onto Fort Henry Road. The road winds its way along the hills, just in back of the river, and then swings to the northeast. About three miles from the main highway is a boat-landing place, called Boswell Landing. As the road curves to the northeast, I turn left onto Boswell Landing Road, which then turns north. I drive to the landing, at the end of the road.

Pulling in to this point of land, which juts out into the river, I look out about 200 yards into the water. Slightly southwest of here is where the submerged fort lies. The sun glistens off of the water as I stand here, looking at the area that is now the grave of a timber and dirt fort, defended by a few men so long ago. Across the river, the entire landscape is green. This color covers from the edge of the river all the way to the horizon. That wilderness has probably not changed in more than 100 years.

It is now getting late in the afternoon, and I am done with the sites that I have set out to visit today. But I feel that I still have enough time to go to Johnsonville, about 30 miles upstream from Fort Henry. This will allow me to cut off some traveling time tomorrow, as I try to get to some of the sites that I was not able to visit yesterday. The trip to Johnsonville will be a cross-country trek on some back roads.

I return to US Highway 79, and turn back to the east. After a few miles, I turn south, onto County Road 232. This road winds its way through the wooded hills and valleys of the area, and brings me to the community of McKinnon. I continue south from here on Whiteoak Road. The road now becomes narrower, and there are no highway markers. I drive along for quite some time.

I can now tell though, by the way the shadows from the woods are crossing over the road, that I am not heading south anymore. It seems to be mostly east, and I think, sometimes north. I am hoping that perhaps I am just rounding some hills, and that the road will turn back to the south. Eventually, I end up in the community of Tennessee Ridge. Finally having an inhabited area as a reference, I check the road atlas to see how I am doing. Unfortunately, I discover that Tennessee Ridge is not south of McKinnon, but east! So somehow, I had taken a wrong branch on one of the many forks that I had encountered during my trek, and end up doing almost a complete circle. With the afternoon winding down, this ends my effort to get to Johnsonville. That site will have to wait until tomorrow. I now have to get back to Nashville, in order to meet everyone at the Science Center.

    I check my atlas again, to find the best way to get back to Nashville. I drive northeast a few miles on Country Road 147, to State Highway 49. Here, I turn southeast, meandering with the highway for about 30 miles, to reach Charlotte. I turn south onto State Highway 48, and shortly, come to State Highway 47, where I turn southeast onto it. This moves me cross-country again, and I arrive at White Bluff. Connecting with US Highway 70, I drive east for about 15 miles, then follow signs to get to the interstate. The traffic here is heavier as I blend with rush-hour drivers. Getting on Interstate 40, at the western outskirts of Nashville, this takes me into the core of the city.

    Arriving at the Science Center, the opening day event is still going on. Although much of the food is gone, there are still some bits left for me to nibble on. As I am still trying to devour my morsels, I am shown around the museum, and the new exhibit that David has helped to create. While we are going from exhibit to exhibit, Sue fills me in on her day. This has consisted of meeting David and Merna for lunch downtown, spending the afternoon with Merna, then coming to the museum for the opening.

    After about half an hour, it is time to go. So we say our farewells to Merna and her family. They have provided me with an extra dimension, which I do not usually get to encounter on my travels. In the past, after I had completed a day of exploring, I had usually confined myself to my motel room, or gone to a restaurant or bar. But this time, there have been some acquaintances, who have been able to show me around the city, allowing me to see things that a traveler usually doesn't have the opportunity of discovering. We have both enjoyed the company of Merna and David, but tomorrow, it will be time to move on.

Saturday, September 14

Sue is a little sad about having to leave Nashville, and has joked about having me pick her up on the way back through. But, it is now time to move on to the next city: Memphis. Today is to entail stopping at small battle sites along the way from Nashville, eventually ending up in Memphis at the end of the day. Sue isn't sure what to expect. She had enjoyed finding Blountville, and she also knows that this type of day is necessary for me to visit all of the sites that I want to. Since she is quite good at reading maps, she will guide me to the vicinities of these sites.

Because of my inability to visit some of the sites that I have on my list while here in Nashville, I know that it will be tough on this day to complete the task of finding them, plus the new ones that are on the itinerary for today. But, if by the end of the day, I only have sites left to do that are near Memphis, then I can backtrack, if necessary, while in Memphis to view them, and will consider the day successful.

So, we set off early on this sunny morning to start our explorations. We leave Nashville heading south on Interstate 65, as far as Franklin. Here, I get onto State Highway 96, heading west towards the town. Already familiar with the area, I turn south onto Mack Hatcher Boulevard, to circle around to the south end of town, while avoiding downtown. At the intersection with US Highway 31, I turn south onto it, picking up the trail here that I had to abandon on Thursday. The first stop is about eight miles south of Franklin, at Thompsons Station. Driving up and over Winstead Hill, we head towards our destination.

Action occurred there on March 5, 1863, during the lull after that Battle of Stones River. A Union force, moving south from Franklin to reconnoiter around Columbia, ran into the Confederate cavalry at Thompsons Station. The Federals attacked, but this movement was stopped by the Confederates. Then the Confederates countered. While one division made a dismounted frontal attack, General Nathan Bedford Forrest used a flanking maneuver to get around the Federal left, and into their rear. It took three attempts by the Confederates to break through the Federal defenses on the high ground, but when this was accomplished, and the way to the north blocked, the Federal force had to surrender.

Although Sue is very good at directing me along the roads and highways, her long-distance sight is not as good as mine. I also have a few years experience at locating roadside signs, and I spy the marker along the highway up ahead on the right, well before Sue does. An overgrown field of wild grass, which appears to be swampy, marks the spot where the battle took place. A tree-topped hill lies beyond this field to the southwest. It is hard to determine if the site looks the same now as it did during the battle, but I would not be surprised if it has changed little over that time. The marker adds that the Federals mainly came to this area in the spring of 1863 to forage for food.

Continuing south, my next stop is Spring Hill, just four miles away. The battle there was the first in the series of clashes as the Confederates entered Tennessee in November 1864, with the objective of capturing Nashville. The Federals had part of their army stationed south of Nashville, around Columbia, while the greater part was in Nashville, building defenses in preparation for the arrival of the Confederates. Positioned on the south side of the Duck River, in the town, and facing the Federal troops on the north side, the Confederate plan was to get between these troops and the ones in Nashville, and fight them separately. They proposed to do this by crossing most of their units upstream from the Federal position, to the east, heading north to Spring Hill, and blocking the main turnpike from Columbia, forcing the Federals to fight between two Confederate armies. While this movement was taking place, the smaller Confederate force in Columbia would feint an attack to hold the Federals in place.

In the evening of November 28, the Confederate cavalry crossed the river east of Columbia, and scattered the Federal horsemen, who were picketing the stream. Next, the Confederates laid a bridge over the river and started to cross in the early morning. They then moved northward towards Spring Hill, on a road that paralleled the main turnpike. The cavalry were in the lead, pushing the Federal horsemen before them. Several messages were sent from the cavalry to the Federal commander throughout the early morning of November 29, but these were ignored because he could still see Confederates to his front, on the south side of the river, and they looked like they were preparing to attack. Finally, he sent two divisions northward towards Spring Hill in the late morning: one to position themselves half way to the town, and the other to continue north to hold the crossroads.

Having the more direct route, the Federal vanguard reached the community of Spring Hill first, and positioned themselves at the crossroads. They were informed that Confederate cavalry was to the north and east. Very shortly, these horsemen appeared in the east, and attacked. Beating back this assault, the rest of the Federal division then arrived. A defensive line was set up in a semi-circle from north to south, around the east side of the town. While this was taking place, the Confederate cavalry continued to attack again and again, but were repulsed each time.

By mid-afternoon, the first Confederate infantry division arrived southeast of town, and formed up to attack. But they did not set up completely parallel to the Federal line. They moved forward towards the Federals on an angle, which exposed their right flank. This exposed flank became the focus of the Federal defenders, and necessitated a retreat by the Confederates.

The other two Confederate divisions came up and moved to the flanks of the original one. However, the commander of the right division became confused as to where the Federal line was, it was not where he thought that it should have been, and thus did not attack. The two divisions to the left were waiting for the assault to commence on the right, and when that did not happen, they did not proceed. Darkness fell without a renewal of the Confederate attack; it would be planned for the morning. Thus, the Federals still held the crossroads. The Confederate troops set up their camps where they had deployed for combat, to the southeast of town.

Finally, the Federal commander had recognized the threat to his rear, and by mid-afternoon on November 29, he started his army northward from Columbia, towards Spring Hill. By the time the vanguard of the army reached the vicinity of Spring Hill, it was dark. To their amazement though, the road was clear to the town. No one in the Confederate high command had thought to block it. Their camps remained in the fields south of town, but to the east of the road. Through the night, the Federals stealthily made their way along the pike, including a five-mile long wagon train. As the last of the army cleared the town, the men who had defended the crossroads through the previous afternoon, pulled out as well, becoming the rearguard. The Confederates had lost their opportunity to bag this Federal army. They would attempt to redeem this error later in the day of November 30, at Franklin.

Coming into the center of the small town, I have not seen any marker pointing to where the battle had taken place. I continue on to the south of town, and find a historic house, known as Rippavilla.

It is supposed to contain driving tour guides for the battle at Spring Hill. But, it turns out to be closed. So, we will have to improvise.

Arriving back at the main intersection of the town, I pull over and get out of the car, walking around to see if I can see anything down the side streets. As I was standing on the corner, a gentleman stops to see if I need directions. I tell him that I am looking for the battle site. He replies that there isn't one. Having a map of the skirmish, I know that it had taken place to the southeast of town, along McCutcheon Creek. So I ask him where the creek is. He tells me to take the road here to the east. It will turn south and come to the creek. I thank him for his information.

Following the man's directions, I drive east from the intersection on McLemore Avenue. After a short distance, it turns south, becoming the Old Kedron Road. As I drive along this road, I notice that the creek is flowing on my right, west. The map that I have has it flowing on the east of the road. This road then makes a sharp turn to the west, and ends at another road, which comes from the northwest. At this intersection, a branch of the creek coming from the west flows into the stream. My map shows that the battle had taken place a bit to the southwest of the confluence of these two creeks. I realize that it is just to the west where the battle had been fought.

The ground is flat here along the creek, but across the road to the west, the land inclines in a long slight grade. The area on the west side of the road is mostly covered with grass, which has recently been cut. There is a small cornfield in the near distance, and a larger one positioned along a plateau, at the top of the hill. Across this field, the battle had unfolded. The Federals would have been positioned along the heights. The Confederates had attacked from the vicinity of where we are standing, charging up the hill to the west, and were repulsed. This is all that I can make out of how the fight developed from the map that I have. I am surprised that for a small town, Spring Hill does not have a marker, or markers, showing the battle site, especially since the skirmish had taken place outside of the town, and the terrain is still the same as it had been during the time of the battle. It has not been modified by urban development.

We now want to proceed to Columbia, about eight miles to the south. I turn northwest onto Kedron Parkway, and this brings us back to US Highway 31, the old Franklin and Columbia Turnpike. Turning south, this takes us to Columbia.

Driving all the way to the center of this town, we again have not seen any markers on our way in. So, we continue to the southern part of the town, to see if there are any there. Not finding any, we return to the downtown core. It is still early on a Saturday morning, and nothing is open yet. So, I cannot ask anyone for information. After more driving around, we attempt to use the map that I have, in order to find where the skirmish had occurred. But the map is a general one of the area, and not specific enough for us to determine where the action might have taken place. I know that it would have been somewhere along the Duck River, but I cannot ascertain where exactly.

The fighting in Columbia was part of the diversion by the Confederates to make the Federals on the north side of the river think that a frontal attack was coming, while in fact, the majority of the army was flanking the Union lines to the east, crossing to the north side of the river. This action had occurred on November 27, 1864.

I cross the bridge on the highway back to the north side of the river. At the intersection with US Highway 412, I turn east, hoping that this road will follow the river. But after about a mile, I realize that it does not. I turn around and head back to the intersection, then continue on to the west. We come to the Duck River again, and watch closely for any markers, but do not see any. At this point, I give up, and decide that it is time to move on to the next stop. But we have lost some time in trying to find this site.

This completes the sites to the south of Nashville that I had not accomplished in visiting on Thursday. So now, I have to head cross-country, to the northwest, to get to a point where I can start on my itinerary for today. The first site is Johnsonville, which I had attempted to get to yesterday, but had failed because I had gotten lost on the backroads in the middle of the deep woods.

We get on State Highway 7, which is the first major intersection that we come to west on US Highway 412, and start to the northwest. We wind our way through the tightly bunched hills of the region, and finally reach State Highway 46. Continuing to the northwest for 10 miles, we arrive at Dickson. Here, I turn west onto US Highway 70, and we proceed for 50 miles to the Tennessee River.

The town that is here now is called New Johnsonville. According to the Tennessee brochure that I have, there is a State Historic Area, where the battle was. The site is three miles north of New Johnsonville. The town was moved when the dams were built along the river and the old town was flooded. But the site of the old town still remains.

Just before reaching New Johnsonville, I see a sign pointing towards the Johnsonville park. I turn north onto Shaver Road, which becomes the Old Hustburg Road. The road ends at the Old Johsonville Road, and we turn left, following the signs. Driving through the trees on a narrow road, it is only a short distance to the end of the road, and our destination.

The battle had taken place on November 4-5, 1864. Confederate cavalry General Nathan Bedford Forrest raided into Tennessee in October. His goal was to block Federal shipping on the Tennessee River, and prevent supplies from reaching Atlanta. Coming south along the west side of the river, he set up his artillery across from Johnsonville, and commenced to bombard the Federal naval gunboats and warehouses along the eastern banks, on November 4. The gunboats returned fire, but the Confederate shelling disabled the boats. To prevent Forrest from crossing the river and capturing the transport boats, the Federals put them to fire. But the fire spread to the surrounding warehouses. Forrest continued to shell the town to prevent the fire from being put out. The next morning, the Confederates bombarded the town again, then departed to the south.

The terrain here is similar to what I had seen the day before at Fort Henry: numerous hills, and much of the area populated by pine trees. Not much remains of the town. The land here is flat and forested, but a steep hill ascends next to the road to the south, and an old house is positioned atop it. Walking along a path that leads into the woods, and towards the river, I realize that this was the old railroad tracks. A map that I have shows a railroad departing from Johnsonville to the east, to Nashville. We come to an old wooden platform, which was probably the railway station, or a warehouse; perhaps one of the ones destroyed by the Confederate artillery. We cannot get out to the river though, to view across to the other side, where Forrest would have set up his artillery. So, we wander around this deserted place for a few more minutes, trying to get an idea of how the town would have been during the battle. Then, it is time to move on.

We return to US Highway 70, and turn west. Crossing the Tennessee River, we turn south onto US Highway 641, which will connect us with Interstate 40. After 15 miles, we reach this point, and head west. Our next stop is to be Parkers Crossroads, twenty miles down the road.

We exit the interstate onto State Highway 22. Just north of the interchange, on the right, is a park, and the start of a self-guided tour of seven points, which mark the main events of the battle here. There is no brochure, but a plaque at each location describes the events at that spot, and explains how to get to the next stop.

The battle took place on December 31, 1862, the same day as the Battle of Stones River commenced, farther to the east. Coming back from a raid into West Tennessee, Confederate cavalry General Nathan Bedford Forrest was pursued by two separate Federal forces, in an attempt to cut him off before he crossed the Tennessee River, to the east. Forrest ran into one of the Federal forces here at Parkers Crossroads.

The Federals initially positioned themselves northwest of the crossroads. Shelling by the Confederate artillery forced the Federals back about a mile, just south of the crossroads, and facing north. Faking a frontal attack, Forrest then sent his men around both flanks, where they got into the rear of the Federal defenders. Some of the Federals turned around to defend against this new threat, creating a box formation. The Federals on the southern side of the box then attacked southward, breaking through the Confederates. They then repositioned themselves at a new line to the south. The Confederates on the south side of the box turned their attention to the Federals who had broken through. Another assault by the Confederates on the northern end of the box had the Federals considering surrender, when the other Union force arrived from the north and attacked, trapping the Confederates between the two armies. When asked what to do, Forrest replied to charge in both directions, which is what was done, and the Confederates escaped.

Leaving the park, the second stop of the tour is to the northwest, where the engagement initially began. I turn south onto the highway, then west onto Rock Springs Road. Next, I veer northwest onto Cecil Walls Road, and after about a mile, come to the next stop.

Atop a wooded ridge, which is still in the same condition today as it was then, the Confederates lined up their artillery. An old trail goes east from the edge of these woods. This was once one of the main roads of the area. Across a field on the east side of the road, known as Hick's Field, the Union forces moved to attack the Confederate line. But the Confederate artillery and dismounted cavalry held off this movement, and shelling from the artillery forced the Federals to retreat back to the crossroads. Today, Hick's Field is full of tall yellow grass.

I return to the crossroads and pass through it to the east, onto Wildersville Road, and quickly come to the next marker. This sign indicates that this was where the crossroads originally was. The north-south highway, known during the battle as the Huntingdon-Lexington Road, and now State 22, has since been moved to the west. It was here at the old crossroads that the Federals set up their next defensive position, after falling back from Hick's Field. Some of Forrest's men also started to move to the northeast.

The next stop is about ½ mile to the east on Wildersville Road, at a cemetery. There was an old well here, and the Confederates watered their horses before continuing around to the east of the Federal line.

I continue on to the southeast, where I then turn west onto Expressway Church Road. As we are driving over the same roads used by the Confederate cavalry, I think of them galloping their horses over these pathways, the trees overhanging them, as they are today, as the men moved onward to their positions.

The Federal line was in the form of a three-sided box: north, east, and south. It was set up in a clearing that is now surrounded by woods. The line ran along a fence on the northern side. The best and closest view of this position is at Stop 5, on the southern side of the box, which is along Expressway Church Road. The Confederate cavalry rode in a clockwise direction along the north and east sides of this line, as we have done, and set up here to the rear of the Federals. The Federals then charged through this position, and moved farther to the southwest.

I continue west, to the end of the road, then turn south, onto State Highway 22. After about ½ mile, we come to the next marker. Here, at what was known as Red Mound, the Union line that had broken through to the south, was reformed. The northern part of the Federal line had remained back to the northeast, along the fence. It was while the Federals were in this situation, and Forrest was demanding their surrender, that the second Federal force arrived on the scene. The land here is flat and open, except for a large knoll that blocks the view of the land to the east, and is probably Red Mound. The mound today is yellow, as it is topped by tall grass that grows upon it.

I return north on State 22, to the last stop of the tour, at a convenience store on the right, just south of the interstate. Facing east, this area gives an overall view of the battle. The northwest corner of the Federal box position was about 300 yards to my right front, southeast of us. As some of the Federal troops had attacked to the south, and ended up at Red Mound, others had remained behind, and were still here, and surrounded when the new troops arrived. Across the open field of wild grass to my front, the dismounted Confederates would have attacked from north to south, but been stopped. The Confederate cavalry would have also passed by here in the other direction, at a full gallop, as they turned their attention from the Federal troops that they had boxed in, to focus on the newly-arrived Federal force that was attacking them from the north. The battle ended with the Confederates scattering to the south, after this charge.

Ending our tour right by the interstate, we get back on it, and continue our trek to the southwest. Our next stop is Jackson, 20 miles away. It is now about mid-afternoon, and there are only two more places to visit. So, I am thinking that perhaps we will be able to get back on schedule before the end of the day. But, that is before we enter Jackson. It will be some time before we depart this city.

We exit the interstate, and drive southeast on US Highway 70, to get to the city. There were two battles that took place in the vicinity of Jackson: Britton Lane, and Salem Cemetery. Driving into the center of the city, we do not see any signs for either battle. So, I stop to inquire about these battles. I know from the Tennessee Civil War brochure that Salem Cemetery is on Cotton Grove Road, and that the Britton Lane Battlefield Association is listed on Carriage House Drive. One person is familiar with where Salem Cemetery is, and gives me directions. I also receive directions on how to get to Carriage House Drive.

Salem Cemetery is located on the eastern side of the town. So we end up backtracking on US 70, towards the interstate. In this direction, we see signs pointing the way to the cemetery, but there had been none as we came from the other direction. At Bendix Road, we turn east. After almost a mile, it changes to Cotton Grove Road, and veers to the northeast. Along this road, amongst a grove of trees on the left, lies Salem Cemetery, and a marker to the battle. As I read the marker, to try to get an idea of the what had happened here, Sue goes off to pursue one of her interests: wandering through the cemetery, looking at the gravestones to see what interesting things she might come across.

The battle had taken place on December 19, 1862, as part of Forrest's raid into West Tennessee. It would be just a few days later that he would battle again at Parkers Crossroads. The Federals set up a blocking action here at the cemetery, as Forrest approached from the east. The Confederates attacked the defensive position, but not in earnest. It was used as a feint to occupy the Federals, while the rest of his troops tore up railroad tracks to the north and south of town.

The cemetery sits atop a knoll, which is raised slightly above the level of the road. Woods and shrubs line the south side of the road, but the vegetation is not dense. The cavalry would have had good maneuverability, if this area today maintains the same type of environment as it did during the time of the battle. Satisfied with my understanding of the skirmish here, and Sue having completed her walk through the cemetery, we proceed to track down the other battle that had taken place at Jackson.

Carriage House Drive is on the north side of the city, at the interstate. I have been told to take US Highway 45 north to the interstate from downtown, and I will find the street on my left, just before I reach it. So, we return back downtown on US Highway 70, coming in from the northeast. At Chester Street, the highway turns to the west, to enter the core of Jackson. I find US 45, Highland Avenue, and turn north onto it. It is about four miles to the interstate. Reaching it, I see Carriage House Drive on the left.

We find the address, but it is a furniture store. We drive along the street for a short distance, to see if there are any historical markers here, but do not find any. So, we enter the store, hoping that someone in here has some information on the battle. It turns out that one of the men who works here is part of the association that is involved with the Britton Lane battle. Unfortunately, he is not working today, nor is he at home. The lady who is attempting to help us phones his residence, to try to find him. She knows of someone else who has been out to the battle site, and calls her. Getting some directions, she then attempts to pass them on to us. She states that the site is difficult to find, and gives directions on how to get to the general area. She thinks that once we are in the vicinity, there will be signs that will help us to get to the actual site. So, off we set.

We have been told that the battle had taken place near the community of Denmark, which is located southwest of Jackson, on some secondary roads. We get on the interstate and head west to the next exit. Here, we go south on US Highway 45 Bypass, until we come to State Highway 1. We then turn west, and drive until we see the airport, about five miles distance. Just past the airport is a road that goes south to Denmark. It turns out to be County Road 223. After two miles, we turn to the southwest at an intersection, staying on County 223. About a mile along, we come to a small cluster of houses. A sign on a church here indicates that it is the Church of Denmark. So we have found Denmark, or so we believe.

We drive back and forth along this road for about 10 minutes, then return to the main highway, then retrace our steps again to the small community, all the time looking for markers to the battle. But there are none. No one is outside at any of the houses, so we can't even stop to ask directions of anybody.

I am about to give up on our search when Sue suggests that we keep trying. Since we have looked all around on this road, I start towards the side road that heads east, about a mile east of the community. Perhaps the battle was along that road. This will turn out to be the Denmark-Jackson Road. But there are no signs to tell us that, and thus, we do not know it at the time. We come to another group of houses. We find someone to ask directions of about Denmark. They are not sure, but they think that it is along another road that runs south from here. This is not detailed enough, nor does this person seem sure enough of that they know where it is, for me to go heading off in that direction. So we continue on to the east.

After a few more miles, we come to another cluster of houses. Fortunately, at one of the houses, it looks like a barbecue party is going on. There are many cars parked along the side of the road, and people are coming and going. We stop a lady who is carrying a large bowl of salad, and headed for the party. Inquiring of her as to where Denmark is, she tells us that we are miles from it, and headed in the wrong direction. This does not surprise me. She also knows the location of the battlefield. As she starts to give directions, I ask her if Denmark is the community just to the south of the airport. She replies no, Denmark is probably about another 15 miles beyond that. So, the church sign had confused us, and we had not yet reached Denmark. She tells us that if we want to get to the battlefield, we should not go all the way to Denmark. But before getting there, we will see an old Post Office building on the right, which is abandoned. It is located at the intersection with Britton Lane. We should turn south onto that road. She says that there are signs along Britton Lane that will show us the way to the battle site. Thanking her, we turn around, now headed in the right direction.

I have become a bit discouraged, especially since the woman has said that we are so far away from the battlefield, having become farther removed from it by heading off in this direction. But, Sue props me up by saying that we have come this far, and looked this long. Since we now know where it is, we might as well visit it. I tell her that that will probably mean that we will be arriving in Memphis in the early evening. By now, I have given up on visiting the last site that I have on my list for today, for the sun is getting low in the west. Sue says that she doesn't mind, and has been enjoying herself in helping me find the battlefield. With that support, we continue on towards our goal.

The woman's directions on getting to Britton Lane are right on, although her distances are off somewhat. We pass back through the community with the Church of Denmark, and continue on to the west for another four miles, 10 less than she had thought. We find the old Post Office building on the right. It is now falling down, but the sign above the door indicates what it used to be. Sure enough, on the south side of the road is Britton Lane, and we turn onto it. We are finally headed in the right direction. After a mile or so, we start to see signs to the battle, and veer left, southeast, to remain on the right road. This road wanders across rolling land of spindly forests as we head in a southerly direction. Cresting a hill, we see the marker for the battlefield on the land to the south.

I had almost given up on finding this site on a few occasions. But, this time Sue had been the persistent one, and had convinced me to keep looking. It has taken us more than 45 minutes to track this place down. I had even thought at times that perhaps, this site didn't really exist. Now, we are both overjoyed to finally find it. As the sun starts to set behind the trees to the west, we get out to explore our discovery.

The battle had taken place on September 1, 1862. A Confederate cavalry raid had commenced out of Mississippi, to try to prevent the Federal army here in Western Tennessee from moving eastward, to join forces with another army that was moving through East Tennessee. Here at Britton Lane, the Confederates ran into a small unit of Federals. After a four-hour battle, with heavy losses sustained on both sides, the raiders withdrew, having accomplished their mission.

The site is actually a small park. Markers indicate the different units that were engaged in the battle, and their positioning. The Federals lined up across the road, on the southeastern slope, facing southeast. The direction from which the attack came is now forested, but during the time of the battle, this area consisted of cornfields, with some woods. The crest of the hill, to the rear of the initial Federal position, was the final defensive line of the Union troops.

Near the bottom of the hill, to the south, lies a log cabin, which is larger than the ones that I have seen in the past. It is a long rectangular structure, with a roof that slants down from the roof line to cover a porch. This verandah extends the full length of the front of the house. The slanting of the roof keeps most of the front of the house in the dark, and since it is also below me, I cannot see into it. This farmhouse, positioned in the middle of the fighting, was used by both sides for a hospital after the battle.

This site completes our touring for the day. I have one more site that I wanted to get in today. It is Fort Pillow, along the Mississippi River, north of Memphis. The fort is about 50 miles directly west of Jackson. But I know that by the time that I reach the site, the sun will have set. However, I don't have a lot of sites to visit in the Memphis area. Thus, I feel that I will be able to fit it in tomorrow. So, instead of driving cross-country to link up with the interstate, trying to use back roads that don't have highway numbers marked on them in the road atlas, I decide to drive back to Jackson, and get on the interstate there. I have had enough experience with the back roads of this area.

The Denmark Presbyterian Church, which is supposed to be down the road, was used as a prison after the battle. Sue is interested in seeing if there is anything there of interest, so we drive on to the southeast for a short distance. We don't find a church. However, we do find another road, and this one heads to the northeast, the direction that we want to go anyway. This is the Steam Mill Ferry Road. So, rather than backtracking along the winding roads that we have already driven across, I take this route. It turns out to be shorter, faster, and straighter, and we end up at US Highway 45, in the southern part of Jackson, where Steam Mill Ferry Road has changed to D Street. This route is certainly easier than the way that we had navigated, even though there are still no signs in this part of town that indicate how to reach the battle site.

We drive north into the center of town, and back out again on US Highway 45, Highland Avenue. Getting on to Interstate 40, we proceed southwest toward Memphis. Our hotel is in Germantown, on the east side of Memphis. So, rather than going all the way into Memphis from the northeast, then back out again to the east, I will cut south before reaching the city. As we get to County Road 177, I veer off of the interstate and onto it, heading south. I'm not sure where in Germantown the hotel is exactly, but I know that it is off of Poplar Avenue. But, before we complete our journey by arriving at the hotel, we stop at a restaurant to eat.

Continuing on southward after our refreshment, we come to the intersection with Poplar Avenue, and turn west. Driving along, we finally spy our hotel, and turn in. It turns out to be close to Interstate 240. This is a bit of a distance from Germantown, as far as I'm concerned, but this area is still considered part of the town, I guess.

It turns out to be another interesting hotel. All of the rooms open upon the central atrium, similar to the Opryland Hotel in Nashville. One thing that we find entertaining is at the front of the hotel, near the entrance, there is a small waterfall, which feeds a little pond. This pond contains about 15 brightly-colored small ducks, which seem to be content on just swimming in the water, and waddling around the shore, oblivious to the people who are moving to-and-fro around them.

This is a nice end to a long day. All-in-all, Sue has enjoyed her first full day of traveling to small battle sites. As she has found out, this includes such things as: hoping that they are still there; not knowing what will found at the sites, if anything; while using nothing more than maps, intuition, some miscalculations, and plenty of luck, to track these places down.

Sunday, September 15

The day is overcast. There are scattered showers to the north and west, but not in Memphis. Showers are predicted throughout the day, although the weather is expected to clear by the afternoon. I can't afford to lose a day because of rain. After watching the forecast, and where it is presently raining, I decide to take a chance on getting to the sites before the rain arrives. My first site is to be Fort Pillow, about 75 miles north of Memphis. It is not yet raining in that area. So I think that perhaps I might be able to get there before it starts. After that, I only have two other sites, both around Memphis, and I should be able to get them later in the afternoon, between showers. Sue would like to play golf. But she will wait to see how the weather develops before she makes a final decision. I depart for Fort Pillow.

Circling the city counterclockwise, from the east to the north on Interstates 240 and 40, I get on US Highway 51 at the northern end of the city, heading northeast. As the highway gets farther away from Memphis, it also moves farther away from the Mississippi River. About 50 miles along the road, at Henning, I turn west, onto County Road 87. I drive on this road for 17 miles, which brings me back to the Mississippi, and Fort Pillow State Historical Area. I turn north into the park and drive through the darkened woods for a couple of miles to reach the Visitor Center. In order to reach it, I pass through the outer earthworks of the fort, partially concealed by the forest. As well as the location of the fort, this park is used for hiking, fishing, and camping.

Arriving at the Visitor Center, I go inside to get a walking tour map of the fort, and also to get a quick glimpse of the museum located here. I had driven through a few sprinkles of rain as I moved north from Memphis. The low clouds are very dark, and although it is not raining here yet, I feel that it will start shortly. So, I do not waste much time in the museum.

The battle occurred on April 12, 1864. In the spring of that year, Confederate cavalry General Nathan Bedford Forrest set out to raid into West Tennessee and Kentucky, in an attempt to break the

Federal lines of communication. During that raid, one of the sites that was attacked was Fort Pillow, high above the bluffs of the Mississippi River. Forrest's men quickly overran the earthworks of the fort, and pushed the Union defenders back to the bluff. But at that point, controversy entered the battle. There are accusations that Union troops, half of them black, were massacred after surrendering.

The fort was initially built and manned by the Confederates. By the spring of 1862, the Federals controlled much of the river, and after a number of shellings of the fort by Union gunboats, it was evacuated. Federal forces immediately took over control of the bastion.

There are three sections to the fort: the outer breastworks; the inner breastworks; and the main redoubt. The Visitor Center is located at the inner breastworks. The fort complex is now completely enshrouded by the woods of the area. Paths have been cut out of the vegetation so that points of interest related to the battle can be examined. As I am standing outside and trying to get my bearings, it begins to rain. So, I move to the car to try to sit it out. Since I am here, I want to visit the fort, and am prepared to wait for some time in order to do that.

After about an hour, it has stopped raining, and the area is starting to dry. It is still overcast, but I hope that the rain holds off for awhile, and I attempt to start the tour. Just behind the museum, to the west, is the inner breastworks, built atop a hill between the outer breastworks and the redoubt. These had been built by the Confederates because the original size of the fort was too large for the troops to defend properly. At the northern end of these breastworks, Forrest watched the attack on the redoubt, about ½ mile to the southwest. Because of the forest here now, I cannot see anything beyond a few feet; so I cannot get any idea of what Forrest would have viewed.

Starting west, down the hill towards the fort, which I cannot see, I come to the area where Confederate sharpshooters fired down into the redoubt. I have no idea what they would have seen from here, or how far away that the fort is. So far, all I've been able to see is heavy woods. But obviously, this area was a lot more cleared then than it is now.

The map at this point gets confusing. There are more points of interest along the river, to the north of the main redoubt, but there does not appear to be any paths to get there. After searching around for a few minutes and not finding any way to get over to that area, I decide that I will just follow the path towards the fort, and only see the sites that are along this route. It has now started to rain again, but since I am inside of the forest, I am protected from getting wet. As I move along though, the path is getting wetter, and so is the ground. So I'm glad that I did not attempt to locate those other points to the northwest, which would have forced me to wander through the wet forest. At the bottom of the hill is a deep gully, which the Confederates had to cross over to reach the redoubt. Today, a bridge traverses this gorge. This area is still all forested.

I come to the redoubt, which is a clearing in the forest. The rain has stopped, which allows me to examine this spot where most of the fighting had taken place. The redoubt sits right against a bluff that, at the time, dropped down to the river. Today, the river has changed course and is located about a mile to the west. The map that I have from the park indicates the approximate location of the river in 1864. The redoubt is not very large. It consists of a U-shaped wall of wood, about eight feet in height, and has the open end to the west. Thus, the defenders would have faced mainly east. The northern and southern ends of the fort are open; there are no gates or anything. A few cannon are placed a various points along the fort. Because of the intrusion of the woods, I cannot see very far beyond the edge of the redoubt, and so I have no idea what the defenders would have seen from this position. At the southern end of the redoubt, just outside of the wall, a hollow in the ground marks the mass grave where most of the Union soldiers were buried. Earth was shoveled down from the walls to bury the dead here. In 1866, the dead were exhumed.

On the north side of the fort, a path starts down the bluff, and I try to follow it. I think that perhaps I can get a glimpse of the river, or a better view of the bluffs. But, after a short distance, I realize that this is not going to be possible. So, I return to the fort.

As I start to head back towards the Visitor Center, it begins to rain again. A couple of small white pup tents have been set up for display, and I take shelter in one of them. Sitting here, waiting for the rain to stop, I think about the men who manned the fort so long ago. On a day like this, would they have been sitting in these small cramped quarters, as I am, passing the day by watching the rain, chatting to buddies, and performing odd chores? It is not possible to stand up in these tiny shelters, so there wouldn't have been much that the men could have done inside one of these tents. I wonder what they would have done, and how they would have passed the days before the battle came.

After about half an hour, the rain lets up, and I take my chances on getting back to the Visitor Center. Once I am in the forest, I am mostly protected from the elements anyway, and I make it back to the car, even though the rain begins again.

On my way back out of the park, I stop at the outer breastworks, to view them. These defenses formed roughly a rectangular perimeter, with the long end running north-south on the eastern end of the earthworks, and the western edge protected by the bluffs. The length of the breastworks was three miles. The roadway enters the outer breastworks at the southeast corner of the fort. Earthen walls make up this perimeter, now hidden amongst the trees. At the time of the war, all trees for ½ mile around had been cut down in front of the fort. They were left there as an obstacle for any attacking force. Today, I cannot see any distance beyond the walls because of the forest.

Leaving the fort, I had not gotten to stop at all of the markers that are identified on the map. This is mainly because there does not seem to be any way for me to get to some of them. Also, the thick woods have prevented me from getting an idea of how the two opposing forces saw the battle, and how it unfolded. This is disappointing, and even though the park is trying to keep the place in a natural setting, it should be viewed more from a historical perspective. Some of the woods should be cleared away, especially from around the main redoubt, where most of the fighting took place.

Almost back to County Road 87 from the Visitor Center, the park road curves out to the bluffs, and overlooks the river. An observation point is here. There is a description on the walking tour map that states what is, and was in this area. One of the items concerns another battle that had occurred near the fort. This one was on the river, at a place called Plum Point Bend. There, the main US Navy flotilla, trying to move downriver towards Vicksburg, met the Confederate River Defense Fleet on May 10, 1862. The Confederates rammed several Federal ships and sunk two, then returned to Memphis. The Federal fleet continued to move southward though, and attacked Memphis within a month.

Plum Point Bend is supposed to be near Osceola, Arkansas, about seven miles upriver. I quickly check my road atlas, but do not see a road that goes to the river on the Tennessee side, opposite Osceola. So, I determine that there is no way for me to get close to that fight.

I turn east back onto County Road 87 to return to Memphis, following the same route that I used to get here. It is raining and I wonder, as I start south on US Highway 51, if I will be able to get in any more sites today. A few miles south though, the highway becomes dry, and it seems to be lighter out. The clouds are still overhead, but do not appear as menacing.

Arriving back in Memphis, I want go to the Visitor Center, to try to get some information on the battles that occurred here. So I continue south on US 51 into the city, which becomes Thomas Street. A new Tennessee Welcome Center has recently opened on Riverside Drive, next to Mud Island, and I steer the car towards that spot. When I reach Lauderdale Street, I turn west onto Adams Street, and come out at the river, and the Welcome Center.

Entering the center, I wander around the different sections of brochures, looking for any information related to Memphis at the time of the Civil War. But I cannot find any. I then inquire to one of the attendants here. He is not able to help me either. He mentions that on Mud Island, there is a Mississippi River Museum that may have a bit on the Civil War, since it is about the history of Memphis, and the river over time. If there is, I don't believe that it will be much, as the focus of the museum seems to cover all of history. So, I come away empty-handed.

I notice though, from a city map that I have, that there is another Visitor Center located on Beale Street, at Fourth Street. So, I decide to try there. I drive a few blocks to the south and park near the center. About four blocks of the street are blocked off to traffic and are open only to pedestrians. As I get out of my car and start along this street, it suddenly clicks to me on where I am. The center is located on Beale Street, the famous area of Memphis known for its blues. So, as I head for the Visitor Center, I take my time to notice the different clubs that are strewn along this stretch, and listen to the various forms of music that emanate from inside of these buildings as I pass them. This is a very interesting little area. Reaching the center, I get no more information here than I had at the first Visitor Center. So, I set off to see if I can locate anything on my own.

I head west to the river, and turn south onto Riverside Drive. I keep glancing over to the river to get a good view of it, while at the same time looking around for any markers that may be in the area concerning the battle. A fight took place somewhere around here on the water on June 6, 1862, between gunboats of both sides. This was the next action to take place after the battle near Fort Pillow on May 10, at Plum Point Bend. Between the two fights though, ram boats had arrived to support the Federal fleet. It was those that did most of the damage during the battle. Of the eight Confederate boats that went into the action, only one escaped and sailed south. The others were either damaged or sunk. The defeat of the Confederate fleet here left Memphis in Union hands.

I am not able to find any markers along this promenade. So, now I want to try to locate where the other battle would have occurred. On August 21, 1864, Confederate General Nathan Bedford Forrest raided Memphis, galloping through the streets and causing general havoc. His purpose was to force the Union army to pull troops out of Mississippi, to return and protect the city. He also wanted to release Confederate prisoners from a prison, and capture some Union generals. He did not expect to capture and hold the city though, his raid was only to be a temporary occurrence. His last two objectives were not fulfilled, and Forrest had to withdraw from Memphis after a couple of hours. But he was successful in his first objective, as the Federals returned troops to Memphis from Mississippi, to protect it.

A lady at the first Visitor Center had mentioned that there was a park named after Forrest, and I take a guess that perhaps that was where some of the fighting may have taken place. I find the park at the eastern end of the downtown area, on Union Avenue, between Manassas and Dunlap Streets. I park on Dunlap Street and wander through this quiet park on a Sunday afternoon. There are not many people here. In the center of the park is a statue of Forrest on a horse, and I wonder how many people here today even know who this person was. I seem to be the only person interested in the statue. I wander along the walkways of this small square of green, looking for any markers concerning the fight that had taken place through these streets so long ago. But I do not find one. So, I conclude that the park is dedicated to Forrest, who had lived in Memphis, and not to the fighting.

Concluding my trek around Memphis, and coming up empty, I head on to my last site of the day. It is now getting late in the afternoon, and I debate on whether to do this site now, or wait until tomorrow. It is located to the east of Memphis and we will have to pass it anyway on our way out of town. But I decide that I will need all of the time tomorrow to visit the sites that I have planned. So, even though this stop may not take very long, not knowing exactly where it is could lose me extra time. Thus, I decide to drive out to it now.

From Forrest Park, I go a few blocks north, to get on Poplar Avenue, and turn east. This is US Highway 72, and it takes me right by the hotel in Germantown. But, I continue on beyond this for another 13 miles to the southeast, to where US 72 splits with State Highway 57. I turn east to continue on State 57, as US 72 heads off into Mississippi. State 57 is also Poplar Avenue in the small town of Collierville, which is my objective.

On November 3, 1863, Confederate cavalry out of Mississippi attacked Collierville, thinking that the garrison there was small. However, it was larger than was thought. The Confederates attacked from the south. A reinforcement of Federal cavalry from Germantown arrived on the scene, and hit the flank of the Confederates, forcing them to call off the battle and return to Mississippi.

I reach the town square at Main Street without finding any markers. I suspect that the fighting would have taken place in the town itself, the part that existed at that time. As the town was smaller then, I deduce that the fighting should have taken place in the downtown core. I have discovered during my trips, that if there is going to be any marker within a small community, and it is not at the battle site itself, that it will probably be in the town square. But, I find nothing here, and turn back towards the hotel, retracing my path on US Highway 72.

I have now caught up again with my schedule, except for Tullahoma, which I will try to get in tomorrow. I have spent a full day traveling around, but have not found much for my effort. I have also saved some time by visiting Collierville today, instead of waiting until tomorrow. For I have found out, by coming to Collierville, that part of the road is under construction. This will probably slow me down tomorrow morning, while trying to get back to here. But now, I am prepared for this.

Arriving back at the hotel, Sue informs me that she had gotten a chance to get in a round of golf, as it had not rained within the city. She had golfed with a couple who informed her of the best rib place in town, which is near our hotel. So, she is all set for a big meal after a full day of golf, and she gets no complaints from me about this idea.

Monday, September 16

This is going to be a long day of driving. How long it is going to be will depend on the amount of time that it takes us to tour the battlefield at Shiloh, and if that leaves us enough time, to swing up to Tullahoma on our journey towards Chattanooga. If we are able to include Tullahoma on our trip, then we will probably be getting into Chattanooga quite late. This is no problem for me, and Sue is up for today day as well.

So we set off for Shiloh, about 90 miles east of Memphis, along State Highway 57, continuing eastward from where I had left off yesterday at Collierville. As I had expected, we lose a bit of time around Collierville because of the road construction, but not much. The highway runs just north of the Mississippi state border. Clouds still linger above us from the heavy rain that we had last night. It was pouring by the time that we headed off to the restaurant, and it continued all through the night. But the sun is breaking through, and drying the roads as we move along. So we expect to have a pleasant drive through this southern portion of Tennessee.

Before reaching Shiloh though, there is one small battle that I hope to find along the way. It had taken place at a location called Hatchie's Bridge. I am not sure exactly where this site is, but I know that it is somewhere on the eastern side of Hardeman County. The Hatchie River runs north-south there. I am hoping that the highway is laid on top of the old road, and that Hatchie's Bridge crosses the Hatchie River along the highway. I have let Sue know of my suspicions, and she is keeping track of our location on the map as we go. She tells me when we are getting near the river, and we start looking for a marker concerning the battle. Sure enough, just before reaching Pocahontas, and the river, I spot a marker on the right side of the road.

The battle had taken place on October 5, 1862. After the Confederates had unsuccessfully attacked the Union force at Corinth, Mississippi, southeast of here, they were retreating along this route, pursued by a Union force. Another Union force was coming from the west to intercept the Confederates. Here at Hatchie's Bridge, the Federal army from the west ran into the retreating Confederates on the west side of the river. The Confederates were pushed back to the east, across the bridge. Before the other Federal army could approach from the east, and get them in a pincer movement, the Confederates found a crossing about six miles further south, and escaped.

The land by the marker is flat and open, with a scattering of trees and shrubs. The highway curves to the left, skirting some high ground in the distance, which is covered along its crest by woods. It was along that high ground that the Federals set up and attacked the Confederates, pushing them back across the river, a few miles distant.

So far, the day has started well. I have found the marker for the Battle of Hatchie's Bridge, or Davis Bridge. The sun is now out in full force, and we continue on State 57 towards Shiloh. Another 25 miles brings us to the intersection with State Highway 22, and we turn north onto it. A few miles along this highway, we come to the Shiloh National Military Park.

Entering the park, we drive along the road towards the Visitor Center, which is located in the northeast corner. Sue intends to tour the park with me, since there are no communities that are close enough for her to do anything else. She feels that she is ready to view a large battlefield. As we follow the signs through the park to get to the Visitor Center, she asks me how long I think that it will take tour the site. I tell her that I estimate that it may take up to six hours to do this, since it is a large battlefield, and I have spent that long at some of the other large parks that I had visited in the past. I think that the length of time surprises her. She says that she is interested in touring a large battlefield, since up to this point, she has only seen smaller ones, which have taken no more than a half hour to see. But she doesn't think that her interest will last for that length of time. So, she suggests that maybe it would be better for her to play a round of golf, if there is a golf course close at hand, while I visit the park. That way, I won't feel rushed if she becomes bored. I tell her that we can check at the Visitor Center to see if there is a golf course that is close. If there isn't, she will then do the tour with me.

Driving along through the woods and green open spaces, we pass cannons and markers that we will be revisiting as part of the tour. One thing that I notice, which I have not seen at any other parks, are large shields placed everywhere, indicating which units, Federal and/or Confederate, were situated at a spot during a particular point in time during the battle. It would probably take days to visit each one of these shields. But if someone is truly interested in knowing in great detail how the battle had unfolded, and what units were involved, then this certainly could be done. This is an added feature that I feel is a good idea.

As we near the Visitor Center, Sue sees the many displays that line the road, and asks if there is a possibility that she may be able to find a bullet. I indicate that a lot of bullets would have been whizzing through the air over those couple of days in 1862. Most of the bullets that were just lying around would have been found by now, but perhaps off the beaten path, there may be a possibility of finding one. She says that if she has to end up doing the tour with me, that her goal is to try to find a bullet. This will help keep her occupied as we go from stop to stop, and I try to get a better understanding of what took place at each point of interest.

Arriving at the Visitor Center, we go inside to get a brochure, and ask a question that the Park Rangers probably do not expect to be asked by a visitor during discussions of the battlefield: is there a golf course close by? As it turns out, there is one located in Adamsville, about 10 miles to the northwest. Sue asks if I would mind taking some time out to drive her up to the course. Since it is her vacation too, I tell her that I will drive her over there, then pick her up afterwards. But she will have to be ready to go when I am, since we have other stops to be make before the end of the day. Acknowledging that she can get in a round of golf as quickly as I can visit the battlefield, we agree that she will play golf while I tour Shiloh. But first, she wants to get a brief understanding of the battle that took place here, since she is at the battlefield. So, we view the exhibits and watch the film on the battle. She is interested in understanding what had taken place across these fields and in the woods that surround her, before heading off to golf.

We now make a mad dash up the road to Adamsville. Arriving there, we ask for directions, and find out that it is close to the park.

So we head back to the south on some back roads. Finding the golf course, I drop Sue off, and we set a time for when I expect to be back to pick her up. The Park Ranger has indicated that it should take about four hours to tour the park. Wishing her luck, I head back to the battlefield, stopping on my way for a quick snack, so that I won't have to break midway through the tour.

The battle took place on April 6 and 7, 1862. After losing Fort Donelson, the Confederates had retreated from Tennessee, and reformed around Corinth, Mississippi. The Federals moved down the Tennessee River under General Ulysses Grant, and also overland from Nashville, under General Don Carlos Buell. The two armies were to rendezvous at Pittsburg Landing, on the west bank of the Tennessee River, before proceeding against the Confederate army. Grant arrived first at Pittsburg Landing, and waited for Buell. The Confederates, with a similar number of men as Grant, decided to strike before Buell could arrive and strengthen him.

The Confederates moved north and were in front of the Federal army by April 4. But foul-ups in preparations prevented them from being ready until the early morning of April 6. There were suspicions by the Federal men in the ranks, and some of the officers, that the Confederates were close, and even some light skirmishing had taken place as patrols ran into each other. But Grant and his commanders remained confident that the Confederates were still in Corinth, and therefore, made no efforts to prepare defensive positions while they waited for the arrival of Buell.

In the early morning of April 6, the Confederates struck the unsuspecting Federals, who had spread their camps over a couple of miles, inland from Pittsburg Landing. A Federal patrol had been sent out to the south on a reconnaissance, to see if there were Confederates in the area. Coming into a field, Confederates emerged from the woods, onto the south side of it. These were skirmishers, proceeding the entire Confederate army, and they fired at the Federal patrol. This fire was responded to by the Federals. Then, more Confederates came into the clearing, and the Federals fell back. They had come across the Confederate army.

The Confederates hit the Federal camps in the south before those men knew what was happening. Many were captured, while others ran to the rear. But the noise of the shooting alerted some Federal units just to the rear of those exposed camps, and a defensive line began to form. After resisting the Confederate attack for more than an hour, parts of that line began to break apart, and the Federal troops were ordered to withdraw to another position to the north, where reinforcements were arriving to aid in the defense of that next line.

As the Federals went about setting up their next defensive position, about a mile to the north of their original encampments, many of the Confederates stopped in the Federal camps to eat the food that was cooking, or grab souvenirs. The Confederate commanders also found that the uneven and heavily wooded ground had broken up many of the ranks of their units. Pieces of different units had reformed, and were fighting together. All order had disappeared. So, it was taking time to reassemble these segments back into units that could be commanded. This long pause was giving the Federals more time to prepare for the next attack.

The focus of that attack would be on the eastern part of the battlefield. The Federals there had formed along an old sunken road, which gave them some protection. There was also brush along this line, and a fence traced beside the road, adding to the safety of the troops. Directly to the south of this Sunken Road was a large open field, which the Confederates would have to cross in order to reach the Federals.

Before the Confederate attack commenced at the Sunken Road, the artillery began to shell that defensive position. Federal guns returned fire. So many shells were being fired, and there was so much noise, that a rabbit came out of the woods, trembling, and snuggled up next to one of the Federal soldiers hunkered on the ground along the road.

Then, the Confederate infantry attacked. As the troops crossed the open ground, the Federal artillery focused on them, breaking up their ranks. As the Confederates got closer, the Federal infantry in the Sunken Road added to the lead already in the air. It was too much for the Confederates, and the survivors withdrew back to the south. Another attack was ordered by a second brigade, with the same results. Arriving at his own lines, one of the survivors called the place where he had just come from the Hornet's Nest, and that's what it became known as. Then, a Louisiana brigade was ordered across the field. Returning unsuccessfully, it was sent back across again, and again, and again, and again, until there was hardly anything left of it. With the Confederate units attacking piecemeal against the

Hornet's Nest, and no coordinated effort, the Federals could focus all of their efforts on that single unit, hitting it from the front and the flanks as well.

On the east side of the Sunken Road, and to the south of it, was a Peach Orchard, and some Federals had positioned themselves there. The Confederate commander, General Sidney Johnston, wanted to take possession of the orchard, and ordered units forward. When they hesitated, he led them. The fighting amongst the flowered trees was intense, and the Federals finally had to retreat back to the Sunken Road. Johnston rode to the rear, and inspected the bullets that had nicked at him. One though, had struck the artery behind his knee, and shortly, he was dead from loss of blood.

To the east and west of the Hornet's Nest, the Federal units were being pushed back. Those to the west were withdrawing to the northeast, towards Pittsburg Landing. To the east of the Peach Orchard was a small Federal brigade, which the Confederates turned their attention to after clearing the orchard of Federals. The Federals were forced to retreat, opening a path into the rear of the Federals, all the way to Pittsburg Landing. But, the Confederate focus remained on the Hornet's Nest, and all of troops congregated there. Eleven Confederate attacks took place across the field over the course of the afternoon; none of them were successful. Then, 62 guns were brought forward, shelling the Hornet's Nest for a half hour.

The repeated attacks and shellings by the Confederates on the Sunken Road had taken its toll. As the Federal units to the east and west of this defensive position had fallen back, the Confederates had been able to attack the flanks of the Hornet's Nest, forcing them back. By late afternoon, the Federal defenses resembled a U. Another attack finally pushed the ends together, and the Federals were surrounded. There was nothing more to do, but surrender. However, this position had held the Confederates up for over six hours. During that time, Grant had pulled together all of the units that had retreated from the fighting over the course of the afternoon, and developed another defensive position at Pittsburg Landing.

The Federal line ran to the west from Pittsburg Landing, for about three miles. At the Hamburg-Savannah Road, the line turned to the northwest, to run along it. By early evening, Buell's army had begun to arrive on the east side of the river, and was ferried across to reinforce the line. Grant focused most of his artillery on the east side of the defenses, next to the river. He felt that that was where the Confederates would attack.

In fact, most of the Confederates were exhausted from over 12 hours of fighting, and had not followed up their success by positioning themselves in front of the new Federal line. They had also spent time in gathering up prisoners from the remains of the Hornet's Nest. But as darkness began to fall, two Confederate brigades were ordered forward, near the river. The Federal artillery demolished the formations, and the fighting ended for the day.

Through the night, in a pouring rain, Buell's troops continued to cross over to the west side of the river. Two Federal gunboats ran along the river, firing shells over the bluffs and into the Confederate lines. Although the missiles were not very destructive to the men, tree branches rained down on the Confederates, and kept them from getting much sleep. The new Confederate commander, General Pierre Beauregard, as well as his lieutenants and most of the men, felt that they had won a victory, and that the Federals would be gone in the morning. Thus, some of the divisions had pulled back a couple of miles from the battlefield, while others milled about where they had last fought. No one though, had posted pickets, nor had most of the men been resupplied with ammunition. But, Grant would not be gone in the morning, and was preparing to attack.

Early on the morning of April 7, the Federals moved forward. With twice as many men as the Confederates, half of them fresh, the Federal attack began to roll over the Confederate defenders, retaking the ground that they had had to give up the day before. But not all resistance by the Confederates was weak. To the west, around a small church named Shiloh, the Confederates held on to the ground that they possessed, then counterattacked. This assault was stopped, and the Federals counterattacked. In this area, both sides repeatedly threw men against the defenses of the other for much of the morning. But the Federal attack was too strong, not only around Shiloh Church, but all across the battlefield. By mid-afternoon, what was left of the Confederate army was retreating back to Corinth.

The tour of the battlefield begins along the river, at Pittsburg Landing, just down the hill to the east of the Visitor Center. Here at the edge of the river, the steamboats had moved back and forth across the water throughout the night, after the first day of battle, ferrying fresh Union troops to this side. These men then marched up the bluff and into the battle-weary lines. The river is not very wide at this point. Of course, during the battle, the river was in flood-stage, as were some of the creeks that flowed into it. A short band of sand lines along the far shore, which ends at a small cliff, which is about six or seven feet high. The top of the cliff is covered with forest. This spot is still and tranquil this morning, but during the night of April 6-7, the commotion that reigned here would have been immense.

Turning around and looking back up the hill, I can easily imagine the continuous marching of organized units of men, as they disembarked from the transports and moved up the road to join their comrades, hidden behind the crest on a large plateau atop the bluff. The sides of the embankment on this side of the river, and the top of it, are now engulfed in trees and undergrowth. At the time of the battle, this area was all open space.

Ascending from Pittsburg Landing, and moving just past the Visitor Center, I come to the next stop: Grant's Last Line. This is the left flank of where Grant had set up his last defensive line during the afternoon of April 6. The line ran west for about 1½ miles, before turning northwest along the Hamburg-Savannah Road, of which only traces remain today. At this spot, the line was bolstered by all of the guns of the Union artillery, since Grant felt that this was the weakest spot. Some of these guns are still positioned here today, and stretch along a ridge that became the defensive line. It is difficult to get an idea of what the troops stationed here would have seen as they looked out towards the Confederates to the south, for the area is now engulfed by forest. At the time of the battle, this was all open land.

Driving on about a mile to the southwest, on what was the Corinth-Pittsburg Landing Road, I reach the Hornet's Nest, at the northern end of the Sunken Road. The Sunken Road meets the Corinth-Pittsburg Landing Road here, which was the main road to Corinth during the war. The Sunken Road runs to the southeast, and eventually curves back to the northeast, to meet the Hamburg-Savannah Road. It is no longer sunken, but has been filled in over the years. It lies tight against a forest on its northern side, the edge of which overhangs the road in places. On the other side of the road is a zigzagging rail fence, which parallels the course of the path. The Federal troops hid behind this fence, and fired at the oncoming Confederates through the railings.

Walking along the road, as the Federal officers would have done, trying to rally the troops, I peer across a field of grass on my right, to another forest growing a few hundred yards in the distance. In front of those trees, the Confederate troops would have lined up and started across the field toward this objective. Eleven times, they would have tramped over this open space, getting within yards of this spot, and eleven times, remnants of those charges would have retreated back across the field, without obtaining their goal. Some of the units made the charge numerous times, for many of the soldiers, one more than they should have. This peaceful field of grass is in complete contrast to the death and destruction that would have been strewn across its breadth on that April day. I cannot look across it without picturing the multitude of bodies that would have covered it, and so I stop for a moment, to give reverence to this section of earth, for what had taken place upon it.

As I walk along the Sunken Road, I continue to peer out across the field laid out in front of me, continuously picturing men forming up at the far tree line, then starting across the open space towards me. Set against the woods on this side, the noise of the attacks would have echoed off of the trees, at least those that remained standing, and it must have been terribly loud along the Union line here. At the far end of this stretch of the Sunken Road, where it crosses the Eastern Corinth Road, a marker indicates that the surrender of the remaining Union troops in the Hornet's Nest had occurred here. This must have been disappointing, perhaps even devastating, to the men who had continuously won victories against so many attacks during the day, to have to finally relinquish this piece of ground. The Sunken Road continues east past the Eastern Corinth Road to the Hamburg-Savannah Road. It was along that stretch that the severest fighting took place. But, I turn around and head back to my starting point.

The next stop is at the other end of the field, and I now get a view of the Confederate side of the battle here at the Hornet's Nest. Amongst the shade of the trees, the men would have waited to form up and march off against a formidable obstacle, which had taken so many of their comrades before them. Or they would have watched with horror at the devastation of their fellow troops, as the latest assault unfolded in front of them. For the Confederate units were sent across this no-mans-land a few at a time, instead of as one large force.

Here as well, is a sample of the 62 Confederate guns from 11 batteries that were finally brought up late in the day, and fired repeatedly against the Union line. This was the most guns ever assembled in North America up to this point in time. The shelling softened the Federal defenses, and the next assault finally forced the surrender of the remaining troops. Standing just in front of the guns, and looking down this line of destruction, the noise and smoke here must have been tremendous during the demonstration, but awesome to watch. Looking across the field at the target of these guns, the Union line would have been a mass of exploding shells, trees, men, and equipment, with carnage taking place everywhere.

The next point of interest is to the west of the Hornet's Nest. The Corinth Road moves westward from the Hornet's Nest, and I follow it to just where it turns to the south. Set at the edge of a forest is the largest of five Confederate Burial Trenches. This one contains the remains of over 700 men, 100 men lying seven deep.

On the east side of the road from the burial ground is Water Oaks Pond. On the second day of fighting, April 7, the Confederates were pushed back to the vicinity of this pond from the north. Here, they counterattacked back across the pond, only to be repulsed. They then had to trudge their way back across the ground that they had just taken, this time in retreat. The counterattack was their last effort at stopping the Federal advance. This small area of wild grass, mostly surrounded by woods, is only a pond during wet weather. So on this day, it is dry. It would have contained water during the battle, but probably was not very deep. However, across this wetness, Confederate soldiers would have tramped in a vain attempt to stop the forward motion of the Federals. This space must have been an area of much confusion, as the men of both sides moved against each other in opposite directions, until the to-and-fro finally subsided to a movement in one direction: to the south.

Just to the south of this pond, on the Corinth Road, sits Shiloh Church, after which the battle is named. The present church that stands here was built in 1949. This small area, cut out of the surrounding woods, was the center of a maelstrom on both days of the battle. On the first day, the Federals regrouped here after the initial Confederate attack. They held this area against continued assaults until they were finally forced to pull back late in the morning, moving to the next line to the north, which connected with the Hornet's Nest. The following day, the Confederates were pushed back across the ground that they had taken on the previous day, putting up a gallant stance here for several hours, before retreating with the rest of the Confederate army.

Continuing south on the Corinth Road for about a mile, I come to the far southwestern corner of the park. Here is Fraley Field, where the battle commenced. At 5:15 a.m. on April 6, Federal scouts moving south, exited the woods at the edge of a farmer's field. There, they encountered the first Confederate troops moving towards the Union camps. Firing commenced on both sides, starting the battle.

Walking to the southern edge of the field, following the route taken by the Federals, I look across a small freshly-mown pasture of about one acre, which has been cut out of the woods. Rolls of hay are scattered throughout. The land rises towards the south end of the field. It was on that high ground that the Confederates fired down upon the Federals, who had just entered the field from the north. Here along the southern tree line of this squared space, the Union troops set up a defensive position, and held up the advance of the Confederates. After about an hour, the Federals moved back to the next field to the north, Seay Field, and continued their resistance. Walking back to the car, which is at the edge of Seay Field, I find that it is larger than Fraley Field, and flat.

Moving about ½ mile to the northeast, this is where the Federals set up their first line of defense upon hearing the shooting between the Confederates and the Federal scouting party, going on to the south, in Fraley and Seay Fields. The ground is high here, but completely covered with forest. It would have been very difficult to set up a line of defense at this spot. The Federals did not last very long here, overrun in a matter of minutes by the Confederates.

Continuing northeast, I come to the location of the Union camps on the Rea Springs Road. They would have been set out amongst the trees, to give the men some protection from the elements. After being pushed back from their first position, the Federals formed a line along their camps here, which held for some time. Eventually though, they had to retreat from this position as well, and reformed at the Hornet's Nest, about a mile to the north.

Although it has started out as a sunny day, clouds have continued to move in as the afternoon has progressed. I viewed very black clouds while at Fraley Field, and heard rumblings of thunder. I had hoped that rain would not commence to fall, but as I finish with this stop, it starts. Rather than waiting here in the car to see if this is going to be a quick thunderstorm or not, I decide to drive back to the Visitor Center. I'll watch the circumstances of the storm from there for awhile, before deciding if I can continue with the tour or not.

So while it rains, very hard at times, I wander around the bookstore. I also wonder if this storm is affecting Sue. I hope not. As I pass the time by looking over books, I find one that I determine will be of use to me as a future reference. Entitled *A Tour Guide to the Civil War*, by Alice Cromie, it contains a list of battlegrounds, landmarks, museums, relics, and other sites related to the Civil War, broken down by state. Within each state is a listing by place, and then all of the items that can be found there. I test it against some of the places where I had discovered things on my own during my trips of the past, places that usually are not listed in any of the other books of this type that I had looked through previously. Those other books had only listed the major battlefields of the war. To my surprise, in most cases there is a listing in this book. There are even a few places identified where skirmishes had occurred in states that I had already visited, and I had been unaware of them at the time.

I also pick up a map of the battlefield, which shows where all of the markers are, what they are, and of more importance to me, how the present day park compares with this place during the time of the battle, particularly what was cleared land and what was wooded. Surprisingly, there is very little difference, which is the way that I prefer it.

As I look out of the window, I can see clearing in the distance, so I decide to wait out the rain. With one final large crash of thunder, the rain ceases, and the sun comes out. That is quite a dramatic end to the storm. I still wonder how Sue has made out during this cloudburst. Letting things dry for a few minutes, I head back to where I had left off. This interruption has lasted about 45 minutes. But, it has allowed me to find a reference book that I will use thoroughly in the future, as I plan and track down battlefields in upcoming states.

The Union Camps display had been at the southern end of the park. The last stops are located a bit to the northeast of that, along the Hamburg-Savannah Road, on the east side of the Hornet's Nest. The first point of interest there is the Tent Hospital Site, at the intersection of the Hamburg-Savannah and Hamburg-Purdy Roads, southeast of the Hornet's Nest. Federal surgeons gathered tents here after the battle, creating one of the first tent hospitals of the war.

Just north of this a short distance, on the east side of the road, is the place of Confederate General Albert Sidney Johnston's death. While directing the attack against the eastern flank of the Hornet's Nest, he was struck by a bullet, which pierced a major artery in his leg, just behind the knee. He died from loss of blood. Here, at the edge of some woods, is the remains of the trunk of the tree that Johnston was standing beside when he was shot.

Entering into the woods, I follow a path downward to the bottom of a ravine. It was here in the shelter of the forest, protected by the ravine, where Johnston actually died. His death was a major blow to the Confederacy, and perhaps altered the outcome of the battle, since he was the commanding-general of the army.

A little further north, on the west side of the road, is where the Sunken Road ends at the Hamburg-Savannah Road. The Peach Orchard is located here, on the south side of the Sunken Road. Angling to the southeast from the Corinth-Pittsburg Landing Road, to the west, the Sunken Road turns to the east to meet the Hamburg-Savannah Road. The orchard contains about eight rows of trees, with about 10 feet between each tree. The trees are rather small, spindly, and are not very tall. Not having seen peach trees before, I cannot tell if this is the way that they are supposed to look, or whether these are freshly planted trees. I know what pear and apple trees look like, and suspecting that peach trees should be about the same size, I tend to believe that these trees are quite young. So, this makes it difficult to get an idea of what the scene here would have been like during the time of the battle. It was said that since it was springtime, the trees were filled with blossoms, which rained down like snow upon the ground and the dead, as the blossoms were cut from the trees by bullets whizzing through the air.

To the south of the trees sits a row of guns, representing the Union line. They are aimed at a forest, which would have been a cleared field during the time of the battle. On the north side of the peach orchard runs a rail fence, which runs next to the Sunken Road. To the north of the Sunken Road, the forest starts up again, similar to the layout to what it was at the west end of the Hornet's Nest. Less than 100 yards to the west, along the Sunken Road, sits the cabin of William Manse George, around which the battle would have swirled on that first day. West of the cabin, the woods take over the south side of the road as well. The road beyond that disappears into the forest, leading to the area that would have sustained the heaviest fighting.

The last stop on the tour is to the north, and on the west side of the Hamburg-Savannah Road, just behind the trees that line the Sunken Road. Here is located a small pond, which became known as Bloody Pond. After the series of attacks along the Hornet's Nest, and in the Peach Orchard, the battle moved farther to the north. Left behind, as the noise and commotion receded from this area, were the wounded and dying of both sides. The pond attracted men who were thirsty for water, with neither side caring that the other side was here too. As the men bathed their wounds, or quenched their thirst, some dying after doing so, their blood changed the color of the water to a dark red. Dying and dead horses also littered the water and its edges. The small pond, set against a backdrop of trees, and surrounded by grass, is still filled with water, and seems a place of peace and tranquillity on this still day.

Unfortunately, the time that I can spend at this stop is cut short, because it has started to rain again. The sun did not remain out for very long, and it has clouded back over. Luckily, this is the last stop, so I have been able to get in the entire tour. This is fortunate, for it does not look like the rain is going to let up for awhile this time.

On the other hand, I am disappointed that there are not more stops and points of interest on the tour. This battle had lasted two days, one of the largest battles in the West, but there are only 14 stops. Much more had happened, and should be included. This tour only seems to cover the highlights. Certainly, in order to explore the site in detail, all of the plaques pertaining to the different units could be visited, but that should not be necessary. Smaller sites than this had had more detail. I feel that I am coming away from this park without as complete an understanding of the battle here as I should have. Indeed, I have seen things that have allowed me to better comprehend the ferocity of the fighting here, but I still feel that I have an incomplete picture.

But, I have visited as much as I can, and since it is now mid-afternoon, it is time to go to pick up Sue. As I drive towards the golf course, the rain starts coming down heavier than it had during the previous rainstorm. I have no idea what condition Sue will be in when I reach the course.

Pulling up to the clubhouse, I think that Sue will probably be waiting inside. But as I get to the door, I notice her coming towards the car from around the side of the building. She is completely soaked through. While she puts her clubs away in the trunk, I get some towels out of the back seat for her.

Sliding into the car, I ask her if she was looking out of the window when I pulled up, since she was heading towards the car. She says that she was just arriving back off of the course, and I had pulled in at the same time. She tells me that it had rained here earlier, as it had at Shiloh, but that she had been near the clubhouse at that time, and was able to duck in to avoid the rain. After it had stopped, she continued with her round. Unfortunately for her, when it started raining this second time, she was at the farthest spot from the clubhouse, and could not get back without getting wet. She had an umbrella, and waited under it for awhile, to see if it would let up or not, but had come to the same conclusion as I had, that it wasn't going to this time. So, already wet, because the umbrella was not of much use in the heavy rain, and thinking that I may be coming along soon, she decided to give up and head back in. Thus, we had arrived at the clubhouse at the same time. Even though she is wet, immensely so, it is warm out. So she isn't too upset at her predicament.

We drive on to Adamsville. But before continuing on our journey, we stop first for a bite to eat. This also allows Sue to dry off a bit, and put on some dry clothes. It certainly will be a golfing day that she will remember, although for different reasons than usual.

Leaving Adamsville, we are heading east on US Highway 64, towards our next stop, Tullahoma. I estimate that it will take us about 2½ hours to get there. Naturally, the sun starts to come out again as we leave town. But we are both in good spirits in spite of this; the rain has not dampened our mood.

Sue spends the time tracking the towns that we pass through on the map, and checking all of the sites listed for Tennessee in the new book that I have bought. As she comes to a listing pertaining to a battle, she describes the skirmish, and where it was. I then comment on if I have already been there, or will be going there. She also describes places out of the book where there are things that she feels are of interest, and that I might want to see. There is only one site that I did not have on my list that Sue has mentioned, and it is between Chattanooga and Knoxville. So, I can research it more over the next couple of days and decide if I want to stop there on our way back home. None of the other sites that she thinks may appeal to me pique my interest, but I appreciate her trying to find more sites for me that I may have missed.

After two hours, we reach Fayetteville. To the east of it, we turn northeast onto State Highway 50. Just before Lynchburg, the highway changes to State Highway 55, as State 50 veers off to the southeast. We then come to Lynchburg, home of the Jack Daniels Distillery. It is a very interesting little town, in the way that it is laid out amongst the hills. In the future, every time we see a bottle of Jack Daniels, we can say that we've been through the town where it is made.

We continue on to the northeast for another 14 miles, and finally arrive at Tullahoma. We now begin to try to find out what had taken place here, and where. The brochure that I have indicates that a pamphlet of the Tullahoma Campaign Driving Tour can be picked up at the Tennessee Backroads Heritage Association, at 300 South Jackson Street.

The highway comes into the town from the west, and turns south onto North Jackson Street before departing to the east. So, it has been easy for us to find Jackson Street. Now, we must locate the Heritage Association, as we turn right onto Jackson Street. Checking the house numbers as we move along, I find that we are headed in the right direction towards the house, but we miss the entrance to the driveway, and have to circle the block.

I turn right onto Carroll Street to do so, and right away see a marker on the left, indicating that graves of Confederate soldiers are located about a mile southwest of here. Completing the circle, we return to the building containing the association. It turns out that the man who knows all of the information pertaining to the Civil War in the area is not around today. But, one of the ladies gives us a brochure of the driving tour and a map.

Looking at the map, the area covered by the backroads driving tour pertains to a number of counties along the south central part of the state, with Tullahoma as the center. Reviewing the list of sites on the back of the map, the tour includes a wide range of historical locations, not just ones related to the Civil War. Going through the list inside the brochure, there is only one Civil War site, and that is Hoover's Gap, at Beechgrove, which I have already been to. I believe that there has to be another driving tour specific to the Civil War, for in the Tennessee brochure that I have, it describes visiting sites related to engagements, camps, and guerrilla activities. But the woman did not seem to be aware of any other tours.

I also find out that there was no battle that actually took place in Tullahoma. The campaign that pushed the Confederates back to Chattanooga from this area, where they had stayed for six months after the Battle of Stones River, was called the Tullahoma Campaign. But except for the fighting around Hoover's Gap, there were no other exchanges of gunfire as the Confederates withdrew towards Chattanooga. So, I guess that I had been confused about this, and thought that there had been fighting in Tullahoma, when it actually referred to the campaign in this area.

I am glad in a way that there are not a number of sites on these backroads for us to get to. It is now after 5:00, and I don't believe that we would have time enough to visit any of them. But before we leave Tullahoma, Sue suggests that we try to find the Confederate gravesite. Since we are here, and it is related to the Civil War, she feels that I should at least see it.

So, we turn southwest onto Carroll Street, and drive to the end of it. We do not see any cemetery. At Westside Drive, we turn south, and go for about a mile, looking for a graveyard, but do not find one. Thus, we turn around and make our way back to Jackson Street. We turn south onto it, thinking that the cemetery may be in this direction. But, nothing is found again. The backroads brochure has a small map of Tullahoma, indicating the location of the gravesite, but it is not marked well enough with street names for us to pinpoint where it is exactly. So, after driving around for about ½ hour trying to locate this site, we give up.

It is starting to get dark, and we are still about 75 miles from Chattanooga. We head northeast to Manchester along State Highway 55, about 12 miles, where we follow the signs and connect with Interstate 24, going southeast. As we get closer to Chattanooga, we start to encounter very large and steep mountains, which have to be climbed over rather than driven around. As it is dark, and now raining and foggy, it is not an overly pleasant journey. It probably would have been very scenic during the day, and under sunny conditions, but we are not able to enjoy this vista.

One interesting thing that happens is that by having to go south around one of the large mountains near Chattanooga, we actually enter Georgia for a stretch of a couple of miles, then reenter Tennessee. This is something that I did not realize that we would be doing, until I see the signs that we have entered Georgia. At first, I think that we have taken a wrong turn somewhere, to end up in Georgia. As it is raining and dark, the visibility is not that great, and perhaps I accidentally veered off onto the wrong highway. But seeing a highway marker, which indicates that we are still on the same interstate that we should be on, I suspect that the mountains have forced us temporarily into Georgia, and my suspicion is somewhat verified when I see another roadside sign that welcomes us back to Tennessee.

Strangely enough, we enter Chattanooga from the southwest instead of the northwest, having to skirt that mountain. Out motel is on Cummings Highway, on the west side of the city, and right on Lookout Mountain, where many of the sites that I want to visit are located. I exit the interstate onto this road, and approach the motel from the west. It is just after 8:00.

Tuesday, September 17

This day is planned for taking me to some of the outlying sites around Chattanooga, while tomorrow will be used for touring the battlefields of the city itself. Sue is going to wait for awhile, then try to see if she can find a golf course in the area to play a round of golf. It has stopped raining, but is foggy along the mountain.

My first stop is to be Anderson's Crossroads, which is not on my map. I know that the site, which doesn't exist anymore, is north of Chattanooga, but I'm not sure on which road. After the Federals had been defeated in the Battle of Chickamauga, south of Chattanooga in northwestern Georgia, in September 1863, they had retreated to Chattanooga. The Confederates occupied the hills to the west, south, and east of the city, blocking all Federal supplies that were coming into Chattanooga from the west. Thus, the Federals were required to take a roundabout way to get provisions into the city. From Bridgeport, Alabama, they used wagon trains to move north along the valley of the Sequatchie River, then at Anderson's Crossroads, they turned southeast, to meander up and over Walden Ridge, and eventually arrive at Chattanooga from the north. It took from eight to 20 days to complete this trip. As many as 16 mules were required to pull the loads up the steep side of the mountain.

The Confederates decided to attempt to halt this traffic. On October 1, the cavalry crossed the Tennessee River, to the west of Chattanooga, and started north along the Sequatchie River. On October 2, at Anderson's Crossroads, they attacked an 800-wagon caravan, burning more than 300 wagons and killing the mules. But the Federal cavalry had been in pursuit, and arrived on the scene, charging into the Confederates. The Confederates fired, then withdrew. They set up another line, which was charged again by the Federals, dispersing some and capturing many more. The Federal horsemen also recovered some of the captured wagons.

Getting on Interstate 24 and heading east, I connect with US Highway 27 and turn north. This takes me through the center of Chattanooga, and I exit the city by crossing the Tennessee River at the north end. The highway veers to the northeast outside of Chattanooga, following along beside the ridge, which is to the west. My plan is to drive as far as Dayton, about 35 miles, looking for any markers related to the battle, although I don't expect to find one on the east side of Walden Ridge. I will then cross over the mountain to the west on State Highway 30, arriving in the Sequatchie River Valley. I will turn southwest onto US Highway 127, paralleling Walden Ridge on the west side, while continuing to look for Anderson's Crossroads.

I drive along US 27, keeping my eyes peeled for any markers. The scenery is very beautiful, with Walden Ridge rising and keeping parallel to me on my left. At Dayton, I feel that I have gone far enough north. So, I turn west onto State 30, taking me over the top of the ridge. Unfortunately, the cloud cover is so low that when I reach the crest, I am in fog, and cannot get a view of the vista. Descending from the mountain, I arrive at Pikeville, and turn south onto US 127. I reach Dunlap without finding any trace of Anderson's Crossroads, so I start towards my next site.

The place that I am looking for is called Sweden's Cove, which is located west of Jasper. I again do not know if this place still exists, for it isn't on my map. At Dunlap, I connect with State Highway 28, and run southwest on the west side of the Sequatchie River for 25 miles, to Jasper. Walden Ridge stays with me on my left as I do so. I know that Sweden's Cove is west of Jasper, and the only road on the map that goes in that direction is US Highway 72. It runs southwest to Kimball, four miles away, and continues southward into Alabama. But, just beyond Kimball is a secondary road, County Road 2, that heads north, and this is the one that I will follow.

As I leave Kimball, I find a road marked as Battle Creek Road. I think that maybe I am on the right track, and turn onto it. It is County Road 2, the road that I am looking for anyway. It winds its way north through the valleys, crisscrossing with Interstate 24. After 10 miles, the road ends at the interstate. I have not found Sweden's Cove along the way, or any marker for a battle.

All I know about the fight is that it had taken place on June 4, 1862. Federal troops were moving eastward to push the Confederates out of East Tennessee, and routed the Confederates at Sweden's Cove during that movement.

So, I still have not found anything as I start towards my next point. But, I've gotten a good view of the scenery around Walden Ridge, on both sides of it. The next site is Brown's Ferry, located just west of Chattanooga. I drive back in the direction of Chattanooga on Interstate 24, and get off at Browns Ferry Road, one exit beyond the turnoff to our motel. I head north on this road for about two miles, to the community of Brown's Ferry, where the road ends. I now try to locate where the battle would have taken place.

It occurred on October 27, 1863. Even though the Federals held Chattanooga, the Confederates were positioned on the high ground around the city to the west, south, and east. The only route for supplies into the city was a circuitous route through Anderson's Crossroads. The Tennessee River turns south on the west side of Chattanooga, then makes an abrupt 180° curve to the north, creating a peninsula of land on the north side of the river called Moccasin Point. Brown's Ferry is located on the west side of the river, across from the northern end of Moccasin Point.

The Federals decided that they could open a more direct supply route by moving across the road on Moccasin Point, and building a pontoon bridge over to Brown's Ferry, which the Confederates controlled. So, on the evening of October 26, the Federals sent some troops across Moccasin Point, while others floated downriver in pontoon boats to land at Brown's Ferry. The pontoon boats would be used to build the bridge across to Moccasin Point. The

Federals in the boats went undetected as they floated down the river. Nearing Brown's Ferry at daylight, they attacked. Initially, the Confederates were able to resist this assault, as they held the high ground just to the rear of the river. But, they were flanked by the Federals, and had to fall back. As this fight was going on, the Federal units at Moccasin Point were ferried across the river to reinforce those already in the fight. This augmented force was able to overwhelm the Confederates, who withdrew to the south. The way to the west, and to supplies, was open.

On a map that I have of Civil War sites, Brown's Ferry Road goes north, then turns east to the river, where the ferry would have been, and the pontoon bridge was built. Coming to the end of Browns Ferry Road, it turns away from the river and continues on to the west. But a small lane goes off to the right, towards the river. I think that this must be the continuation of the old part of the road. I drive up and over a hill, and come to the end of the road. A driveway turns up to the left and climbs to the top of another hill. A fence, thick brush, and trees block the way to the river. I am very close, but cannot see, nor get to the river. I have found the place where the skirmish had taken place, but no markers are here. So I'm not sure how the battle had unfolded.

I have only one more small site to visit in order to complete my list for today. This site, Wauhatchie, is right in this area. Because I have not found much on my travels, it has not taken me very long to finish my agenda. It is now just after 10:30. So, I decide to start my tour of the battlefields around Chattanooga. This will include Lookout Mountain, which is also in this vicinity. Since I am right below Lookout Mountain, I decide to visit that site first before going to Wauhatchie. I return south on Browns Ferry Road to Cummings Highway, and turn east. But before continuing on, and because I have to drive right past the motel to get up the mountain, I stop in at the motel to see if Sue has gotten away to golf. If not, I can give her a ride to the golf course.

As it turns out, she is still in the room, and quite glad to see me. There are no golf courses in the area, and since I had already left, she thought that she would be stuck in the room all day. So with me showing up, she now has an opportunity to come with me and see some Civil War sites, which is better than sitting in a motel room watching TV.

The booklet that I have indicates that the Visitor Center for the Chattanooga Battlefields is located at Lookout Mountain. So, that is where I need to start, to get information on the battles that took place around the city. We head east and follow the signs, turning south onto Scenic Highway, and proceed to ascend the winding narrow road up the mountain. The signs are not marked well concerning the park, and about 2/3 of the way up, a sign indicates that we have reached the Craven House. I am not sure if this is where the Visitor Center is located or not, so we pull in and stop at this point. It turns out that the Visitor Center is not here, but at the very top of the mountain. However, not knowing that at this time, we explore this site before proceeding.

The battle on the mountain had occurred on November 24, 1863. After the Federal defeat at the Battle of Chickamauga in Georgia in September 1863, the Federals had retreated to Chattanooga, and the Confederates had occupied the high ground around the southern perimeter, holding the heights to the west, south, and east. Federal General Ulysses Grant had been ordered to Chattanooga in mid-October to eliminate the Confederate siege. Additional units were sent to the city to aid Grant in his task. But, before he could begin offensive operations, he needed to feed the starving troops that were already in Chattanooga. Thus, the maneuver at Brown's Ferry had taken place, in order to open the supply route to the west, which became known as the Cracker Line.

After some preliminary movements and fighting, Grant was ready to take the heights to the east of the city from the Confederates. This ridge, which runs north-south a couple of miles to the east of Chattanooga, is called Missionary Ridge. One Federal army was positioned at the northern end of it, and ready to strike. A second army, which was located in Lookout Valley, on the west side of Lookout Mountain, was to move around the mountain at its northern end, and occupy Rossville Gap, to the southeast. This pass through Missionary Ridge was located at the southern end of the Confederate lines. They were to ignore the Confederates stationed on Lookout Mountain.

On November 24, the Federal movement around Lookout Mountain began. While part of the force crossed Lookout Creek near where it flows into the Tennessee River, at the northern end of the mountain, the other half of the army was sent a few miles to the south to ford the creek. They were then to turn north, and link up with the northern component, round the mountain, and turn towards Rossville Gap. But the day was foggy, and the southern contingent, after crossing the creek, continued westward, starting up Lookout Mountain. They then turned northward, moving around the mountain along its slope, and finally connected with the other section below, at the northern end. As the units on the side of the mountain started to the east, they ran into Confederates positioned at the Craven Farm, and fighting began.

Lookout Mountain angles upward from its base, then near the crest, a rock wall runs almost vertical to the top, where a large flat plateau exists. The Craven Farm rests near the base of this vertical wall, on the northern slope. The Federals positioned their right flank against the wall face, and formed their line down the slope to attack the Confederates. As fighting took place over the farm, in the fog, Confederate reinforcements arrived. To their consternation, the Confederate gunners atop the mountain could not depress their guns over the precipice to support their comrades. At times, the fighting ceased completely because neither side could see the other. But, the Federals continued their attacks. The Confederates gave ground, setting up at a second, then a third, defensive line to the east. As the Federals were beginning to run out of ammunition, darkness descended, halting the fight for the day.

Through the night, from the valley below, soldiers on both sides could see the campfires of the men on the side of the mountain, showing the positions of the two foes relative to each other. But the Confederate commander, General Braxton Bragg, decided that the men on Lookout Mountain could not defeat the Federals positioned against them, and pulled his troops back to Missionary Ridge through the night, to reinforce his line there.

As at Shiloh, there are large colored plaques marking the positions of the troops as the battle unfolded. While I am here at the Craven House, I am not aware that the Federals had been advancing along the western side of the mountain from the south, rounding it here to attack from the west. Without much information on the battle at this point, I assume that the Federals had moved up the slope from the north to assault the Confederate defenders. Thus, I will find the battle here confusing.

The position of the plaques shows the fighting as moving from west to east, across the open ground around the Craven House.

This seems odd to me, but again, I do not know the details of how the battle unfolded here at this time. There are no brochures for me to pick up at this spot.

The Craven House was destroyed by the fighting, and by Federal artillery fire from the valley. But it has been rebuilt, to show what it looked like. It faces east. It is a two-story white wooden structure, with a verandah along the length of the front, and one of the sides of the house. A small slanted roof of shingles, supported by small beams at the outer edge, covers the porch. A stone chimney occupies each end of the house. The land around the farm has now been reclaimed by the forest. At the time of the battle, the surrounding area would have been cleared.

There is a path that runs into the woods on the west side of the house, and leads to some of the Confederate rifle pits. There are numerous trails here for hiking, which go in different directions around Lookout Mountain. Some of them are more than five miles in length. The sign here indicates that the rifle pits are just over a mile away, so we start our trek through the woods.

The trees are quite tall along the slopes here, but are somewhat spindly. Even though they are high enough not to allow the sun onto the forest floor, we can see for some distance. There is also not much brush to hinder out movement, but we have to watch out for the numerous rock outcroppings, so that we don't stumble over them. Because of the steepness of the slope, it is difficult to wander very far away from the path.

As I walk along, taking in my surroundings, I wonder what the Confederates had witnessed as the Federals approached, and how much noise had echoed through the forest as the two sides fired back and forth at each other. There probably was some vegetation here then, but much of it may have been cleared away for defensive purposes.

Reaching the remains of the rifle pits, I am still puzzled to find that they had been dug in a north-south direction, instead of the east-west direction that I had expected. The pits are now mostly long narrow grooves in the ground. I finally realize that the action of the battle must have taken place in an east-west direction, with the Federals coming from the west. But I am still puzzled as to why the Federals had attacked from that direction, instead of straight up the slope from the north. I will find out the explanation to this over the next day. I illustrate to Sue what had taken place here, along the ground that she is standing on: how the rifle pits were dug; the direction of the attack; the Confederates pushed back to the Craven House; and all of the fighting that would have occurred here as the battle moved on. We then return along the path towards the Craven House, following in the footsteps of the soldiers as the battle progressed.

We continue southward towards the top of the mountain. Near the summit, the road turns back to the north, and we follow it to its end, at Military Park, situated at the north end of the plateau. A residential area has also been built atop the mountain. We go into the Visitor Center and view some exhibits. I pick up a map here, which covers all of the sites for Chattanooga, and for Chickamauga as well.

Walking through the park, set up with benches, flowers, and shrubs, it resembles more of a public garden than a military battlefield park. Arriving at the edge and looking northeast, we get a view of what the Confederates would have seen while stationed here on the mountain: a beautiful picture of the land below, including the city, now sprawling across the landscape; the Tennessee River twisting and turning, eventually passing in front of us just beneath; and the peninsula of land created by the river, Moccasin Point, which juts out to our front, today still mostly covered by forest, with some industrial development on it, and a golf course along the western side. Some of the Confederate siege guns are located here, but certainly the terrain on top of which they sit would have been different during 1863 than the pavement that they are now placed upon.

Moving over to the northwest side of the lookout, we peer down on the land below, still mostly forested. Muddy Lookout Creek moves in underneath the mountain from the south, disappearing from our sight. On the high ground to the west of it, between the creek and the Tennessee River, which turns back to the north here, the Federals assembled to move around these heights to the north, and had also set up their guns to pound the Confederate defenses on the mountain. All along that area, I can picture the movement of thousands of Union soldiers proceeding to and fro, forming up in ranks to prepare for an advancement up the slopes towards me. At least at this time I think that it will be towards me. In actual fact, the movement from that spot would be around the mountain. The Federal troops that ascended the mountain did so farther to the southwest. It is sunny today, and there is a clear vista before us. But the actual motion of the Federals on the day of the battle would have been obscured by fog; the Confederates commanding these heights would not have been able to see any of the Federal movement below.

A museum is located here. Within it are some of the pictures that have been taken atop the mountain over the years. Stairs in front of the museum allow us to climb down to a path, which goes in front of some of the cliff wall. The cliff prevents people from reaching the top of the mountain by ascending the northern slope. This rock face is more than 100 feet in height. The Federals would have proceeded along in front of this cliff, and the Confederates above would have had no ability to fire down upon them with cannon, because they could not lower the guns to that sharp of an angle. Climbing back up, and again passing by the vista laid out before us, it is hard not to take one more look before moving on to our next stop.

The next area to explore is the battle at Wauhatchie. This is in the vicinity of Lookout Mountain. The battle had taken place on the night of October 28; the day after the Federals had captured Brown's Ferry. As part of the plan for taking and holding Brown's Ferry, the Federals had marched units from Bridgeport, Alabama to support the action at the river, although they had not arrived in time, and as it turned out, were not needed. During October 28, the Federals fortified their position around Brown's Ferry, including sending a division three miles to the south, to Wauhatchie, along the railroad coming in from the west. But the Confederates wanted to retake Brown's Ferry. Instead though, the decision was made to attack the lone Federal division at Wauhatchie, and it would be done during the night, a rare type of battle during the Civil War.

The Confederates moved west along the road, around the northern face of Lookout Mountain. At the crossroads where the road went north to Brown's Ferry and south to Wauhatchie, they posted some units to prevent the Federals at Brown's Ferry from reinforcing those at Wauhatchie during the attack. The rest of the Confederates then turned south towards Wauhatchie.

The Confederates came out of the dark and attacked the unsuspecting Federals. But, these surprised men held firm against the assault. The Confederates regrouped, focusing on the Federal right flank, where the few guns of the defenders had been placed.

However, the Federals held on again, but by that time, the ends of their lines had been pushed back so that some of the men were positioned almost back-to-back. They also started to run out of ammunition. The commander ordered his men to use the bayonet if another attack came. But it did not. The Confederates had given up on the attempt to eliminate this Federal position.

In the meantime, the Federal units at Brown's Ferry had heard the fighting to the south, and started on their way to reinforce their comrades. However, they ran into the Confederates positioned on high ground around the crossroads. They attacked this line again and again in the dark, moving up the steep slopes of the hill, but repulsed each time. Finally, a bayonet charge was ordered. The first attempt was held off. The Federals formed again and forcefully made their way to the top of the knoll. Upon cresting the hill, and moving forward to attack the Confederates, the defenders fled. By morning, the Federals had retained their possessions around Brown's Ferry and Wauhatchie, and the Cracker Line could start bringing supplies into Chattanooga.

There are four stops listed on the park map relating to the Wauhatchie battle. Stop 1 is located off of the Brown's Ferry Road, just south of Interstate 24. We descend Lookout Mountain on the Scenic Highway to arrive back at Cummings Highway. We turn west onto it. Driving just over a mile, and crossing Lookout Creek, we are following the path of the Confederates. We turn north onto Browns Ferry Road. The road that we want is just before the interstate. Finding it, it turns out to be Parker Lane, and we turn east onto it. The lane is about ½ mile in length, and curves to the north just after we turn on to it. Reaching the end of it, we are at the first stop.

This spot is called Tynsdale's Hill. It is related to the fight at the crossroads, as the Federals moved south from Brown's Ferry to reinforce those at Wauhatchie. The Federals attacked up the hill and eventually routed the Confederates. The heaviest part of the fighting took place right here. We are looking at the hill from the north, as the Federals would have seen it during their attack, and it rises steeply in front of us. We, though, see it more clearly today than the Federals would have during the night attack. The hill now contains tall grass, and is topped by a cluster of trees. There is a fence that prevents us from getting to the top of it. From the crest of the knoll, the land also slopes downward to the right, and then rises again, creating a gully that runs between the hills. On the night of the battle, the slopes were wet and slippery, and great effort was used on the part of the Federals to scale this mound. But it was finally done, and the Confederates were routed.

The second site is located a little more than a mile south of the junction of Browns Ferry Road and Cummings Highway. So, we return to this intersection, then continue southward. The road at this point is called the Wauhatchie Pike. The marker is supposed to be just before a left curve, after crossing a creek. I cross the creek, which is Black Creek, and start looking for signs. The road curves to the left, then to the right. I know that I have now missed any marker and so, I turn around. I watch closely, but do not see any signs. I then spot a large stone monument next to the railroad tracks on the left, west, side of the road. It is parallel to the road and thus, is not easy to see. I had been looking for a newer type of marker with a description of the fighting here, as we had found at Tynsdale's Hill.

The stone monument is large, with a square metal plate in its center, on the reverse side from the road. Upon the plate are words stating that the Union line was struck here by the Confederates. Thus, this would have been where the Battle of Wauhatchie had taken place. But there is no map, or any more details laying out where I am standing, or how the battle had unfolded. Therefore, I do not know if I am on the Federal or Confederate side of the lines, near earthworks, where the heaviest fighting had taken place, or anything else. I cannot determine anything from the landscape either. The land here is flat. Beyond the tracks to the east, except for some trees, it is mostly grassland, which runs all the way to Lookout Creek, about ½ mile away and nestled in next to the western slope of Lookout Mountain. The land to the north of here is heavily forested, but probably would have been mostly open land during the time of the battle.

Site 3 is situated at the northern part of the fight, near the crossroads from where we have just come, about ½ mile to the east of Tynsdale's Hill. It is just south of the Interstate, and appears to be beside that highway. The map doesn't show any other road that goes to it. Thus, there does not seem to be any way for me to get to it, and I do not attempt to try.

Site 4 is located about ½ mile southeast of Site 2, along Lookout Creek. But again, there is no road leading to this site. So, we are not able to get to these last two sites. If there are ways for us to get to them, they certainly are not indicated on the park map. I find that the park brochure, as it relates to the sites around Chattanooga, is good for identifying where the points of interest are, but very poor for descriptions of what happened at these sites, and for indicating how to get to them. Some of the streets and roads are not even labeled. There are no details at all on Wauhatchie, except for the markings on the map.

Finishing with the battle at Wauhatchie, it is only early afternoon. So I decide to continue our tour of Chattanooga. We return north to Browns Ferry Road, and take that to get on Interstate 24, going east. This gets us quickly to the downtown part of the city. We exit onto Broad Street and head north. At Main Street, we turn southeast, and drive for about three miles, until we reach Orchard Knob Avenue. Here, we turn northeast and go almost to the end of it, stopping at East 4th Street. On our left is a small park. This is Orchard Knob.

In late November 1863, Grant was positioning his men into place to strike Missionary Ridge, which is on the east side of Chattanooga. As he was doing so, he had received rumors that the Confederates were withdrawing from the heights. His main units though, were not yet ready. They were still moving into position towards the north and south ends of Missionary Ridge. But Grant wanted to test the Confederate defenses, to see if they were in fact still there. He decided to strike at the Confederate forward position to the east of town, on a wooded hillock called Orchard Knob. The main Confederate defenses were atop Missionary Ridge, about a mile further to the east.

On November 23, Federal units moved out of Chattanooga and positioned themselves in the open plain before the knob. At first, the Confederates thought that they were watching a dress parade. Then, as the Federals drew nearer, they realized that they were about to be attacked, and scrambled into their defenses. But the Federal assault was overwhelming. In a matter of minutes, not only did the Federals test the Confederate defenses, which indicated to Grant that the Confederates were still there, but they also took Orchard Knob, with the Confederates withdrawing back to Missionary Ridge.

At the time of the battle, this high hill was situated in the middle of a flat plain, between Missionary Ridge, a mile to the east, and

Chattanooga, a mile to the west. Now, this site is deep within the heart of the city. It was also wooded then, whereas today, it is a park. Because of the surrounding residences, it is difficult to get an idea of how this hill would have stuck out amongst the flat countryside in 1863. The land rises quickly from the streets below, which envelop Orchard Knob. The park still contains many trees.

We follow a path up to the top, where we find large stone monuments of different shapes, and cannon that litter the grassy top. Numerous trees mingle with the memorials. The markers here, unfortunately, indicate the positions of the Federal artillery during the battle for Missionary Ridge, which took place a few days later, on November 25. This was also Grant's position, where he watched the battle from on that day. There are no indicators for the battle that took place here on November 23. Because of the trees that grow on the crest of the hill, I am not able to see towards the west, and the approach that the Federals would have made to reach the Confederate positions here. Nor am I able to look to the east, to view the ground over which the Federals marched to reach the base of Missionary Ridge on November 25.

It is now late in the afternoon, but I feel that we still have time to drive along the stops on top of Missionary Ridge. The park map shows that we can take East 3rd Street, just a block to the north, and head southeast until we reach the end of it. At that point, we turn northeast onto a street that is not labeled, and it will take us to the northern end of Missionary Ridge.

This does not turn out to be the case. We drive east on East 3rd Street until we reach Glenwood Avenue, the last street that we come to that goes to the north. I turn left onto it, and start to the northeast. After some blocks, it curves to the left, ending at Chamberlain Avenue. I turn north onto this street to continue my quest of getting to the top of Missionary Ridge. I keep looking to the east to see if I can see a road that leads up to the ridge, but there does not seem to be any. I reach the end of Chamberlain, at Wilder Street, and turn east onto it. I do not seem to be getting any closer to my objective. Wilder Street ends after a couple of blocks, at Campbell Street. This is getting frustrating. I am right at the foot of Missionary Ridge, but can't find the path up it. At Campbell Street, I look to the right, and see that that road seems to lead up the heights. So I turn onto it, and sure enough, I see it rise up the ridge in front of me. I am not impressed with the map from the park service. It looked as easy as going to the end of East 3rd Street and turning left. That was not the case, and I am not sure what street the map was referring to.

Campbell Street ends at the top of Missionary Ridge. Crest Road runs along the heights. I am to follow it southward, stopping at different points that are marked on the map. The first one is Sherman Reservation, just to the left of the intersection of Crest Road and Campbell Street. I turn onto Crest Road and stop by a path, which will take me up to a high hill above the road.

The battle for Missionary Ridge had occurred the day after the battle of Lookout Mountain, November 25, 1863. The Confederates were aligned along the ridge for about six miles, peering down on the valley below, and Chattanooga. Grant's plan was for the Federal troops to attack both flanks of the Confederate line, then he would send in a frontal assault across the valley from around Orchard Knob, and up the slopes. The troops to the north were already in place. Those to the south were still getting there on the morning of November 25, having fought upon Lookout Mountain the day before. The units in the valley to the west of Missionary Ridge had been the ones that had taken Orchard Knob on November 23.

The Federal troops to the north were commanded by General William Sherman. He held the heights one hill over from the northern end of the Confederate line. The Confederate defenses faced west at the northern end of a hill, known as Tunnel Hill, then turned to the north and east to prevent the Federals from getting into their rear. The height was called Tunnel Hill because a train tunnel had been built through it. The Federals had to descend from the hill that they were on, move through a valley of open ground, then scale Tunnel Hill.

At mid-morning, Sherman started the attack. As their movement commenced through the open valley, the Confederate artillery fired into the Federal ranks. As most of the Federals began their ascent up the northern slope, some units moved to the south, to attack the Confederate line by climbing the western slope. Nearing their objective, the Confederate infantry added to the lead that was already in the air.

On the northern part of the line, hand-to-hand combat took place. The Federals had to withdraw behind a knoll to regroup. On the western slope, the Federals were stopped before making it to the defenses. Thus, a gap opened between the two attacking lines of Federal assailants. Reinforcements were called up to close the gap. They did so, but could not push forward. The two sides stood and hammered at each other all along the western and northern parts of the line. With no change in the battle by mid-afternoon, the Confederates on the north side leaped over their earthworks and attacked the Federals. After some minutes of hand-to-hand fighting, the Federals broke to the rear. Exposing the flank of those along the western end of the battle line, those Federals were forced to withdraw as well. The northern end of the Confederate defenses had held.

The Federal attack on the southern end of the Confederate defenses did not begin until mid-afternoon, just as the fighting at Tunnel Hill was diminishing. It had taken most of the day to get from Lookout Mountain, repair a bridge over Chattanooga Creek, and reach their start-off point. Once the attack began though, it did not take long to produce results. The Confederates were quickly cleared from Rossville Gap. This allowed the Federals to turn to the north and move into the flank of the Confederate line, while at the same time, other units pushed up the slope from the southwest. With Rossville Gap open, more Federal troops moved to the east, getting into the rear of the Confederates. There were no Confederate reinforcements available in the center to send to the southern end of the line; they had been sent to support the defenders to the north during the fighting there. All that the Confederates at this end could do was withdraw slowly to the north, while firing into the advancing Federals.

At this point, Grant was not aware that the fight at the northern end of the line was almost over. Seeing the Federal success on the southern end of Missionary Ridge, he ordered forward the Federal units around Orchard Knob to aid those fighting at the northern end of the heights. But these men were only supposed to go to the base of the mountain, and halt after taking the rifle pits. Grant believed that this would prevent the Confederates from reinforcing those facing Sherman. On the Confederate side, the men in the rifle pits were under orders to fire once if the Federals attacked, then withdraw up the slopes to the main line. As the Federals neared, this was what happened.

Moving into the Confederate earthworks at the base of the ridge, the Federals found that they were exposed to fire from above. Not wanting to remain in this situation, they started to move up the slopes, without orders. Grant watched this from Orchard Knob and at first, was angry that men were moving without orders. But as they clambered over rocks and through brush up the slope, Grant decided to wait to see what would happen. With the Confederates from the rifle pits scampering up the side of the ridge in front of the Federals, those Confederates atop it could not fire down on the approaching men in blue without hitting their comrades. Thus, the Federals were able to continue their pursuit, mostly undisturbed, and the farther they got up the slope, the more confident they became.

All along the heights, Federal units started to reach the crest. Confusion ensued as retreating Confederates reached the top of the hill and ran into those that were already stationed there, immediately followed by the Federals. Thus, many Confederates only fired once or twice before running down the eastern slope, not giving much opposition. Resistance in the center of the Confederate line crumbled quickly, and a retreat began. Nothing that the officers could do could stop this panic. At the same time as the Federals arrived from the west to the center of the ridge, units fighting their way northward along the crest reached this area as well.

Unaware of the unfolding of events in the center and southern end of the line, the successful Confederate defenders at the northern end were informed that they must withdraw before they were surrounded. They thus became the rearguard. With fighting coming to an end along the heights, the Federals turned to the east to pursue the Confederates, who were racing down the eastern slope. But darkness would prevent many Confederates from being captured.

As has been my experience with this brochure from the Park Service at all of the other sites that we have been at today, there are no descriptions of what took place at the points of interest atop Missionary Ridge. It shows where the markers are, but does not give any information on their significance.

The first stop is called Sherman Reservation. This was the high ground atop Tunnel Hill, held by the Confederates at the northern end of the ridge. Union troops under Sherman stormed this position all day without any success. They were initially stationed atop the next hill to the north. They had to scramble down that one and across the open valley between the two heights before ascending up this hill.

This area is now completely covered in woods, except for a grassy spot that has been cut out of the forest, and has a few guns positioned upon it. The trees make it difficult for me to get an idea of the terrain here: to see across to the other hill that was first occupied by the Union troops, or to get an understanding of the problems that the Federals would have encountered in trying to scale these heights. During the time of the battle, most of the land here would have been open fields, with some clusters of trees.

I start south along Crest Road, which is built along the summit of Missionary Ridge, moving to the next stop. The heights have now been built up with housing, which on the one hand is understandable, since the view of the city from here is beautiful. But it is also unfortunate that this landmark upon which fighting had taken place has been intruded upon. Markers of troop positions, both Union and Confederate, are scattered across the top of the mountain, similar to those I had encountered at Shiloh. Most of these though, sit on lawns of the houses. Because of the narrowness of the road, it is also difficult to stop anywhere. There are very few places to pull over, even in the vicinity of the points of interest.

I am not able to stop at the Phelps Monument, the next point of interest, just over a mile to the south of Sherman Reservation. Thus, I cannot determine the significance of it. So I continue on.

I find though, that I am able to pull over a short distance beyond it. There are no houses here, and I am able to look back across the front part of the slope, up which the Union troops would have clamored as they assaulted the heights. This area is now completely covered with trees, as in most cases, is the entire slope of the ridge. Houses have been built along the crest, but the slopes themselves remain inaccessible to construction. The tree cover that exists today would not have been around during the time of the battle, or at least not to the same extent. Up to this point, the vegetation has also prevented us from getting a clear view of the valley below. We have not been able to make out what the Confederates would have seen: the slope of the ridge, up which a large mass of men in blue would have scrambled; nor have we been able to get a clear view of the city. But here at this spot, we are able to see some of the city, and most of the valley formed by this ridge and Raccoon Mountain, to the west. The land on the western side of the valley is mostly covered with trees, and as the sun starts to set, a haze has formed along the horizon.

The next stop is called Delong Reservation. Here is where the first Union troops reached the pinnacle of the ridge. A small park has been set up that commemorates this deed.

I continue southward, past the markers for Turchin Reservation and Ohio Reservation. For there is still nowhere for me to pull over, so that I can determine what events took place at those two spots.

The following point of interest, which I am able to examine, is called Bragg Reservation. The Confederate general commanding here was Braxton Bragg, and this was where his headquarters was set up, near the center of the Confederate defensive position. The Confederate cannon positioned here could not lower their barrels enough down the slope of the ridge to get any clear shots at the ascending Federals, thus allowing them to continue their assault of the heights without much resistance.

This is the last stop atop Missionary Ridge, but we continue southward for another three miles along the crest of the mountain, looking at the scenery below as we drive along. We come down off of the ridge at Rossville, located just inside the Georgia border. There is supposed to be a marker here for the Iowa Reservation, but I do not see it.

This concludes our tour around Chattanooga. What I had expected to take two days, I have finished up in one. I have been continuously behind with my itinerary for most of the trip, having had to constantly modify my daily agenda in order to get in all of the sites on my list, which had included extending some of the days with extra hours. But in the end, I am actually done early. It seems a bit ironic, and funny. Oh well, those things happen. I would rather be done early though, then have to rush to complete everything that I wanted to see.

We follow Rossville Boulevard north, in rush-hour traffic, to reach Interstate 24. Here, we get on the interstate, which will take us westward back to the motel.

Wednesday, September 18

Because I had finished up all of the sites that I wanted to visit around Chattanooga yesterday, our plans have changed. Since we have the motel booked for another night, I thought that we would stay here for one more day. But, Sue felt that if I was done seeing everything that I wanted to, we might as well start back for home. I agreed to this, and so we will leave today.

But, there are a few things that we will do before departing. The first one is that I want to visit The Battles for Chattanooga Museum. I know that this will not take very long. So after that, we will play a round of golf. We know that a golf course exists on Moccasin Point, near where the Battle of Brown's Ferry had occurred; we had seen it from the top of Lookout Mountain. We both think that it will be interesting to wander around the area where Union troops were bivouacked, and perhaps get a better chance to see the Brown's Ferry location from the other side of the river; all this while playing a round of golf. Then, we will grab a quick snack and start our journey back to Ottawa, traveling as far as we can today.

The day is sunny, but a bit cool. By going to the museum first, this will allow it to warm up before we start our round of golf. The museum is located near the base of Lookout Mountain, on the northeast side on Tennessee Avenue. We check out of our motel and head east on Cummings Highway, curving around the northern base of Lookout Mountain. At the intersection with West 37th Street, we head southeast on that, then turn south onto Tennessee Avenue at the next intersection. The museum is on the east side of the street.

The presentation gives a reenactment of the battles around Chattanooga, on a three-dimensional electronic map. I had read that this should be the first thing to do before touring the battlefields, but I felt that there would be presentations done at the parks. This had not turned out to be the case, and I should have started my tour at the museum.

It gives an excellent detailed account of the different battles that took place here in October and November of 1863. It is shown on a board with all of the correct landscape of the area surrounding Chattanooga. Thus, I am able to get a better understanding of how the terrain looked during the time of the battles, and what the troops on both sides were up against. The show lasts about 35-40 minutes. The map lights up in different areas as a narrator describes what is occurring in that vicinity during a specific point in time.

It is an excellent presentation and, as I stated, I should have started my touring of Chattanooga here. With a complete overview of the events, I would have known more about what I was seeing, as I visited the different spots. I certainly would have known about the direction of the battle at Lookout Mountain while I was standing there, instead of having to figure it out as I went along. Although the presentation is more detail than Sue needed to know, she also has found it interesting, and is impressed with the intricacy and detail put into the making of the model landscape.

Finishing up here, we proceed to Moccasin Point, to enjoy a pleasant game of golf in the warm sun on this bright September day. We head a block north on Tennessee Avenue, to connect with Broad Street. This takes us to US Highway 27, where we get on it to cross the Tennessee River, to the north side of the city. We get off of the highway onto Elmwood Drive, heading south. This connects with Pineville Road, which continues on to the south. As it enters the peninsula, the road changes to Moccasin Point Road, moving along the east side of the land. We then see the golf course on the west side of the road, and turn in.

After our time of relaxation, we are ready to begin our trek back home. It is now early afternoon as we return back to downtown Chattanooga along US Highway 27. At the connection with Interstate 24, we turn east onto it. Just after crossing over to the east side of Missionary Ridge, we turn northeast onto Interstate 75. We are now pointed towards Ottawa.

But, our trip is not yet completely over. While going through the new book that I had purchased, which lists different sites within a state where something of interest related to the Civil War had occurred, Sue had found that a skirmish had occurred at Lenoir City. Located about 30 miles southwest of Knoxville, and along Interstate 75, we have decided that we will make a stop there, to see if we can find anything.

The book states that there is a marker along US Highway 11, in the town. Not knowing on which side of the town the marker will be, I depart the interstate at the exit before Lenoir City. Thus, we should not have to backtrack, and will get back on the interstate to the north of town. The road that I exit onto is Sugar Limb Road, and we head southeast to connect with US 11. At the intersection, we turn northeast onto the highway, and drive a couple of miles to reach the town.

A battle occurred here on November 15, 1863. The Confederates were heading towards Knoxville from Chattanooga, which would result in their attack on the city later in the month. Part of the Federal army had come out from Knoxville to meet the Confederates, but had begun to withdraw back to the city without a fight. The Confederates, becoming aware that there was a small Federal force in front of them, pushed on, catching some of the Federal rear units at Lenoir City, then called Lenoir Station, and getting into a fight. But the main Federal force had been able to withdraw towards Campbell's Station, and the two armies would meet there the next day.

Driving slowly through the town, neither one of us spots any markers, and we exit the community. Not giving up yet, I then turn around, to have another try at finding something. I turn right onto Kingston Street, and drive a short distance, still without finding any marker. So, we decide that we are probably not going to discover anything here concerning the battle, and continue on with our journey homeward. At the east end of town, I turn north onto US Highway 321, which brings us back to the interstate. We then turn northeast again towards Knoxville.

We will end our stay in Tennessee exactly as we had started it. Sue wants one more look at the cemetery in Blountville, and the family that had their slaves buried with them. She wants to get a few pictures so that she will have a copy of exactly what the gravestone says, and the name of the family that had done this.

After almost two hours of driving, as we near the Virginia border, we arrive at our exit, and turn south onto State Highway 37. Entering the small community, which was our first stop almost two weeks, and many miles ago, we proceed to the graveyard, on the hill overlooking the town from the west.

We wander through the grass as I follow Sue to the site that interests her. She shows me the markers, and the size of the plot. The parents are in the middle, with the children on the right, and the slaves on the left. After a few moments of observing the area again, and Sue taking some pictures, we move on.

While stopped for a bite to eat, I look at the road atlas, and decide that I want to try to make it as far as Roanoke, Virginia. Tomorrow, we will stop at my brother's place, outside of Utica, New York, and in order to not arrive there too late, I feel that we need to get as far as Roanoke tonight. The other factor for tomorrow is that, if it is a nice clear day, I want to take a short detour across the Blue Ridge Parkway, to show Sue the spectacular vistas that I had seen last year.

So, on into the night I drive. It is a clear night, and the traffic is light. Thus I am making good time. Sue gets sleepy, but tries to force herself to stay awake, so that she can talk to me and make sure that I don't start to dose off. I appreciate her efforts, but when I'm driving, I do not usually get sleepy. However, she eventually succumbs to sleep, and I continue on, arriving at Roanoke around midnight.

Thursday, September 19

Today arrives clear and warm, as I had hoped. Starting out early, we drive down the Shenandoah Valley with ease. I turn off of the interstate at New Market, the place where a battle had taken place in 1864, and where Sue had seen guns positioned off in the distance on our way down to Tennessee. We do not want to spend too much time driving through the mountains, and this is the last entrance into the Blue Ridge Mountains before the northern end.

Heading east on US Highway 211, we cover the distance along the Valley floor, then commence our twisting and turning slow ascent up the western side of the Blue Ridge Mountains; probably covering a route used more than once by Stonewall Jackson to confuse the Federals during his 1862 campaign. At the intersection with Skyline Drive, as it is known at the northern end of the scenic route, we enter Shenandoah National Park, and turn north to follow the crests of the Blue Ridge Mountains.

The views are not disappointing. The more spectacular views are on the western side, looking down into the Shenandoah Valley. As we near the end of the trail, the additional vista of Massanutten Mountain rises before us, splitting the Valley in two. Sue finds this brief detour well worth our time, and as an added bonus, she spots some deer grazing along the side of the road.

Exiting the mountains at Front Royal, we drive through the town. I am already familiar with this community, having been here last year as part of my Shenandoah Valley and West Virginia trip. We head north out of Front Royal on US Highway 340/522 to reach the interstate. Here, we turn westward onto Interstate 66, driving for 10 miles to return to Interstate 81. We veer onto it, to the northeast, to continue our homeward journey.

During our trek today to upstate New York, we do as we had done on our trip southward: listen to music and have some good conversation. But during our conversations this time, we have some new things to discuss and replay. It has been quite an enjoyable two-week period for both of us. We have both done what we had set out to do: I visited Civil War sites, and Sue played some golf. We also had enjoyed our visit with her relatives, and saw some new cities. As well, we had shared our pursuits with each other. I had played some golf, something that I had never done on any of my trips before, and had met some new people, who had been very hospitable and shown me some things that I probably wouldn't have seen if I was on my own. Sue had explored small towns and villages, which she had never heard of before, gone trekking through the woods in search of the Civil War, and found an interest in slavery and the people who lived during that time.

With all of these added features, this trip ranks as one of the best ones that I have been on. Certainly there were more parts of this trip that were non-Civil War related than any of the others. This trip is also the longest to date, in terms of distance. Upon reaching home, I will have put almost 5000 miles on the car. Some of my other trips, in which I had traveled from home by car, had been over 3000 miles, and one had approached 4000 miles, but this is probably one record that I will not break. Most of the states that I have left to journey to are too far for me to travel to by car.

Even with all of the additions that I experienced on this trip, there are lots of memories that go with the battle sites that I visited in Tennessee. Other than Virginia, Tennessee saw more battles fought on its soil than any other state; thus, my reason for thinking of Tennessee as the "Virginia of the West". Whereas the battles in Virginia were fought under a few campaigns that took place over the course of the war, Tennessee had numerous battles occurring at the same time, under the direction of different campaigns. The battles fought in the western part of the state could have nothing to do with any battles unfolding in the eastern part of the state. At the same time, there might be raids going on somewhere else, as the cavalry roamed across the rolling hills of the central part of the state. It was certainly harder to keep track of all of the goings-on within this state. On top of that, there was the loyalty question:

which side were the people faithful to. So as well as the objective of destroying the other army, a further goal was control of the land and the people. This was certainly a much more complex environment than the war fought in the East.

    Now I have added another state to my list, and have gained more insight into the events that occurred during the Civil War. As with all of my visits in the past, and as is to be expected, this state was different from any of the others. Some of the types of events that had taken place here, I had not encountered before; part of that was because of the people, and part of that was because of the landscape. I had found the landscape of Tennessee to be as variable as I had expected. The eastern part of the state was very mountainous. I was surprised though, that Knoxville was not surrounded up close by mountains, although it was in a mountainous region. The rolling hills of the central part of the state were higher, and more numerous, than I had expected. The western part of Tennessee, near the Mississippi River, was not as flat as I had thought. Now I have more memories to add to the ones that I already have, and the landscape of Tennessee will stay with me as I continue to read about the battles that were fought across its soil.

Looking east in Third Creek valley, just west of Fort Sanders, Knoxville

Looking southeast from behind a Federal gun in the Round Forest, Stones River

Looking east from the Federal defensive position atop Vaught's Hill

Looking south towards Shy's Hill from where the Federals formed to attack

Looking west towards Federal campsite atop hill at Hartsville, where the heaviest fighting took place

Looking northwest down the Cumberland River from the Lower Battery, Fort Donelson

Looking west towards Federal position atop the hill from Old Kedron Road, Spring Hill

Looking southwest from the Federal position within the Hornet's Nest at Shiloh

Bibliography

Civil War Sites Advisory Commission *Report on the Nation's Civil War Battlefields, Technical Volume 2: Battle Summaries*, 1993 http://www.cr.nps.gov/abpp/battles

Conservation Fund *The Civil War Battlefield Guide* (Boston, 1990)

Cromie, Alice *A Tour Guide to the Civil War*, 4th ed. (Nashville, 1992)

Kentucky Department of Travel Development *Official Kentucky Vacation Guide* (Frankfort, 1996)

McPherson, James M., ed. *The Atlas of the Civil War* (New York, 1994)

Missouri Division of Tourism *Missouri Travel Guide Getaway* (Jefferson City, 1995)

Perryville Battlefield State Historic Site and U.S. Army Armor School *A Guide to the Perryville, Kentucky Civil War Battlefield* 1996

Roth, Dave "The General's Tour: The Battle of Stones River" *Blue & Gray Magazine* Special Publication, 1993

Scalf, Henry "The Battle of Ivy Mountain" Chapter VI in *Historic Floyd, 1800-1950* (Prestonsburg, c1950)

Tennessee 200 *A Path Divided: Tennessee's Civil War Years* (Nashville, 1996)

Time-Life Books, eds. *The Civil War*, 28 vols. (Alexandria, Va., 1987)

Index

Anderson's Crossroads, 253-254, 255
Arcadia, 54
Arcadia Valley, 10, 54
Athens, 43, 44

Barbourville, 69
Bean Station, 132-133
Beechgrove, 170, 172-173, 252
Belmont, 7, 8, 9, 45, 48-49
Big Blue River, 25, 26, 27-28
Big Hill, 88-89, 90
Blountville, 125-130, 131, 273
Blue Springs, 130-131
Boonville, 34-41
Boonville, First, 35, 37-40
Boonville, Second, 35-36, 41-42, 55
Brentwood, 186-187
Britton Lane, 223-227
Brown's Ferry, 255-256, 257, 261-262, 271
Bulls Gap, 130, 131-132
Burkesville, 72-73
Byram's Ford, 26, 27-28

Cairo, 6-7, 8, 9, 46-47
Campbell's Station, 142, 145, 273
Carthage, 21-23
Chattanooga, 121-122, 136, 139, 142, 167, 171-172, 197-198, 236, 252-254, 255, 256, 257-272, 273
Collierville, 235
Columbia (Missouri), 4, 33

Columbia (Tennessee), 172, 187-188, 215, 216-217, 218-219
Columbus, 7-8, 48-49
Cumberland River, 175, 198, 199-201, 204-205, 207, 209-210
Cynthiana, 85-86
Cynthiana, First, 85-86
Cynthiana, Second, 86

Dandridge, 133-135
Dover, 207, 211-212

Fair Garden, 135-136
Fort Anderson, 6,7
Fort Craig, 92, 94-95, 96
Fort Davidson, 54-57
Fort DeRussy, 8
Fort Dickerson, 141-142
Fort Donelson, 207-212, 239
Fort Henry, 133, 198, 207, 212-213
Fort Negley, 174, 178-180
Fort Pillow, 227, 229-232, 234
Frankfort, 64, 75, 83-85
Franklin, 168, 178, 187-196, 215
Franklin, First, 196
Franklin, Second, 187-196, 217

Glasgow, 41-43, 55

Hartsville, 198-206
Hatchie's Bridge, 236-237
Hickman, 8-9
Hodgenville, 100-103
Hoover's Gap, 169-173, 252

Ironton, 54, 55, 57
Island No. 10, 52-54
Ivy Mountain, 106-108, 109

Jackson, 223-225, 228
Jefferson City, 25
Johnsonville, 198, 213-214, 219-221

Kansas City, 4, 23-25, 28, 30, 33
Kentucky River, 74, 75, 84-85
Knob Creek, 103-105
Knoxville, 121-122, 125, 129-130, 131, 133, 134, 136-144, 145, 167, 198, 273, 276

Lebanon, 74, 82-83, 86, 97
Lebanon, First, 82
Lebanon, Second, 82-83, 86, 97
Lenoir City, 272-273
Lexington (Kentucky), 6, 64-65, 74, 83, 84, 86-87, 94; Old Frankfort Pike, 117; Paris Pike, 86; Todd House, 110-116
Lexington (Missouri), 30-32
Lone Jack, 28-30
Lookout Mountain, 253, 256-261, 263, 266, 267, 271-272
Louisville, 64, 75, 84, 90, 94

Merna, 37-40
Memphis, 121-122, 215, 227, 228, 229, 233-235
Memphis, First, 232, 234
Memphis, Second, 234
Middle Creek, 105-106, 108
Mill Springs, 69-70, 71-72
Missionary Ridge, 257, 258, 264, 265-270, 272
Mississippi River, 3, 4, 5-7, 9, 10, 43, 45-51, 52-54
Missouri River, 4, 24, 32, 34, 40-42, 50

Mossy Creek, 133-134
Mount Sterling, 109-110
Munfordville, 92-96
Murfreesboro, 147, 167-168, 169, 170, 171, 199, 200
Murfreesboro, First, 167-168
Murfreesboro, Second, 168

Nashville, 121-122, 145, 146, 147, 150, 151, 155, 157, 168, 172-186, 187, 190, 196-197, 199, 207, 208, 214, 216, 220, 239
New Madrid, 10, 51-54
Newtonia, 20-21
Newtonia, First, 21
Newtonia, Second, 21

Ohio River, 7
Orchard Knob, 264-265, 266, 267, 268
Ozark Mountains, 10, 54

Paducah, 6, 7
Parkers Crossroads, 221-223, 224
Pilot Knob, 10-11, 54-57
Plum Point Bend, 232-233, 234

Richmond, 87-92, 94
Rowlett's Station, 96

Salem Cemetery, 223-224
Sedalia, 32-34, 41, 55
Shiloh, 197, 236, 237-249
Spring Hill, 186, 187-188, 196, 216-218
Springfield, 4-5, 9-11, 12, 14, 22
St. Louis, 4-5, 9-10, 11, 30, 44-45, 55, 57, 59
Stones River, 147-166, 167, 169, 171, 199, 215, 221, 252
Sweden's Cove, 254-255

Tebb's Bend, 96-100

Tennessee River, 198, 207, 212-213, 219-221, 239, 241-243, 254, 255-256, 257, 260, 272
Thompsons Station, 215-216
Tompkinsville, 73, 97
Tullahoma, 151, 170, 172, 196, 197, 235, 236, 250-252

Vaught's Hill, 169-170

Wauhatchie, 256, 261-264
West Liberty, 108, 109
Westport, 21, 24-27, 28, 34, 55
Wildcat Mountain, 65-69
Wilson's Creek, 11-20, 30, 58

www.ingramcontent.com/pod-product-compliance
Lightning Source LLC
Chambersburg PA
CBHW050337230426
43663CB00010B/1898